Morality in the Making

WILEY SERIES IN DEVELOPMENTAL PSYCHOLOGY

Series Editor
Professor Kevin Connolly

The Development of Movement Control and Co-ordination
edited by J. A. Scott Kelso and Jane E. Clark

Psychobiology of the Human Newborn
edited by Peter Stratton

Morality in the Making:
Thought, Action, and the Social Context
edited by Helen Weinreich-Haste and Don Locke

Further titles in preparation

Morality in the Making

Thought, Action, and the Social Context

Edited by

Helen Weinreich-Haste
University of Bath

and

Don Locke
University of Warwick

JOHN WILEY & SONS LTD

Chichester · New York · Brisbane · Toronto · Singapore

Library of Congress Cataloging in Publication Data:
Main entry under title:
Morality in the making.
   (Wiley series in developmental psychology)
   Includes index.
   1. Ethics—Addresses, essays, lectures. 2. Moral development—
Addresses, essays, lectures. I. Weinreich-Haste, Helen.
II. Locke, Don. III. Series.
BJ1012.M6355   170'.42   82–2749

ISBN 0 471 10423 X   AACR2

British Library Cataloguing in Publication Data:
Weinreich-Haste, Helen
   Morality in the making.—(Wiley series in
   development psychology)
   1. Ethics
   I. Title   II. Locke, Don
   171'.2   BJ319

ISBN 0 471 10423 X

Photoset by Paston Press, Norwich
Printed in the United States of America.

List of Contributors

GLYNIS M. BREAKWELL is lecturer in Social Psychology at the University of Surrey, and Director of the Young People In and Out of Work Project, Nuffield College, Oxford. This project examines aspects of the social psychology of young people entering the labour market, especially the unemployed, those on government schemes, and young women in 'sex-inappropriate' jobs. Dr Breakwell is also engaged in research on the development of identity of individuals and groups, particularly in conflict. Her writings include *Social Psychology: A Practical Manual*, *Threatened Identities*, and *Social Work: The Social Psychological Approach*, and contributions to several books and journals.

NICHOLAS P. EMLER is lecturer in Psychology at the University of Dundee. His research interests include the development of moral reasoning, psychological factors in delinquency, and the role of social interaction in cognitive development. He has published in journals in Britain and America and contributed chapters on moral development to various books.

TOM KITWOOD lectures in the School of Science and Society at Bradford University on the social relations of science and technology, and coordinates a research project on aspects of the Social Psychology of Industrialism. He is author of a number of writings concerned with values, education, and the field of Science-and-Society, including *Disclosures to a Stranger* (1980) an account of adolescent values in advanced industrial society. Having worked for a period in Africa, he is particularly interested in the phenomena of rapid social change.

PETER KUTNICK is Lecturer in Education (Social and Developmental Psychology) at the University of Sussex. He has published articles on child development, socialization, and the social effects of schooling. His current research interests include moral and social development, social interaction, and the development of cooperation amongst children.

DON LOCKE is Professor of Philosophy at the University of Warwick. He has published three books on the theory of knowledge, a philosophical biography of the political theorist and novelist Willaim Godwin, and a number of articles in professional journals. His major research interests are the philosophy of action and moral philosophy, two areas which coincide in the topic of moral psychology.

ROGER STRAUGHAN is Lecturer in Education at the University of Reading. He has also taught in primary and secondary schools, and at a College of Education. He is secretary of the Philosophy of Education Society of Great Britain, and has written on various philosophical aspects of moral education.

DAVID M. THORNTON is a Senior Psychologist in the Home Office Prison Department, and works in the Young Offenders Unit. He has done research on moral development, and on cognitive and personality variables associated with criminality and delinquency.

STEPHANIE P. THORNTON is Lecturer in Developmental Psychology at the University of Sussex. Her research is in cognitive development, focusing on processes of change in children's problem solving.

IAN VINE is Lecturer in Social Psychology in the School of Interdisciplinary Human Studies, University of Bradford. His current research interests include the ontogenetic and cultural-historical bases and development of morality, the psychological bases of belief systems, sociology, spatial behaviour and crowding, and theoretical models of human nature. He has published several papers in journals, and is joint editor with M. von Cranach of *Social Communication and Movement*. He is an Associate of the British Psychological Society.

HELEN WEINREICH-HASTE is Lecturer in Psychology at the University of Bath. Her research interests are moral, social, and political development, the relationship between career and life, plans and values, and social psychological aspects of sex roles, in particular the nature and effect of stereotyping. She is also interested in the social image of science. She has contributed to various journals and books, on these topics.

DEREK WRIGHT is Professor of Education at the University of Leicester. His main research interests are in the psychology of child development, religion, and moral education. He is Associate Editor of the *Journal of Moral Education*, and author of, among other things, *The Psychology of Moral Behaviour*. He organized the international conference in 1977 which was seminal in the inception of MOSAIC.

MOSAIC

MOSAIC (The Morality and Social Action Interdisciplinary Colloquium) is a mixed group of psychologists, philosophers, and educationalists sharing a common interest in the psychology of morals, and a common concern to pursue its problems across the usual disciplinary boundaries. It arose from a conference on Moral Development and Moral Education in the summer of 1977, and has met regularly and informally since then for intensive round-table discussion of the issues which form the underlying themes of this volume: the development of moral and social cognition, the relationships between moral thought and action, the nature and sources of moral judgment and moral behaviour, the impact of moral conceptions on the group and the individual, the nature of morality itself.

But we have no agreed solutions to these problems, nor even a common perspective on them. What unites us, rather, is the belief that new insights can be gained by bringing our different perspectives and traditions into conflict and interaction with each other. This book is therefore the outcome of an exercise in communal thinking by a group of individuals, not all of whom have contributed chapters themselves. Each chapter has been moulded and modified by the comments, critical and constructive, of other members of MOSAIC, and by the need to explain its conclusions to those who do not share its assumptions. In short it, like us, is a mosaic: a collection of differently-coloured pieces put together to form a pattern, but a pattern that may vary with the perspective, and the preconceptions, of the beholder.

Foreword

Scientists, and perhaps more especially social scientists, are sometimes rebuked for studying trivial questions and more often for failing to pay sufficient attention to important contemporary issues. Often these complaints are ill-judged and ill-informed but sometimes they have substance and then it is important that the scientific community be responsive. Morality and the development of moral competence are obviously of great importance and philosophers, educationalists, and psychologists have been interested in these issues for a very long time. Although there is an extensive and important literature, especially on stages of moral development, the study of moral behaviour has not attracted its fair share of attention and effort in mainstream psychology. There are many reasons why this is so; it is too value-laden, it seems vague, it presents difficult conceptual problems, it is certainly complex, and behaviourism, the principal theoretical framework of twentieth-century psychology offers little to the study of moral behaviour.

The three philosophical doctrines which have a bearing on moral development and which are represented in psychological approaches to the subject (the doctrines of original sin, innate purity, and the idea of an infinitely malleable *tabula rasa*) are of limited use since they do not fit the facts. So we have then a subject matter which is complex and multi-faceted, where people may quite easily be discussing different issues in the mistaken belief that they are the same. The concepts we use, the available data base, and the theoretical framework within which to consider morality and the development of moral behaviour all require close and careful attention. With such a formidable agenda an approach which crosses existing disciplinary boundaries is necessary and this is what MOSAIC set out to provide. The psychological issues discussed in these essays are informed by criticism from philosophical and educational standpoints. As the editors make clear, no comprehensive solutions to the problems of moral behaviour and its development are offered; instead the group hopes that by raising old issues in an interdisciplinary context new questions, rather than new answers to old questions, will emerge. G. K.

Chesterton's Father Brown put our difficulty well enough. 'It isn't that they can't see the solution. It is that they can't see the problem.'

The essays contained in this book have a relevance and importance well beyond the boundaries of developmental psychology. Philosophers and educationalists and many others concerned with this central set of issues in human behaviour will find much to arrest and arouse their interest.

KEVIN CONNOLLY

Contents

Section I   Moral Thinking—The Cognitive-Developmental Approach

Section II   Moral Behaviour—The Relation between Thought
and Action

Introduction

Morality, according to Shaw's character Dubedat, consists in suspecting other people of not being legally married. Certainly if you ask the average passer-by about morals, he or she will probably think of one of three things. There are first individual peccadilloes, especially of the sexual kind that figure so prominently in the tabloid press, but also including lying, promise-breaking, and other minor dishonesties: the sort of sins that most people commit at some time. Then there is the grand guignol of the moral world, those dramatic forms of deviance which have always horrified, but also enthralled, the averagely law-abiding sinner: spectacular robberies, rape, murder, terrorism, and genocide. And finally there are the more diffuse, de-individualized forms of anti-social behaviour which increasingly affect most people directly or indirectly, whether as victims or observers: vandalism, hooliganism, teenage violence at football grounds or on public beaches, riots, and political violence.

When people complain of a decline in public morality, in the schools and in the streets, it is probably this third category, the 'collapse of law and order', rather than promiscuity, murders, or organized crime, that they have most in mind. Here, they insist, something must be done, and there is no lack of suggestions as to what that something should be. The very phrase 'when law and order breaks down' is a revealing one. It might refer simply to the fact that people do not do what the authorities tell them to; but it also implies a failure of internalized constraints, the inability of some people to control themselves as the rest of us do. So the moral seems plain: we must train people to behave themselves, to control their impulses and observe the norms and conventions of civilized society. But if, in the meantime, these internal controls are inadequate, then we must increase the external constraints, legal enforcement and the threat of punishment.

In fact there is no reason to expect that these methods will be any more successful in controlling the third form of immorality than they have ever been with the other two. Of course we can punish our children, shame our friends, fine and imprison our fellow citizens, as we have always done. But these perhaps have more effect on what we will *regard* as acceptable behaviour than on individual action as such. Despite extensive efforts to make people chaste, honest, and truthful, we have learned to live in, and even enjoy, a world of moderate immorality. If the grand guignol crimes are relatively rare, it may only be because they do not fall within the normal range of temptation of most healthy and adjusted people. We do not, on the whole, abstain from murder from a fear of the consequences, or because we have been taught not to kill. The circumstances of our ordinary lives typically preclude murder arising as an option for us. If we are driven to it then, self-defence aside, it is typically the result of extreme emotion towards someone close to us whom we, perhaps temporarily, find intolerable. Under those circumstances anything may be possible, even—and perhaps especially—for the most self-restrained of us. As the statistics demonstrate, you run more danger of being killed by your nearest and dearest than by a total stranger.

The de-individualized anti-social behaviours of contemporary concern also lie, on the whole, outside the range of normal temptation, except under the pressure of social circumstance or particular group norms. Riots do not break out spontaneously, nor are they merely triggered by chance occurrences; they require a background of disaffection and alienation. Teenage hooliganism may, like duelling, have more to do with symbolic acts of honour and display, with the presentation of self and the maintenance of prestige both for the group and within the group, than with violence and aggression as such. This is not necessarily to find such behaviour excusable, let alone acceptable. The ancient adage that to understand all is to forgive all does not preclude a desire to change things, to ensure that they need not happen again. The moral is not that we have to tolerate social disorder, violence, and lawlessness as the product of our circumstances and not ourselves. The moral is that we have to understand these phenomena—more to the point, we have to be able to explain them—before we can hope to modify or affect them.

Yet the unfortunate fact is that we know almost nothing about why people behave morally or immorally. Despite the competing claims of everyone from sociobiologists to psychoanalysts we lack any agreed and comprehensive account of why people in general behave as they do, individually or together. But the study of moral behaviour in particular has, until recently, been relatively ignored, especially within orthodox psychology, as too indefinite, too value-laden, and, perhaps, too complex. Research was conducted covertly even within the portals of behaviourism, under such headings as the conditioning of anxiety or guilt, the social transmission of values, or the acquisition of norms, habits, and skills. These investigations did not examine the nature of morality, but simply assumed that 'immoral' was equivalent to 'deviant'. The function of the psychologist was therefore to account for this socially deviant behaviour, by reference to the contingencies of socialization. The assumption was that both pro- and anti-social behaviour, and their associated beliefs, were inculcated into a passive individual through reward and punishment; the desired outcome would be self-motivated restraint, and the self-monitoring of behaviour by reference to internalized cultural values. The label 'social learning theory' says it all: the acquisition of morality is a branch of learning theory, with conditioning the primary mechanism; and what is thus learnt or acquired is essentially social, the conventions and expectations of the group.

But morality cannot be reduced to social norms. It is, on the contrary, something in terms of which social norms can be, and ought to be, criticized. The identification of 'moralization' with socialization presupposes a particular view of morality, and of the role of moral training, which has as its goal an individual who is self-controlled and law-abiding. This is in marked contrast to the dominant philosophical tradition, at least since Kant, that moral maturity consists not in conformity but in autonomy, the ability to decide for oneself and act on one's own judgement. Of course the assumption is that the autonomous individual will also be self-controlled and law-abiding, but only to the extent that morality requires: in a conflict between law or social expectation and morality, the latter will take precedence. And underlying these different conceptions of morality are different conceptions of human nature, one which sees the human being as inherently sinful, as needing to be kept from evil by the combined forces of social pressure and internalized constraints; the other which sees the human being as tending naturally to the good, as needing to be free, independent, and self-governing, in order to discover what is right and act accordingly. It is still an open question which of these ancient conceptions is correct. No doubt the truth, as often, lies in some combination of the two.

But neither is morality simply a matter of what people do, of how they behave. Similar behaviours, breaking a law or keeping a promise for example, can be profoundly immoral in one context and supremely moral in another. Individual motivation is relevant too. What one person does from a sense of duty or obligation, another may do for reasons of pure self-interest, and the morality of their conduct varies accordingly. Hence we cannot study morality without taking account of the various reasons, justifications, and rationalizations which lead people to behave as they do: morality is also a matter of what people think, and in particular of what they think they ought to do. Behaviour can be identified as moral only by reference to the agent's beliefs and understanding, both about morality and about what he is doing.

Yet for many psychologists attitudes and values have often been of interest only as 'mediating variables', having significance merely as potential predictors of behaviour. In other words, an attitude is explicable, and justifiable as an object of study, only insofar as it can be related directly to the primary process, behaviour. First consistency theories and latterly attribution theory have made inroads on this assumption, dealing with attitudes and beliefs as subjects of study in their own right, even if they are seen as providing only a post-hoc justification of behaviour.

Increasingly there is interest within psychology in cognitive processes as such, in contrast to the previous bias towards motivational factors. This shift of attention forces the psychologist to confront a wide range of new issues. The important questions of cognitive development concern the individual's understanding of the physical and social world, and here the reasoning process is primary, whether in the form of problem-solving or in the form of construal, the organization of understanding. And once we begin to take seriously the view that the person is an active, thinking being, rather than a passive creature controlled directly by contingencies of reward and punishment, then we have to take account of moral thought a well as moral conduct. Once we recognize that morality is not simply a matter of social conformity, we see also that the explanation of moral thought and behaviour must go beyond the assimilation of social norms and social skills, to the understanding and elucidation of morality itself. We need to know what morality is, and how different individuals understand it, before we can identify, explain, and ultimately, one hopes, promote moral thinking and moral action.

Philosophers, of course, have discussed these problems for centuries, but without arriving at any generally agreed solutions. But that may be because the questions are not wholly philosophical. An anthropologist—or, one day perhaps, an astronaut—faced with some alien community, the Ik of Northern Uganda for example, whose values, if they have any, seem radically different from ours; a psychologist, faced with subjects who seem prepared to administer massive electrical shocks to their victims because they feel they ought to do as the experimenter says, or with school children who insist that lying and cheating are wrong, but do it just the same; a teacher presented with a curriculum which includes 'moral education', or merely faced with the conflicting behaviour of children from a variety of social and ethnic backgrounds, and wondering what, if anything, he ought to do about it; any private individual struggling to reconcile personal need with moral obligation—all of these may find themselves asking 'But what *is* morality, after all?', and the answers they need need not be the same.

But it is also apparent that these fundamental questions of morality cannot be answered in purely philosophical fashion, without reference to the empirical facts. Moral philosophy is idle and empty if carried on in isolation from the facts of human development, and implictly or explicitly the major moral theories, from Aristotle to Sartre, are also theories of human nature: it is because man is as he is, they argue in effect, that morals are as they are. Philosophers have traditionally operated with a 'rational man' conception of humanity, as suspect for its intellectualism as for its sexism. The dominant questions of much contemporary moral philosophy have been: what form of morality would it be rational to adopt? what form of morality would a rational man choose to support? But we are not, for the most past, rational in the philosophers' sense; and we do not choose our moralities, if we choose them at all, for those sorts of reasons. Our morality is not, accordingly, that of the philosophers' rational man. If morality consists, for example, in acting only on that maxim through which you can at the same time will that it should become a universal law of nature, then there is precious little morality, even among philosophers.

There is, moreover, a difference in interest, in emphasis. The philosopher is primarily concerned to understand morality, to define moral judgments and analyse moral concepts. The psychologist is more concerned to explain morality, to discover its function and origins, at both an individual and a social level. But asked in a new context, old questions may yet acquire new answers. The definition of morality may be one thing in a philosophy seminar, quite another when we probe the thought of the average 13-year-old. And in seeking to understand the latter, we may learn something new about the former.

There thus arises a subject area, or overlap of subject areas, which we might call 'the psychology of morals'. What is morality? Where does it come from? Why do people accept it, if they do? How do they understand it? How far does it influence their behaviour? These are questions of enormous theoretical interest and practical importance to which we hardly begin to know the answers. They are questions whose answers require both philosophical analysis and psychological explanation.

The contributors to this volume, for all their other differences, share the belief that morality cannot be explained or understood without bringing together the varying perspectives of philosophers and psychologists, both social and developmental. Philosophical theories can be criticized for their psychological implications (see Kitwood, Chapter 12); psychological theories for their philosophical assumptions (Emler, Chapter 3); philosophical distinctions can be used to justify a psychological position (Thornton and Thornton, Chapter 4), psychological data to illuminate a philosophical problem (Straughan, Chapter 7); and sometimes the influences can run in both directions: psychological concepts are used to support a philosophical thesis which in turn has implications for psychological theory (Vine, Chapter 2).

Inevitably there are problems of communication across these interdisciplinary boundaries, and what appears an answer from one point of view may seem an irrelevance from another. What, for example, is the point or purpose of a theory of morality? The philosopher will be looking for a definition, some set of necessary and sufficient conditions, which enables us to distinguish morality and moral judgment from other social phenomena and forms of discourse. The developmental psychologist will want to understand the nature of moral development, not so much what makes it moral development as how it works, what processes it involves and what functions it serves. The social psychologist, similarly, will be concerned with the function of morality and moral judgment, and especially their social utility, serving both individual and group needs, rather than their role in personal development. All of these have to be distinguished from the moralist proper who wants, more concretely, some account of the things that are moral and immoral, and why. And underlying all these concerns is the prior theoretical question of whether and how far they can ultimately be separated: of whether some presuppose others, and if so which.

These differences of approach will also be reflected in the answers provided. When the philosophically-minded confront the question 'What is morality?' they naturally seek an answer which sets a definitive limit to what is to count as moral: this attempt to circumscribe the moral domain is evidenced, for example, in the approaches of Vine (Chapter 2), Thornton and Thornton (Chapter 4), and Locke (Chapter 6), though while all agree on the need to keep this definition neutral as between competing moral viewpoints, the conclusions they draw as regards the possible contents for different moralities are very different. But from a developmental point of view Weinreich-Haste (Chapter 5) argues that narrowly philosophical criteria of morality disguise the psychological processes involved, inasmuch as the empirical phenomena demarcated by the philosophical definition in fact overlap with other aspects of social and interpersonal development. And from a social-psychological perspective Breakwell (Chapter 13) tacitly assumes a more functional and relativistic position, where the key isue is not what moral judgments are, but what they do.

Similarly, when we confront the issue of thought and action, there is for philosophers like Straughan (Chapter 7) and Locke (Chapter 9) a clear conceptual distinction between judgment and behaviour: what people think they should do is not necessarily what they do do. The problem, accordingly, is to explain how and why the two connect in practice, which is one aspect of the traditional philosophical problem of *akrasia* or weakness of will, the failure to translate moral principle into action. But for psychologists like Wright (Chapter 8) and Emler (Chapter 11), in very different ways, the problem runs in the opposite direction, not from moral thought to action, but from action to moral thought or moral character generally. In re-assessing Piaget, Wright is concerned with the developmental issue of how action gives rise to thought; underlying Emler's discussion is the broader methodological issue of how far overt behaviour can justify the ascription to the individual of specifically moral characteristics, be they personality traits or levels of moral judgment, which might then enable us to classify, and perhaps even explain, the behaviour in question. The problem of bringing these different approaches to grips with one another is in part theoretical, in part empirical. First, tentative, steps in this direction are taken by Locke (Chapter 9) and Kutnick (Chapter 10).

With these differences of background and concern to separate us, we have not pretended to provide any comprehensive or consistent solution to the problems which unite us. Each chapter is an independent contribution to its particular topic, though informed by discussion of, and disagreement with, the contributions of others. The psychologist, forced outside his technical terminology by the incomprehension of the philosopher, may find it difficult to view that terminology, and the theories it encapsulates, in the same light again; the philosopher, asked to relate his abstractions to the facts of human development, may find the received truths of moral philosophy less easy to receive. By raising traditional issues in this interdisciplinary context, we hope not merely to suggest new answers, but to raise new questions.

HELEN WEINREICH-HASTE
DON LOCKE

SECTION I

Moral Thinking—The Cognitive-Developmental Approach

Psychological accounts of morality will vary according to the theoretical model and methodological preferences of the particular psychologist. The psychologist whose preference is for strictly observable behaviour and contingencies will concentrate on what can be seen as the antecedent and consequent conditions of specific behaviours. The psychologist who is interested in consistency of behaviour will explore enduring personality traits or repeated patterns of behaviour and response. The psychologist who is concerned with the effects of social, rather than individual, factors in morality and deviance will experiment with or observe naturalistically the effects of group influence upon behaviour. The psychologist who is concerned with the understanding of rules and norms will explore the reasoning of the individual.

For many, though not all, of the contributors to this volume an interest in the psychology of morals focuses in particular on cognitive-developmental moral theory, as exemplified in the work of Jean Piaget and, especially, Lawrence Kohlberg. This is for two related reasons. The first is that both Piaget and Kohlberg are explicit that the questions they raise are philosophical as well as psychological and educational. As Kohlberg has put it himself, he is interested in the child as a developing moral philosopher. But also, more fundamentally, their approach sees moral thinking as primary, in that moral behaviour cannot be studied, or even identified, in isolation from moral thought. Behaviour is moral or immoral not just because society or the experimenter classify it as such; we have also to take account of what the agent thinks of himself as doing, and why.

Accordingly the first section of this collection is devoted to cognitive-developmental moral theory, both exegesis and criticism. In his classic paper 'From Is to Ought: or how to commit the Naturalistic Fallacy and get away with it', Kohlberg uses philosophical criteria of morality and moral judgment to interpret the empirical data, then draws from those data conclusions about both

1

the philosophical and the psychological adequacy of certain forms of moral thinking. The developmental progression, he argues, validates both the philosophical definition and the psychological theory, as well as justifying a particular moral position. Predictably, therefore, Kohlberg has suffered the wrath of both parties: the psychologists criticize his measures and his methodology, the philosophers criticize his arguments and assumptions. But these criticisms, including those in this volume, cannot obscure the immense importance of his recognition that his chosen subject matter not merely benefits from, but positively demands, the interaction of psychology and philosophy.

Some understanding of cognitive-developmental moral theory is therefore necessary for several of the discussions that follow. In the opening chapter Helen Weinreich-Haste provides an outline introduction to Kohlberg's position, the research findings which support it, and the problems which it generates.

The following chapter, by Ian Vine, is primarily concerned with a much broader and more fundamental issue, the nature and definition of morality itself. Vine offers an account which while allowing for some variability between different moralities, nevertheless ties morality to a particular sort of content which, he argues, follows necessarily from its social and biological function. But this definition also has implications for a theory such as Kohlberg's. Philosophers have traditionally distinguished two levels of moral assertion and opinion, the ethical and the meta-ethical. There is first the level of substantive morality, of particular opinions about what is right or wrong, what ought or ought not be done, and why. But there are also questions about the nature of morality and moral judgments, the objectivity or relativity of moral values, the relevance of reason and emotion to moral belief and moral truth. The latter, it is often suggested, are the proper subject matter of philosophical ethics. Substantive moral opinions belong to the rhetoric of everyday life, where the philosopher, as such, has no special authority or expertise. But, unsurprisingly, separation between the two proves difficult to achieve in practice, and may not be desirable in principle. Nevertheless the psychological study of morality can be affected by philosophical as well as moral assumptions, by taking as given the dominant values of the society under investigation, for example, or assuming that moral values can have no status outside of the particular society in which they are adopted. It is at this meta-ethical level that Vine criticizes Kohlberg, arguing that his theory stems not so much from a particular moral viewpoint as from a more philosophical misconception about the nature of morality and the status of moral value.

In the chapter which follows, however, Nicholas Emler carries these criticisms further, down to the level of substantive ethics, in an investigation of the pervasive ideology which underlies Kohlberg's theory in particular, and much North American social science in general. Interestingly, the individualism and rationalism which Emler identifies as key elements in this ideology, are also sources of the philosophical position criticised by Vine, suggesting, once again, that the two levels, the ethical and the meta-ethical, interact. But Emler's essay is not merely an exercise in bias hunting. The implication, both of his argument and of the empirical evidence which he assesses, is that in attempting to abstract from the content of particular moral judgments, Kohlberg may have succeeded only in replacing moral content with a content which is more broadly ideological, even political. The suggestion that so-called moral development is only an aspect, or a symptom, of some more broadly-based form of cognitive development is taken up again in Chapter 5.

Faced with such criticisms as these, cognitive-developmental moral theory can proceed in either of two ways. The first is to meet the criticisms from within, by modifying or reconstructing Kohlberg's theory so as to justify or avoid the disputed philosophical or ideological claims. This is the approach adopted by David and Stephanie Thornton in Chapter 4. They begin by offering a detailed defence, against Emler's criticisms in particular, of the empirical claims on which the cognitive-developmental theory is founded. They argue that the evidence is that changes in cognitive operations are associated with the different stages in the development of moral reasoning. What is disputable, they suggest, is Kohlberg's interpretation and explanation of these facts. Accordingly they offer an interpretation of morality and moral development in terms of the recognition of collective interests, an interpretation which is both more restricted than Kohlberg's, avoiding the accusation of moral or ideological partisanship, and also closer to that proposed by Vine in Chapter 2. It remains, nonetheless, a more rationalistic conception of morality than Vine's, if less individualistic than Kohlberg's: the emphasis is on understanding *collective* interests rather than the individual interests of others; but it is also on *understanding* those interests rather than, as with Vine, enabling practical solutions to particular conflicts of interest.

A second, more radical, approach is to meet the criticisms of Kohlberg's own theory by attempting to set his empirical discoveries within a wider, and consequently rather different, context. This is the strategy adopted by Helen Weinreich-Haste in the chapter which concludes this first section. She argues that an obsession with philosophical criteria of morality and distinctively moral judgment has obscured the psychological reality, that moral development is rather to be construed in terms of the development of more general social cognition. Moreover, this emphasis on 'the moral' has disguised the nature of the psychological processes involved, and the evidence provided by the empirical studies. In particular, setting moral development within the wider context of social cognition obliges us to reassess the developmental process, as less static and stage-structural than orthodox Kohlbergian theory maintains, and more open-ended and dialectical in nature.

The question raised here is fundamental for the psychology of morals. Is there any reason to suppose that the philosophical distinction between the moral and the non-moral marks a significant psychological difference? Is there a distinctive form of behaviour, separable from other behaviours, which can be labelled 'moral behaviour'? Is there a distinctive form of cognition, moral cognition, following its own distinctive development through its own distinctive stages, separate from political, religious, or social cognition generally? Or does the philosophical distinction merely mark a difference in the content of judgment and reasoning, making no essential difference to how those judgments and reasonings are to be explained? Nevertheless in the preceding chapter David and Stephanie Thornton concentrated on the development of moral understanding in the sense of a developing understanding of the nature of morality, and in particular the ability to distinguish the moral from the non-moral. And this, it might be argued, does presuppose the philosophical distinction. Indeed it might be held to be precisely the development of some such philosophical understanding: they are concerned, in effect, with the individual's development of a theory of morality, what Kohlberg has called the child as moral philosopher. Perhaps there is a difference here between a developing understanding and recognition of those factors which are moral, which may be part of some wider form of cognitive development, and a developing understanding and recognition of the fact that they are specifically moral considerations, which involves a distinctively moral understanding. Some of these questions will be taken up again in the chapter which opens Section II.

Morality in the Making
Edited by H. Weinreich-Haste and D. Locke
© 1983, John Wiley & Sons, Ltd.

CHAPTER 1

Kohlberg's Theory of Moral Development

HELEN WEINREICH-HASTE

There are several ways of asking the question, 'How do people become moral?' It depends both on how 'moral' is defined, and on how one approaches development or 'becoming'. Psychologists on the whole have been reluctant to address the first issue; the divisions between them, therefore, have mainly arisen from different paradigms of development. The 'moral' has tended to be equated with that which is socially accepted, behaviour which conforms to the requirements of good habits, control of impulse, and the acquisition of appropriate values. The emphasis of such an approach is on the cumulative learning process by which cultural values are transmitted to the child, and on the mechanisms of conditioning which promote the development of guilt anxiety.

In contrast, the cognitive-developmental approach assumes that the individual develops through active cognitive interaction with the physical and social world, and that what is manifested in the expression of morality is the way in which the individual has made sense of the moral world. The emphasis is less on moral actions, and more on moral intentions and on ethical understanding. Within this model, there is much more scope for an explicit definition of 'the moral', and Kohlberg's theory of moral development is both a highly developed theory of developmental processes, and a theory about morality. It is in fact Kohlberg's contention that the two are integrally related to each other, and that this approach creates a bridge between philosophical and psychological issues in morality (Kohlberg, 1971).

In many ways, Kohlberg's work is an extension and elaboration of Piaget's study of moral development in young children (Piaget, 1932). However, there are some important differences. Piaget addressed the question of how the individual, who perforce must initially acquire his or her knowledge of moral rules through an authority relationship, comes to be able to make autonomous moral decisions and to base understanding of morality not on a unilateral respect for authority, but on mutual respect between persons. Piaget's study mapped the transition from a heteronomous morality to an autonomous morality, and demonstrated the cognitive shifts which occur as the child comes to a more complex appreciation of the function of rules, the nature of justice and the importance of intention. But while Piaget's main preoccupation in his monograph was with the social processes which facilitate that transition, his successors have tended to focus on limited aspects of his original studies, and especially on the *cognitive* aspects of his work on morality. In fact Piaget did not make the same claims about 'stages' of moral reasoning that he developed in the logical domain; it is through subsequent replications that a more cognitive-developmental framework has been applied to his work on morality (Lickona, 1969; Weinreich-Haste, 1982). Piaget's theoretical and empirical work on moral development is discussed by Wright, in Chapter 8, and by Kutnick, in Chapter 10.

The Six Stages of Moral Reasoning

Some twenty-five years after the publication of Piaget's monograph, Kohlberg undertook a study of the moral reasoning of adolescent boys aged ten to fifteen, fifty-eight of whom have now been followed longitudinally, being tested every three years until 1976. In contrast to Piaget, Kohlberg's interest has been almost entirely in the development of moral reasoning, the changes and transformations which occur over time in how the adolescent understands, interprets, and integrates moral and legal rules, rights, and obligations, and most particularly, the nature of justice. Kohlberg's method, again in contrast to Piaget, is to present moral dilemmas involving classic confrontations between legal and moral obligations, authority and contract, and private and public responsibilities. The dilemmas are followed by a series of questions designed to elicit the individual's moral thinking on a wide range of issues, practical and theoretical. The most widely-quoted dilemma is given in Figure 1. Probe questions for this dilemma will explore such issues as duty and rights, obedience to the law and punishment for law-breaking, and so on.

On the basis of these investigations Kohlberg (1958, 1969, 1976) has discovered a developmental sequence of moral reasoning, consisting of six stages

---

In a country in Europe, where there was no free Health Service, a woman was near death from a special kind of cancer. But there was one medicine which the doctor thought might save her. It was a kind of radium medicine which was being developed by a chemist in a nearby town. The medicine was expensive to make, but the chemist was charging ten times what it had cost him. He paid £100 for the ingredients, and he was charging £1000 for a small dose of the medicine. The sick woman's husband, Heinz, went to everyone he knew to try to borrow the money, but he could only raise £500, half of what it cost. So he went to the chemist and asked him to let him have it cheaper, or let him pay later, but the chemist said, 'No, I discovered the medicine, and I'm going to make money from it.' So Heinz got desperate and thought of breaking into the man's laboratory to steal the medicine for his wife.

FIGURE 1   The story of Heinz (British version)

which are held to have the same characteristics as Piaget's stages of logical-cognitive development. That is, the stages are invariant, occurring in all individuals in the same order and with no stages omitted, though individuals may vary in the rate at which they develop from one stage to another, and not all will reach the same final stage; the stages are held to be culturally universal and independent of the social context, though societies may vary in the extent to which they facilitate moral development, or enable the higher stages to be attained; and the stages are held to be qualitatively, not merely quantitatively, different, involving changes of *kind* and not merely of *degree* in the subject's moral understanding and ability to resolve moral problems. Thus the six stages form a developmental hierarchy of increasing integration and differentiation, in which each stage integrates and transforms the preceding stages.

Let us consider the stages of moral reasoning as laid out in Figure 2. Even on a prima facie basis, they clearly represent a progression from simplicity to ethical and conceptual complexity. The first level reflects reasoning based on extrinsic considerations such as reward and punishment, and an unreflective acceptance of rules, codes, and labels. Even though the individual may argue that the law can be broken in a particular case, the law itself is never questioned. An example of Stage 1 reasoning about Heinz could be that if Heinz stole, he would be a thief—a simple labelling of deviancy. Alternatively, the Stage 1 thinker might argue that he should steal for such irrelevant and extrinsic reasons that his wife might be a rich person with lots of possessions. At Stage 1, there is no real recognition of any conflict; only one aspect of the situation is oriented to, whether this is the rule or some essentially irrelevant aspect of the person such as their wealth.

With the development of stage 2, there comes a recognition of the possibility of conflict between the rules and individual needs. The resolution is couched in terms of instrumental outcomes—if Heinz steals he will probably be caught and they will all be worse off; if he does not steal, his wife will die and be lost to him, so he should steal and hope to get away with it.

There is a shift between pre-conventional and conventional reasoning in how rules are understood. At the conventional level, the individual understands the function and origin of rules as social utilities, but there are many kinds of rules, and much of Level II thought is engaged in assessing the conflicting demands of laws, moral rules, and natural justice. Stage 3 reasoning on the Heinz dilemma reflects a conflict between normative role expectations—a *good husband* would act to save his wife is possible; and legal constraints—a *good citizen* obeys and upholds the law. With Stage 4 comes a significant change in the understanding of *society* as an abstraction: if Heinz steals, his action and its consequences may set a precedent which could undermine the legal system and affect the wider society, not simply the group of individuals directly involved. If the Stage 4 thinker advocates that Heinz should steal, it is because marriage as an institution places obligations on the partners for mutual support, irrespective of the feelings they have, or alternatively, because there is a moral *rule* to preserve life which is of greater importance than the legal constraint against stealing.

Level I   *Pre-conventional*
Stage 1   Heteronomous Morality

> Orientation to punishment and obedience for its own sake. Avoidance of damage to persons and property. Focus on extrinsic characteristics (e.g. physical damage, status, wealth) rather than on psychological or intrinsic motivation, such as intention.

Stage 2   Individualism, Instrumental purpose, Exchange

> Focus on immediate personal interests of self and others. Pragmatic resolution of conflicts between needs and rules. Orientation to 'fairness', equal exchange, deals.

Level II   *Conventional*
Stage 3   Mutual Interpersonal Expectations, Relationships and Interpersonal Conformity.
> Living up to role expectations of 'husband', 'wife', 'daughter', 'citizen', etc. Being good, virtuous, having good traits are important. Caring for others and keeping mutual relationships. Awareness of shared feelings, seeing other's point of view.

Stage 4   Social System and Conscience

> Fulfilling contractual duties. Laws to be upheld except in extreme cases where they conflict with other fixed social duties. Public, social function of laws and contracts understood; general orientation to maintaining social system.

Level III   *Post-Conventional, Principled*
Stage 5   Social Contracts or Utility and Individual Rights

> Awareness of relative nature of values and options. Rules to be upheld because they are part of agreed social contract. Individual freely and democratically enters social contract; if laws or rules do not serve democratic or social utility ends, should be changed by democratic process. Some principles, e.g. life, liberty, seen as absolute.

Stage 6   Universal Ethical Principles

> Following self-chosen ethical principles; if laws conflict with principle, principle overrides laws. Moral should dictate legal, not vice versa. Principles are universal principles of justice; equality and respect for the human dignity of the individual. Sense of personal commitment to these principles. Perspective that any rational person would recognize the universality of these principles.

FIGURE 2   Stages of moral reasoning

Post-conventional reasoning marks a shift to a more relativistic understanding: the individual can recognize that rules vary across different societies, and can see the functions that rules serve, irrespective of their form. Broad moral principles, rather than culturally-derived rules, are the criteria by which the legal rule should be legitimized. Where there is conflict between the legal and the moral, the moral should almost always take precedence, because the law should serve the moral principle. Legal rules are supported on the principle that, on the whole, they represent the greatest good for the greatest number, and they are, generally, the product of democratic social contract. Bad laws should be changed, not just defied, though it is also recognized that public defiance of a law may call attention to its inadequacies. If it is argued that Heinz should steal, it is because the right to life must always transcend the right to property. If it is argued that Heinz should not steal, the justification is that maintaining the social contract is of greater benefit to society, and therefore more important, than specific individual cases. It is relatively rare that a post-conventional thinker does argue against Heinz stealing; the social contract argument is generally presented as a caveat, a matter of general principle, rather than as an objection to Heinz's action.

Developments in Kohlberg's Model

The empirical validation of these stages has taken several forms. They were originally derived from the reasoning of Kohlberg's original Chicago sample of adolescent boys, and the distribution of stages in this study can be seen in Figure 3. It is apparent that post-conventional reasoning is rare, and that Stage 6

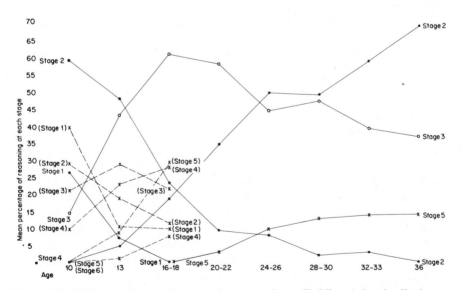

FIGURE 3   Mean moral reasoning at each stage and age: Kohlberg's longitudinal sample.
— 'standard form' (revised) scoring method—cross-sectional and longitudinal data 1957–1976.
.... 'sentence rating' (original) scoring method—1957 sample: cross-sectional data only
Reproduced from material reported in Colby, Kohlberg, Gibbs, and Lieberman (1983)

hardly exists. Stage 6 reasoning has always been essentially a *telos*, a goal or ideal, the hypothetical ultimate expression of justice-based moral reasoning. Reformulations of the coding method have taken place partly as a consequence of the increase of data accruing from the follow-ups of the longitudinal sample, and partly from the increasing rigour of the analytical techniques.

In the initial study, the coding took two forms, an overall 'global' measure in which each story was assigned a single stage score, and a breakdown of the interview into sentences each of which was assigned a stage score. The latter method produced more precise coding, but also of course a greater variation in scores. Thus an individual would have most of his scores in one stage, but with appreciable scatter across adjoining stages (Kohlberg, 1958; Weinreich-Haste, 1977). Subsequent revisions of the coding method have led to more homogeneity of scoring. Partly this is through the use of a larger unit of analysis, mostly it is due to the shift towards the scoring of *structure* rather than *content* (Colby, 1978; Colby *et al.*, 1983). Structural scoring takes into account the underlying assumptions the individual holds about the social system and the function of rules, roles, and rights. For example, the statement 'if there were no laws there'd be chaos' might reflect a simple vision of Armageddon: the existence of law defines order, and the absence of law defines anarchy, a topsy-turvy world. Alternatively, the individual might be taking a more differentiated view in which he or she understands the function of the judiciary and legislature, and appreciates the ways in which the law does impose social order. Another example of a similarly rhetorical statement whose interpretation depends upon context, is 'saving lives is the most important thing.' This may be nothing but the expression of a normative platitude, or it may be a fundamental principle whose implications for other principles, and for moral and legal rules, has been fully considered.

These modifications in scoring have been designed to move away from manifest expressed opinion, and towards underlying structure. The revisions have considerably improved reliability of scoring, and have also reduced the variation of scores within individuals. The effect of the revisions on the overall pattern of results, however, has been slightly to depress the scores. In particular, this is true at the higher stages; there are no Stage 6 subjects in the longitudinal sample, and the few who do operate substantially with Stage 5 reasoning have a considerable amount of Stage 4 mixed with it (Colby 1978; Colby *et al.*, 1983). At the other end of the scale, however, greater attention to structure has altered the scoring of some adults' reasoning. As the longitudinal sample grew up and went to college, where they were exposed to alternative perspectives, several individuals experienced what might best be described as an acute attack of relativism. Their reasoning, as coded by manifest content, appeared to regress from Stage 4 to Stage 2, which created problems for the supposed irreversibility of the sequence (Kohlberg and Kramer, 1969).

Careful scrutiny of this reasoning, however, indicated that although the subjects expressed extreme pragmatism, and apparently were wholly instrumental in their conclusions, the arguments they presented depended upon a sophisticated and complex understanding of the social system, quite different from the simple instrumental view of the world which younger Stage 2 subjects demonstrated. These subjects came to be regarded as 'Stage 4½', as intermediate between Stage 4 legalism and the integrated, utilitarian, relativism of Stage 5. These events were an important impetus to revision of the coding methods.

One implication of this however is that some early research evidence, for example that derived from studies of the relationship between moral reasoning and political action, may have coded as 'Stage 2' reasoning which should more properly be seen as '4½' (4/5 in present coding forms). Although this would not substantially alter the interpretation of the correlations between moral reasoning and political action, the conclusions which could be drawn about the distribution of moral stages among adults may need to be revised (Broughton, 1978). Overall, the material now available on adult moral reasoning suggests that most adults operate with Stage 3 or Stage 4 reasoning, while post-conventional reasoning is quite rare. This obviously has a number of implications: one is that the lack of data at this level makes it somewhat difficult to study in detail, and inevitably some of the conclusions about the parameters of post-conventional reasoning must be tentative. Thornton and Thornton (Chapter 4) and Emler (Chapter 3) consider some of these issues in detail. The evidence of behavioural correlates of post-conventional reasoning, which I shall consider shortly, indicates that something of importance is happening, but the full understanding of the nature of post-conventional reasoning perhaps must wait upon more data. Another implication concerns Stage 6: it is still regarded as the apotheosis of moral development, the final form of justice reasoning, but it remains an abstraction. It is Stage 6 which has attracted most of the philosophers' criticisms, and the criticism of psychologists who object to Kohlberg's definition of what constitutes 'morality' (Locke, 1980; Puka, 1976; Peters, 1971, 1978). The lack of an empirical base to anchor these issues has led to a number of confusions about whether these criticisms fundamentally undermine the *developmental* theory, or whether they are a commentary upon simply one aspect of it. I shall return to this later in the chapter (see also Weinreich-Haste, Chapter 5).

The Correlates of Moral Reasoning

There have now been a large number of correlational studies, which have addressed two questions: what are the processes involved in the development of moral reasoning, and what does stage of moral reasoning predict? Research on the processes of moral development has tested the extent to which the model fulfils the requirements that the stage sequence is hierarchical, irreversible, and that each stage integrates the previous one. Ultimately, the longitudinal data answered most of these questions, but there were a number of studies by Kohlberg's students, notably Rest, Turiel, and Blatt, which experimentally tested aspects of the model. Rest and Turiel found that people preferred the stage with marginally greater complexity than their current mode of thought, and they reinterpreted material of higher stages in the terms of their current stage. Blatt (and subsequently others) found that exposing the individual to discussion with others of a stage higher than themselves, and promoting 'socratic interaction', produced movement upwards over a period of time (Turiel, 1966; Rest et al., 1969; Blatt and Kohlberg, 1975). These studies were important contributions to the understanding of development; they also had practical spin-offs for the development of intervention programmes in moral education (Mosher, 1980).

Stages of moral development may be adequately validated by such studies, and their cognitive-developmental status established, but moral reasoning does not exist in isolation. Firstly, it seems to depend on the development of logical operations. Several studies have indicated that the development of Stage 4 moral reasoning requires formal operations (Kuhn et al., 1977; Colby, 1984), and that the development of Stage 2 reasoning requires concrete operations (Smith, 1978).

It is not surprising that logical operations should be a necessary but not sufficient condition for the development of moral reasoning; there is a strong cognitive element involved in Kohlberg's theory, in particular in the changing comprehension of 'society' and 'law'. Kohlberg has argued that the translation of logical operations into moral operations requires another intervening step, role-taking. 'Role-taking' is a difficult concept—in particular there is frequent confusion between 'I feel what you feel' and 'I can put myself in your position and see things as you do'—and different approaches to moral development have focused on different meanings of the term (Lickona, 1976). Selman has resolved both the conceptual and the empirical problems by studying *social perspective-taking*, the capacity to take the perspective of the other (the second of the above definitions), and in a series of studies he and Walker have established that stages of social perspective-taking are a necessary but not sufficient condition for the development of the parallel stages of moral reasoning (Selman, 1980; Walker, 1980).

To some extent the research on the behavioural correlates of moral reasoning extends the theory of moral judgment development; to some extent it is a concession to the commonsense argument that moral judgment must be validated by moral action. Other chapters in this book (especially Section II) address this question in detail. There have been several studies of the relationship between moral reasoning and both pro- and anti-social behaviour, and also between moral reasoning and political behaviour. To summarize this material, it appears that there is not a good correlation between moral reasoning and anti-social behaviour (though see Emler, Chapter 3, for discussion of this issue). There have been several studies however that indicate that delinquency and crime (as measured amongst convicted populations) is associated with lower stages of moral reasoning (Blasi, 1980; Rest, 1979); and Thornton (1977) has found that the type of crime for which the person has been convicted relates to moral stage ⌊offences committed without regard to possible negative consequences to the self being associated with more advanced moral reasoning.⌋

The evidence for a relationship between moral reasoning and pro-social behaviour is stronger. Studies of promise-keeping indicate that higher-stage reasoners—particularly post-conventional reasoners—are more likely to keep promises (Rest, 1979). In studies of bystander intervention (helping others when doing so requires counter-normative behaviour, or resistance to authority pressure) it is the post-conventional reasoners who respond and act on behalf of the distressed (McNamee, 1977; Milgram, 1965). Studies of student protest behaviour show that to some degree moral stage predicts political action. This is partly context-specific however: where there was a definite moral issue at stake, as in the Berkeley Free Speech Movement in 1964, post-conventional thinkers aligned themselves actively with the protest position; when the issue was less clearly a moral one, it was more likely to be the 'Stage 2' anti-authority subjects who were actively involved (though in the revised scoring system, many of these people are now reclassified as Stage 4½, or 4/5, which effectively places them on the transition point to post-conventional moral reasoning (Kohlberg and Candee, 1981)) (Haan et al., 1968; Fishkin et al., 1973; Rothman and Lichter, 1978).

The body of research represented by the examples above clearly validates some predictive relationship between moral reason and moral action (see Chapter 7). It also demonstrates a relationship between reasoning on moral issues, and reasoning on social and political issues. Some of the implications of this are discussed further in Chapter 5.

Educational Implications

Over the last decade interest has shifted somewhat away from the correlates of the theory and towards practical applications. The most obvious application, apart from contributing to the explanation of social and political behaviour and attitudes, is in moral education. The work of Blatt and others has suggested that moral development can be stimulated through classroom discussion of moral dilemmas, and especially by exposure to conflicting moral opinions, which introduces disequilibrium into the current way of thinking, and so hasten the move to a higher stage (Blatt and Kohlberg, 1975; Rest, 1973; Turiel, 1966). Clearly this approach can be used across a wide range of curriculum subjects— history, social studies, English—and not only in the discussion of specific moral and social issues. Mosher (1980) has collected material on a number of such intervention methods.

A further development arose from Kohlberg's findings that institutions have an implicit stage of functioning. In other words, the norms of an institution, the way in which authority relationships and peer interaction operate, themselves reflect assumptions about the maintenance of order and the nature of rules and rights, and these assumptions are enacted and responded to by all members of that institution. Kohlberg therefore began to experiment in prisons and, most particularly, in schools, with a 'just community' approach, in which participatory democracy is practised, and in which the members are actively involved in reflecting upon their moral and rule-making decisions (Mosher, 1980; Wasserman, 1976, 1980). These 'just communities' operate as units within the larger institution; pupils who became part of the 'school-within-a-school' take a proportion of their curriculum in this setting, and the rest in the normal school context.

There is of course nothing very novel about participatory democracy in progressive educational (or even correctional) institutions, and indeed part of Kohlberg's approach derives from work on moral atmosphere and moral reasoning in the kibbutzim (Reimer and Power, 1980). The novelty lies in the explicit commentary upon moral processes. As others have found, this kind of participatory democracy in the classroom is demanding on the resources of all its members. However, demonstrably both the just community and the socratic discussion methods in the classroom produce results. On average, the pupils in these programmes progress one stage in about two and a half years, which is better than occurs among 'control' subjects.

The Defining Issues Test

The extensive use of the moral judgment development measure in correlative studies, and as an evaluation measure in intervention programmes, has led to some modifications of method. Clearly, presenting nine dilemmas in a clinical interview setting is time-consuming to administer and to code. Kohlberg and his associates have therefore developed three parallel forms of the measure, Forms A, B, and C, each of which uses a different three dilemmas to address essentially the same moral issues. Many issues have used this format in written form, rather than interviews. This method produces codeable material, but inevitably of less range and depth than an oral interview. The great difficulty of streamlining the method, either for convenience of coding or for the more dubious goal of conforming to conventional psychometric demands, is that it is quite inconsistent with a constructivist model to use any method which relies upon recognition or upon evaluative opinion. If one is analysing the way the individual constructs meaning and makes sense of the moral and social world, one must elicit that construction from the individual. Attitude measures will reflect what he or she agrees with, not how he or she understands. One possible solution is to offer multiple choice versions of the same opinion expressed at different stages of reasoning; the possibility however is that the individual will prefer higher stage thought to his or her present stage (as Rest's and Turiel's studies demonstrated) or even that the impressive-sounding language which is inevitably associated with the post-conventional stages will give weight to these statements even if they are only partially understood.

Rest has attempted to overcome these obstacles and has developed a multiple-choice questionnaire measure by which he taps what the individual perceives to be the *defining issues* in the moral dilemma, a method which focuses on a central concept rather than upon agreement or disagreement. In the Defining Issues Test (the DIT) the individual is asked to rate how important a number of considerations should be in deciding what the right course of action is. The DIT has now been widely used, particularly with large samples. It proves to be a reasonably valid measure of moral judgment maturity, in the sense that it appears to be measuring much the same thing as Kohlberg's method. But it does not provide a satisfactory basis for typing subjects by stages, and it is also overwhelmingly the case that people score higher on the DIT than on Kohlberg's measure, which suggests that it is impossible to overcome completely the problem of preference for more abstract or complex forms of words. It therefore is a valuable measure where comparisons of *samples* are being made, but it may be of less use as a measure of individuals (Rest, 1979).

Criticisms

There have been several criticisms of Kohlberg's theory, many of which will be examined or elaborated in the next four chapters. These criticisms can be divided into basically three types: those directed mainly at the cognitive developmental model, and tending to focus on methodology; those which accept the cognitive-developmental paradigm, but object to the way Kohlberg defines 'morality', and those which reject the whole exercise, usually on the basis that moral development research should attend to other factors than reasoning. Obviously there is considerable overlap amongst these areas of criticism.

One of the major methodological critiques has been by Kurtines and Greif (1974) who argued that some of the early studies were inadequate tests of hierarchy and irreversibility, and concluded that Kohlberg's case was not proven. But although they have some basis for their critical conclusions, their review is substantially diminished in value because it largely misses the point of what a developmental theory is about, and they oriented to the theoretical model as though it were a psychometric approach to individual differences (Broughton, 1978).

Critics who accept the cognitive-developmental model as an account of the developmental process have nevertheless been sceptical about the way Kohlberg defines and interprets the moral domain. Many of these criticisms have focused on the way that Kohlberg's definition of justice as the core of morality may be a Western bourgeois preoccupation, and that attempts to claim its universality may be a potentially pernicious form of cultural bias (Simpson, 1974; Sullivan, 1977). In Chapter 4 Emler considers the ways in which Kohlberg's theory is vulnerable to the biases of individualism, rationalism, and liberalism. Another, related, criticism arises from Kohlberg's specifically articulated argument that the evidence or moral judgment *development* is a confirmation of the *moral adequacy* of Stage 6 (Kohlberg, 1971, 1973; Locke, 1979). In Chapter 2 Vine explores the argument that this position makes Kohlberg into an ethical realist, in contradiction to the constructivist or moderate constructivist position which is traditionally the essence of cognitive-developmental theory. A third line of argument which also tries to disentangle Kohlberg's theory of development from his theory of morality is provided by Thornton and Thornton in Chapter 3 and by Weinreich-Haste in chapter 5, both of which suggest alternative interpretations of what Kohlberg is actually measuring.

Critics from outside the paradigm have tended to focus on Kohlberg's theory of morality, though they extend this criticism to the whole exercise of dealing with moral development in terms of moral reasoning. Both psychologists and philosophers of various theoretical persuasions have attacked Kohlberg for ignoring affect, and for paying inadequate attention to social and cultural factors both in the developmental process and in the criteria which culturally define the moral domain. Broadly speaking, psychologists have concentrated on the developmental processes and on socialization, and philosophers on the limitations of the moral theory as expressed in its hypothetical complete form, Stage 6 (Alston, 1971; Lickona, 1976; Peters, 1971; Trainer, 1977).

So far Kohlberg's theory has withstood its critics by virtue of the strength of the empirical support for at least the first four stages of the developmental sequence. The correlates of moral reasoning indicate that it is not a phenomenon which is isolated and irrelevant to other issues, though the exact nature of the determining or cotermining relationships needs considerable attention. Currently, Kohlberg and his associates are looking at whether *responsibility*—the extent to which the individual feels him or herself personally responsible for enacting the analytical conclusions of moral reasoning—is the significant intervening variable between reason and action. Other research is widening the definition of the moral; in particular, Gilligan has found that women tend to think about the moral dilemmas in a different way, focusing more on relationships and interpersonal responsibility and less on rights and rules (Gilligan, 1977, 1982).

However, the criticisms expressed in this volume and elsewhere underline the present limitations of both the theory and the database, while at the same time recognizing the great importance of the theory in changing and expanding the way in which psychologists and philosophers have come to look at what it means to 'become moral'.

References

Alston, W. P. (1971). Comments on Kohlberg's 'From Is to Ought'. In T. Mischel (Ed.), *Cognitive Development and Epistemology*, Academic Press, London.
Blasi, A. (1980). Bridging moral cognition and moral action; a critical review of the literature. *Psychological Bulletin*, **88**, 1–45.

Blatt, M., and Kohlberg, L. (1975). Effects of classroom moral discussion upon children's levels of moral judgement. *J. Moral Education*, **4**, 129–62.

Broughton, J. (1978). The cognitive developmental approach to morality. *J. Moral Education*, **7**, 81–96.

Colby, A. (1978). Evaluation of moral developmental theory. In W. Damon (Ed.), *New Directions in Child Development* (I): *Moral Development*, Jossey Bass, San Francisco.

Colby, A., Kohlberg, L., Gibbs, J., and Lieberman, M. (1983, in press). A longitudinal study of moral judgement. *SRCD Monographs*.

Colby, A. (1984, in preparation). The relationship between moral and cognitive development. In L. Kohlberg, D. Candee, and A. Colby (Eds), *Research in Moral Development*, Harvard University Press, Cambridge, Mass.

Colby, A., Kohlberg, L., Gibbs, J., Speicher-Dubin, B., Candee, D., Hewer, A., and Power, C. (1983, in preparation). *The Measurement of Moral Judgement; Standard Issue Scoring Manual*. Cambridge University Press, New York.

Fishkin, J., Keniston, K., and Mackinnon, C. (1973). Moral reasoning and political ideology. *J. Personality & Social Psychology*, **27**, 109–119.

Gilligan, C. (1977). In a different voice; women's conception of the self and morality. *Harvard Educational Review*, **47**, 43–61.

Gilligan, C. (1982). *In a Different Voice*, Harvard University Press, Cambridge, Mass.

Haan, N., Smith, M. B., and Block, J. (1968). Moral reasoning of young adults. *J. Personality and Social Psychology*, **10**, 183–201.

Kohlberg, L. (1958). The development of modes of moral thinking and choice in the years ten to sixteen. Unpublished Ph.D. thesis, University of Chicago.

Kohlberg, L. (1969). Stage and sequence; the cognitive-developmental approach to socialisation. In D. A. Goslin (Ed.), *Handbook of Socialisation Theory and Research*, Rand McNally, Chicago.

Kohlberg, L. (1971). From is to ought; how to commit the naturalistic fallacy and get away with it in the study of moral development. In T. Mischel (Ed.), *Cognitive Development and Epistemology*, Academic Press, New York.

Kohlberg, L. (1973). The claim to moral adequacy of a highest stage of moral judgement. *J. Philosophy*, **70**, 630–46.

Kohlberg, L. (1976). Moral stages and moralisation; the cognitive-developmental approach. In T. Lickona (Ed.), *Moral Development and Behaviour*, Holt, New York.

Kohlberg, L., and Kramer, R. B. (1969). Continuities and discontinuities in childhood and adult moral development. *Human Development*, **12**, 93–120.

Kuhn, D., Langer, J., Kohlberg, L., and Haan, N. (1977). The development of formal operations in logical and moral judgement. *Genetic Psychology Monographs*, **95**, 97–186.

Kurtines, W., and Greif, E. B. (1974). The development of moral thought; review and evaluation of Kohlberg's approach. *Psychological Bulletin*, **81**, 453–70.

Lickona, T. (1969). Piaget misunderstood; a critique of the criticisms of his theory of moral development. *Merrill-Palmer Quarterly*, **16**, 337–50.

Lickona, T. (1976). *Moral Development and Behaviour*, Holt, New York.

Locke, D. B. (1979). How to improve your moral thinking. A critique of the stage-structural theory of moral reasoning. *J. Moral Education*, **8**, 168–81.

Locke, D. B. (1980). The illusion of stage six. *J. Moral Education*, **9**, 103–109.

McNamee. S. (1977). Moral behaviour, moral development and motivation. *J. Moral Education*, **7**, 27–32.

Milgram, S. (1965). Some conditions of obedience and disobedience to authority. *Human Relations*, **18**, 57–76.

Mosher, R. (1980). *Moral Education: a first generation of research and development*, Praeger, New York.

Peters, R. S. (1971). Moral development; a plea for pluralism. In T. Mischel (Ed.), *Cognitive Development and Epistemology*, Academic Press, New York.

Peters, R. S. (1978). The place of Kohlberg's theory in moral education. *J. Moral Education*, **7**, 147–57.

Piaget, J. (1932). *The Moral Judgement of the Child*, Routledge, London.

Puka, W. (1976). Moral education and its cure. In J. R. Meyer (Ed.), *Reflections on Values Education*, Wilfrid Laurier University Press, Ontario.

Reimer, J., and Power, C. (1980). Educating for a democratic community; some unresolved dilemmas. In R. Mosher (Ed.), *Moral Education: a first generation of research*, Praeger, New York.

Rest, J. R. (1973). Patterns of preference and comprehension in moral judgement. *J. Personality*, **41**, 86–109.

Rest, J. R. (1979). *Development in Judging Moral Issues*, University of Minnesota Press, Minneapolis.

Rest, J. R., Turiel, E., and Kohlberg, L. (1969). Level of moral development as a determinant of preference and comprehension of moral judgements. *J. Personality*, **37**, 225–252.

Rothman, S., and Lichter, S. R. (1978). The case of the student left. *Social Research*, **45**, 535–609.

Selman, R. (1980). *The Growth of Interpersonal Understanding*, Academic Press, New York.

Simpson, E. L. (1974). Moral development research; a case of scientific cultural bias. *Human Development*, **17**, 81–106.

Smith, M. E. (1978). Moral reasoning; its relation to logical thinking and role-taking. *J. Moral Education*, **8**, 41–50.

Sullivan, E. E. (1977). A study of Kohlberg's structural theory of moral development; a critique of liberal science ideology. *Human Development*, **20**, 352–376.

Thornton, D. (1977). Stages of moral reasoning and types of criminal behaviour. Paper read to the International Conference on Moral Development and Moral Education, Leicester, England, August 1977.

Trainer, F. E. (1977). A critical analysis of Kohlberg's contributions to the study of moral thought. *J. for the Theory of Social Behaviour*, **7**, 41–63.

Turiel, E. (1966). An experimental test of the sequentiality of developmental stages in the child's moral judgements. *J. Personality and Social Psychology*, **3**, 611–618.

Walker, L. J. (1980). Cognitive and perspective-taking prerequisites for moral development. *Child Development*, **51**, 131–139.

Wasserman, E. (1976). implementing Kohlberg's 'just community' concept in an alternative high school. *Social Education*, **40**, 203–207.

Wasserman, E. (1980). An alternative high school based on Kohlberg's 'just community' approach to education. In R. Mosher (Ed.), *Moral Education; a first generation of research and development*, Praeger, New York.

Weinreich-Haste, H. E. (1977). Some consequences of replicating Kohlberg's original moral development study on a British sample. *J. Moral Education*, **7**, 32–39.

Weinreich-Haste, H. E. (1982). Piaget's moral psychology; a critical perspective. In S. Modgil and C. Modgil (Eds), *Jean Piaget; Consensus and Controversy*, Holt-Saunders, Eastbourne.

Morality in the Making
Edited by H. Weinreich-Haste and D. Locke
© 1983, John Wiley & Sons, Ltd.

CHAPTER 2

The Nature of Moral Commitments

IAN VINE

> 'There is, as I see it, no single non-analytic moral thesis that is not
> contestable, and is not being contested . . . men are, and cannot help
> being, moral partisans . . . consequently, to speak of particular per-
> sons or doctrines as moral or humane or rational is to risk saying
> nothing that is demonstrably true, except to those already committed
> to certain favoured partisan teachings.'
>
> (Margolis, 1971, pp. 4–5)

In the study of morality, just as with other aspects of human activity, the sole
task of biological and social scientists has traditionally been seen as establishing
contingent and 'value-free' empirical facts about how and why people come to
feel, think, and behave as they do. By contrast, philosophers and moralists
have assumed responsibility for elucidating the meanings of moral concepts, for
specifying criteria of adequacy for alternative conceptions of morality, and for
seeking to establish whether some moral ideals are objectively superior to
others. But recently such comfortable doctrines and divisions of labour have
increasingly come under attack. There is, for example, renewed interest in the
possibility of deriving from our shared biology and adaptive needs some form of
objectively valid 'evolutionary ethic' (e.g. Cattell, 1972; Lorenz, 1974; Wilson,
1978)—but unfortunately these writers' ignorance of the associated philosophical difficulties (Flew, 1967) has proved to be a major obstacle to valid analysis
and to the acceptance of their prescriptions. Yet a minority of social scientists
has at least made serious efforts to come to grips with conceptual and evaluative
problems that obscure the relations between prescriptive ethics and empirical
data on moral activities and processes (e.g. Boyce and Jensen, 1978; Edel and
Edel, 1968; Kohlberg, 1971, 1973). Kohlberg in particular has rejected the

traditional philosophical view which makes it impossible to derive prescriptive conclusions from factual premises, although his arguments remain controversial.

On the other hand, some moral philosophers have at last begun to take seriously the relevance to ethical analyses of empirical discoveries about human nature and its social nexus (e.g. Brandt, 1976, 1979; Midgley, 1978). For ethical theory must be applicable to real people in their real social contexts if it is to progress further, to provide meaningful solutions to actual moral disputes and dilemmas. And it is evident that such features as our investigative methodologies, the contingent facts and logically necessary truths they reveal, our evaluative and conceptual presuppositions, stipulative definitions, theoretical interpretations, and prescriptive conclusions, actually interpenetrate in highly complex ways.

So researchers within the human sciences who study morality and related topics must at least become more explicitly aware of the conceptual and often implicitly evaluative assumptions underpinning their theories and practices. As Lickona (1976) observes, further substantial progress in the psychology of morals must depend upon more serious consideration of debates about what 'morality' itself actually *is*, including conceptual disputes about its fundamental forms and functions. Indeed, if our personal moral partisanship, to which Margolis (1971) bluntly refers, should even extend to how we define basic moral terms, then it is quite essential for empirical scientists to be alert to associated moral philosophical problems. Otherwise it will be impossible for any data to resolve conflicts between competing theories impartially.

In this chapter I shall present and defend one particular set of starting assumptions for a theory of some social psychological aspects of moral development. I shall also show how these conflict in significant ways with some often less explicit, and in my view less acceptable, psychological and philosophical presuppositions in Kohlberg's influential theory of morality. This highly rationalistic and individualistic cognitive-developmental approach currently dominates research on the moral development of the person. But I shall argue that, despite attempting to come to terms with descriptive and prescriptive ethical issues more thoroughly than has any other psychological theorist, Kohlberg has actually relied upon a quite unconvincing ethical stance that makes his theory untenable, at least without serious modification. In contrast to Kohlberg, I shall stress how our commitments to moral codes and principles arise out of our fundamental social experiences; and then consider how far moral maturity might still be identified objectively with acceptance of some particular ethical system, or with universal forms of moral reasoning. For present purposes I take for granted the general case for taking progressive changes in cognitive structures to be a major aspect of moral development, as Piaget and Kohlberg claim, while acknowledging that alternative approaches may also have much to contribute to an eventual inclusive theory of our moral psychology.

Realism, Constructivism, and the Status of Morality

Any large-scale theory of human nature and its relation to the world must take a stand, at least implicitly, on several quite fundamental background issues. First there are ontological questions as to what has truly authentic existence as the basic stuff of reality. But these are followed closely by epistemological problems about how we ourselves come to know that reality, and to know that we know it. With regard to the material world, most modern thinkers agree in adopting a 'realist' ontology, whereby only physical matter and associated forces exist autonomously in space-time, in contrast to Platonic notions which postulate the real existence of immaterial 'ideal forms' of things. The thorough-going physicalist also denies any possibility of a supernatural world of 'spiritual' entities, like gods or ghosts. And 'empiricist' epistemology holds that we can come to know the features of the real physical world essentially through the exercise of our senses (aided in some cases by both technology and rational reflection). Under suitable conditions this experience yields objective knowledge of things as they actually are and would continue to be even if no-one actually perceived them. We perceive this reality directly, more or less passively coming to discriminate what is there outside our own minds awaiting discovery.

Against such a realist ontology combined with an empiricist epistemology, classical varieties of 'idealism' and 'rationalism' currently fare very poorly. The sceptical view that we can be certain only that our minds have real existence, or that the world as we know it is nothing but a mental creation, slides too readily into a philosophically incoherent solipsism. The successes of natural science, based on materialist and determinist assumptions, make it difficult to claim that even human beings are in essence anything 'more' than very complex configurations of matter in motion. Dualistic ontologies which see minds as anything but dependent products of physical brains are generally discredited. And epistemologically, merely introspective intuitions are suspect if they smack of the possibility of innate knowledge (Chomsky notwithstanding), or claim to tell us truths about the world which cannot be assessed empirically, or postulate a 'free-will', that can break the strict chains of physical causation to which physical entities are subject.

Yet the empiricist must concede that we can only come to know those selected aspects of the physical world which, by virtue of evolutionary contingencies, our senses are adapted to perceive. Even then we do not typically respond directly to physical stimuli; for we at least rely heavily on induction and unconscious inference in interpreting information. When we consciously deliberate about the world our mental processes or structures clearly contribute still more to our knowing. And when processing social information, any inference which depends upon attributing states of mind to other persons unavoidably entails making even stronger unproven assumptions about their status as rational agents with mental structures essentially similar to our own. Furthermore, although the free-will versus determinism debate remains unresolved, commonplace facts about our subjective experiences strongly suggest that the effects of our values and choices can extend to influencing how even the physical world is perceived, as well as colouring our social perceptions. Realists cannot readily deny the genuine existence of mental experiences, of our cognitive structures and processes, or of their effects in and on the world, even when they insist on interpreting the causal chains in terms of a physicalist and reductionist assumption. It thus involves no great leap of faith to conclude that we are actually active construers of reality, who necessarily select, enrich, and order even our sensory experience in systematic but somewhat idiosyncratic ways (Kelly, 1955)—although these must be partially constrained by intrinsic commonalities within human nature itself, and by the external world.

An extreme 'constructivist' epistemology might hold that we can 'know' nothing about reality outside ourselves except as what we actively create in the form of the mental models, constructs, or schemas through which we interpret external stimulation. Such a humanly conceived knowledge may be bounded by requirements of personal and social coherence, consistency, and communicability; but for any constructivist there is still no direct route to immediate knowledge of 'raw' external reality itself, in the sense in which things may exist independently of human perceptions of them. Furthermore, many phenomena will not in fact *have* any such existence outside of human mental structures and the behaviours they give rise to, although such a view need not necessarily involve rejection of a realist ontology for material objects. (Only the extreme ontological constructivist is likely to claim that the physical world is purely a figment of human minds.)

A more moderate and plausible view avoids both extremes. The thoroughgoing person–environment interactionist view of human development, long represented in the 'genetic epistemology' of Piaget (e.g. 1972a, 1972b), is now being taken more seriously in accounts of human cognition proposed both by general psychologists (Neisser, 1976), and by biologists (Lorenz, 1977). These perspectives may be identified as varieties of a moderate constructivist epistemology and ontology. A mass of data now supports the general claim that we do in a significant sense personally and actively create our own cognitive structures, and deal with the world in terms defined by these. However, this active and progressive structuring is quite strictly constrained and modified by uniformities within nature itself, and by social, cultural, and historical factors which impinge unavoidably upon our course of development. Broadly speaking, one's mental structures do come to reflect humanly significant features of the world outside one's individual self, or we would be unable to cope with it as effectively and adaptively as we do.

By far the most problematic and complex application of this moderate constructivist perspective clearly arises in connection with our knowledge of phenomena which concern human social life, rather than the merely inanimate or biological worlds. Even ontologically, much of our experienced reality is a *social* reality that is humanly and collectively constructed, although it often imposes itself upon us with a potency that seems as inexorable as that of physical forces. Despite the apparent autonomy and fixity of social institutions they are, at least in part, the product of revisable human choices. Berger and Luckmann (1967, p. 146) wrote provocatively that 'all symbolic universes and all legitimations are human products, their existence has its base in the lives of concrete individuals, and has no empirical status apart from these lives.' And Berger and Pullberg (1965) have argued that we inevitably 'objectify' human products just by categorizing them. But the process of self-alienation whereby we also 'reify' them as autonomous features of fixed, objective reality is not, in principle, humanly inevitable—as the facts of deliberate, self-consciously instigated social change remind us.

Everyday social experience also allows each of us some measure of innovation and negotiation in attaching meanings to human actions, and in both interpreting and changing their associated intentions, effects, and social implications (Harré and Secord, 1972). Yet we should never forget that these basic capacities to modify our own and other persons' cognitive-affective mental structures are themselves developed under strong adult guidance during infancy (e.g. Lock, 1978; Richards, 1974). Our basic modes of social understanding and intervention, as well as the norms, roles, and other cultural institutions these generate, are thus very definitely social products in large degree, rather than purely personal mental constructions. And the intersubjective inertia of socially constructed realities means that for some purposes at least, and in the short term, we often have to regard them *as if* they were independent features of the natural world.

Thus far, I shall assume that the case for a moderate constructivist perspective on social reality is relatively uncontroversial. Rather less obvious is whether all elements of that special class of normatively prescriptive constructs by which we evaluate and regulate our social actions and shared lives are *purely* socio-cultural creations—or whether at least some values and norms have a more distinctively binding source. Some broadly consensual 'order of values' permeates the life of any society and most of its members; and as Kelvin (1969) argues, our basic human need for predictability and order in our interactions with others can in general suffice to explain the emergence of shared intra-societal values as intersubjective constructions, expressing a culture's common goals and priorities. But does such an order and its embodiments within the social system ever have more than purely local validity, contingent upon some current measure of consensus within the culture? Can a merely consensually constructed order of values ever be legitimately held to create obligations towards or from members of other societies, not party to the same cultural goals, contracts, shared meanings, and so forth? Are there any intrinsic constraints on the valid social construction of value orders, arising from human nature itself or even from some autonomous source external to us? Is there some discoverable set of absolute criteria by which these value systems can themselves be compared and evaluated? Are some of the latter then better than others in an objective sense?

In particular, is that subset of values, norms, and principles we label 'moral' (rather than merely 'conventional') of special epistemological and ontological status, set apart from culture–specific social constructions as matters for *discovery* rather than social invention?

For those explicitly conventional, and culturally very variable, normative phenomena such as role expectations, codes of manners and etiquette, institutional rules, and culturally defined legal codes, the most plausible perspective is still the moderate social constructivist one. All these surely have real existence only in so far as people do continue to believe in them collectively, even if it is an objective requirement of harmonious social life that they should take some one agreed form or other, as collective beliefs and shared, action-guiding mental structures, in a given society at a given time. In developmental terms, a society's existing value order may initially be internalized holistically by the child, as an invariant feature of social experience to be accommodated to just as physical realities must also be taken as given. Yet we must each actively interpret our social experience even to infer what such norms are. Indeed it is this flexibility of assimilation by individuals that permits the degrees of innovation which allow norms to shift over time, and to change adaptively as social needs change.

Where the social constructivist viewpoint is likely to be challenged is precisely in the realm of *moral* norms and values. Piaget (1932), in his early and incomplete but seminal theory of moral development, gave a significant but distinctly limited role to social factors in the development of moral understanding. Social experience does influence the child's developing moral conceptions; but it acts basically by stimulating personal rational reflection, which is itself the immediate source of an autonomous moral perspective (cf. Wright, Chapter 8). Some contemporary Piagetians take the 'socialization of thought' more seriously (e.g. Voyat, 1978; cf. Kutnick, Chapter 10); but still understand mature moral commitment as going beyond a merely arbitrary social consensus. For Piaget, moral maturity involves acknowledging the prescriptive force of specific principles of justice, and concern for others' welfare, which are impartial, timeless, and universally applicable. In the final analysis such a conception of morality makes it a product of the individual's reason, shared with other mature moral thinkers because of the universal rational demands of moral logic itself. This rationalist and individualist emphasis is still stronger in other cognitive-developmentalists like Kohlberg; and at least superficially it represents a move towards the realist end of the realism-constructivism dimension as regards the ontological status of moral values.

The advantage of claiming that morally mature individuals will normally come to agree in their rational and reflective personal constructions of the form and content of their basic moral codes, and even in the principles by which they justify these, is of course that the evaluative relativism implied by extreme social constructivist accounts of moral understanding and commitment can thus be avoided. Alternative theories of moral development typically fail, as in the case of simple learning theories analyses, to explain convincingly why some individuals espouse moralities at variance with that of their own culture, and hold these to be superior to the prevailing code. This fact is especially significant when the most conspicuous external reinforcement pressures militate against adopting a different moral perspective from that of one's primary social groups. Other approaches, such as psychodynamic theories, may explain the phenomenon—but only in terms of irrational or maladaptive processes, rather than the rational construction of an ideal human ethic.

The constructivist who is convinced that morality is *not* an arbitrary matter, and that there is some uniformity in the ethics adopted by the saints, martyrs, and moral heroes of human history, confronts an awkward choice in seeking to explain how morality can be distinguished from norms and social regulations of other kinds, to be viewed as somehow superordinate to these, legitimately transcending mere social consensus. If such beliefs are not illusory, must they entail a departure from constructivism if we are to account for the fact that particular basic moral principles are often held to be absolute and pre-emptive rather than just culturally sustained, universally valid rather than subject to social re-negotiation? And in philosophical terms are such moral commitments rationally justifiable?

One apparent solution is simply to reject ontological constructivism in the field of moral values. If one assumes a realist ontology, in which certain codes, or principles, or ends of conduct, and certain means towards ends, simply *are* morally good or bad, in an evaluatively objective, transcendent sense, then the morally mature individual is simply one who has actually discovered these independent moral truths and seeks to live by them. Unlike other norms, they are not human creations at all. I shall identify this extreme objectivist view of values as *ethical realism*. It is most clearly exemplified in Platonism, in which the 'Form of the good' is seen as the valuative aspect of ultimate reality itself. Moral reality is thus a given, in no way contingent upon our actual moral conceptions, yet being prescriptively binding for all human action. Traditional theological views which identify perfect ethical ideals with the will of a god, knowable through the grace of divine revelation, are essentially analogous in their realist assumptions. Ethical realism presumes that there exists some independent, non-human criterion that specifies which ends we ought to pursue; and it typically holds that one such standard applies without exception to all persons in all cultural contexts and epochs.

In contrast, the ontological *ethical constructivist* must insist, with Mackie (1977), that moral codes are made by and for human beings; but need not hold that moralities are indistinguishable from other normative social constructions which become reified and treated as if they had independent status. In principle, the constructivist can even admit an element of discovery in the recognition of morality and obligation. This is partly because moral codes embodied in culture are initially encountered as given social facts. But also there may be universal and intrinsic human needs and motives, sympathies and concerns, social experiences and laws of psycho-logic, to provide the foundations upon which constructive moral reflection must be based. Cognitive-developmental accounts of morality presuppose that such factors play a major role in generating universal sequences of individual moral development. Yet they need not asume that such development involves progressive approximations towards an intuition or empirical discovery of transcendental ethical realities which are in any sense supra-human, timeless, or inexorable.

Moderate ethical constructivists can allow that there are many natural facts about human beings and their environment, including social pressures, which may very heavily constrain and funnel in a common direction the cognitive-affective moral constructions of all or most individuals—at least under ideal conditions. For Piaget (1932), logic and the possibility of ideal rational consensus define the optimum forms of moral rules; but since he regards logic as a symbolic abstraction of our actual thought processes ('the axiomatics of the operations of thought', Piaget, 1972b, p. 81), morality still remains a human creation. It is just that the rational constraints are in his view so strong that our moral constructions progress towards one unique and universal form. Unless this form of analysis can be ruled out altogether, it is inappropriate to equate every variety of objectivism about moral values with ethical realism. An attempt to summarize and clarify such distinctions is presented in Table 1, which contrasts ethical realism with the moderate ethical constructivism outlined here.

Table 1   Ethical realism versus ethical constructivism

ETHICAL REALISM

1. *Ontology*

   Social institutions and regulations in general may be flexible human constructions; but underlying a subset of these, distinguished by the form or content of the prescriptions in question, are rules and principles which are specifically moral. The ethical values these embody are absolute, universal, and transcendent—i.e. they are authoritative, autonomous, and unalterable, being in no way dependent on human choice and circumstances. They give rise to pre-emptive obligations upon us, irrespective of any contingent facts about our natures and forms of social life. As the prescriptive aspect of what is ultimately real and meaningful in the world, they are naturally binding on any rational being, and prescribe a solution for every moral dilemma.

2. *Epistemology*

   These ultimate values are assumed a priori to be objectively discoverable, at least within limits imposed by the imperfections of the human mind's interpretative processes—either through rational reflection, intuitive revelation, or discovery processes involving inductive inference from empirical facts available to our senses.

Table 1   continued

3. *Moral maturity*

This consists in coming, by whatever route, to recognize these ultimate values and associated principles and rules, and in living strictly according to them at whatever personal or social cost. Irrespective of contingent circumstances, anything less constitutes moral failure or ignorance, and a betrayal of our human potential and responsibility.

ETHICAL CONSTRUCTIVISM

1. *Ontology*

All norms and values, even moral ones, are flexible human constructions. They only exist, and have validity in prescribing action, is so far as people do accept and choose to live by them. Thus moralities may be created, abolished, or altered as the human condition alters. They can only be evaluated in relation to the natures, commitments, and broader life-goals of individuals or social groups, and by criteria which relevant parties agree to accept. They can be more or less objectively binding on rational beings, according to how effectively they do in fact serve terminal values which all persons do share, irrespective of their cultural, historical, and ecological contexts or idiosyncratic constitutions, or could be rationally persuaded to share.

2. *Epistemology*

All social institutions and regulations are at first discovered experimentally under social guidance. But they are interpreted actively, and somewhat idiosyncratically, within limits imposed by the child's general mode of cognitive functioning. Subsequently they are progressively transformed and differentiated, reflecting social experience and cognitive-affective development. This restructuring changes one's substantive conceptions of and commitment to the moral norms, as well as their mode of justification by reference to underlying values. Conceptions of their scope, prescriptive authority, and relevance to underlying values may develop until they are seen as overriding other norms and values and having universal human application and validity.

3. *Moral maturity*

This consists in reaching the most comprehensive perspective on the nature and justification of morality, and a corresponding active and rational commitment to one's code, of which one is plausibly capable, given one's constitutional capacities, socio-cultural experience, and opportunities to acquire and process relevant information. The form and content of a mature morality may thus evolve as human cultures evolve, although it may have limited invariant features as well.

In practice, however, many moral objectivists do rely a priori on ethical realist assumptions in both ontological and epistemological respects, and I shall seek to show that Kohlberg's theory is tainted in just this way, partly as a result of giving insufficient weight to the social aspect of ethical constructivism, and partly because he misidentifies the nature of morality itself. Piaget is less susceptible to this criticism, if only because he lays greater stress on the development of the individual's moral structures as depending upon actual social relationships and shared experiences. Of course, if this is so then the likelihood that every person will be in a position to construct his or her morality within a single species-typical mould is in practice reduced—but that fact at least helps to account for the lack of actual universal moral consensus. And still it does not rule out the future possibility that, if certain basic aspects of social life and human nature are truly universal, and if mature thought does have universal structural features, then moral understanding and commitment *could* evolve towards some single universal code, which might then be called 'objectively' optimal for human beings to live by.

But to demonstrate this, even theoretically, would be a major enterprise which remains to be executed. To be done convincingly it would require extensive interdisciplinary collaboration, and its attainment might arguably rank as one of the highest human achievements. So far it has scarcely been attempted, except at a speculative level. And in the meantime, it would be foolish simply to assume the end result. If we simply make the *assumption* of complete ethical objectivism, as distinct from admitting that we are all moral partisans (who like to believe that our own moral code will be the one which actually concurs with this hoped-for objective ethic), there is a serious danger that we thereby unconsciously slide into ethical realism. In view of the conspicuous philosophical objections to ethical realism (e.g. Mackie, 1977; Margolis, 1971), many of which create obstacles for even a constructivist objectivism, it seems unwise to base a theory of moral development on the hypothesis that there is a single transcultural form of moral maturity that embodies a unique and demonstrable objective ethic. Despite the attractions of such a theoretical course, we risk biasing our view of development at every stage if our intuition is incorrect.

I have dwelt at length on these issues because they are often overlooked. In a troubled and morally confused world the ethical realist perspective retains considerable popular appeal, even to social scientists, although it is rarely acknowledged explicitly. If we are to do without its dubious assumptions we must at least seek to discover a reflexive psychological theory to explain and do justice to the strong belief that there are indeed objective moral obligations which can be rationally defended, and that this sense of morality is not simply an arrogant cognitive fiction, or a wishful fantasy which cloaks mere prudence.

Piaget's developmental perspective on morality appeared to hold some promise as the foundation for an account of how we acquire moral commitments in the ways that we do, including convictions about their objectivity. Unfortunately, as his approach has been developed in Kohlberg's hands, it has become vulnerable to charges of ideological bias towards a particular, culture-specific, set of values (cf. Emler, Chapter 3); and it thus fails to do justice to the moral reasoning and conduct of those who reject these in a principled way, and espouse alternative ethics. I shall claim that Kohlberg's unsubstantiated and unacknowledged ethical realism, which in fact meshes poorly with the general Piagetian constructivist approach to moral cognition, is largely responsible for the theory's weaknesses. Although Kohlberg has developed a theory with considerable appeal to moral educators, it has serious social psychological and philosophical defects. Before analysing some of these weaknesses it is necessary, however, to return to the fundamental questions of what 'morality' actually is, and why people have to invent it.

The Nature and Functions of Morality

Any characterization of what morality is and does is made more difficult by the fact that the term 'moral' can have a very wide reference. In this broadest sense one's moral code specifies and relates all the rules and principles of action which impinge upon one's most basic goals, and those of others, and which one feels obliged to bring to bear in evaluating choices of conduct. In these terms the moral realm can be taken to encompass all facets of human life, and arguably one ought by definition always to do what one's own morality prescribes. But then the 'good life' becomes so inclusive that investigating morality becomes scarcely distinguishable from the conceptually and empirically problematic study of values in general (Kitwood, 1977).

In a narrower sense, more relevant to most ethical theorizing and practical moral problems, we can profitably identify a central core of morality which concerns more specific aspects of conduct and character, and which offers only one set of considerations amongst others for deciding what one ought rationally to do. Arguably though, moral obligations are overriding considerations, at least in most contexts. In fact the strictest conceptions of moral duty make it unconditional, so that one's obligation to follow it is unequivocal, even—and perhaps epecially—when it conflicts explicitly with one's own direct interests. Clearly morality is not just about knowing *how* to apply and follow a particular code of rules and principles which set limits on the ends and means of action. It refers centrally to our attitudes and commitments to such ways of regulating conduct. In the words of Piaget (1932, p. 9): 'The essence of morality (is) the respect which the individual acquires for these rules.' To accept a moral code is to acknowledge a special kind of motive, a prescriptive standard that normatively constrains the pursuit of particular immediate desires (Pahel, 1976).

It can also be argued that what is 'good' for human beings can only be understood (except by the extreme ethical realist) as some function of what individuals actually want and need for their satisfaction (Midgley, 1978). But Midgley insists that what is *morally* good must be settled in terms of criteria for rationally modulating our desires themselves, the internal conflicts amongst these, and conflicts between our personal interests and those of others. Such an emphasis on the role of impartial reason in delineating the prescriptions properly inherent in a moral code, and indeed in allowing us to compare alternative codes, is acknowledged by the majority of ethical theorists. And it suggests that commitment to a code is ultimately to be justified by commitment to basic values, like rationality itself, that are taken as being a fundamental requirement for a meaningful life.

However, it is also clear that our actual respect for a moral code by no means arises solely through the exercise of individual reason. Psychologically, it depends heavily on our respect for and attachment to other persons and social groups. In content too, moral codes concern our relations with others—the areas of conduct where conflicting interests have to be weighed and resolved. Although some moralities lay their stress on developing virtues of character, the primary referents of morality appear to be socially oriented. Hampshire (1978, p. 7) suggests that: 'A morality is, at the very least, the regulation of the taking of life and the regulation of sexual relations, and it also includes rules of distributive and corrective justice: family duties: almost always duties of friendship: also rights and duties in respect of money and property'. Empirically, moral codes do function to regulate such basic, universal features of social life. In essence morality is a device to protect the interests of others and promote altruism (Nagel, 1970). Commitment to a moral code involves affirmative recognition of one's shared humanity with those to whom it is applied.

The essential reference of moral codes can thus be summed up as follows: they regulate conduct which affects the most central concerns and interests of both the agent and other persons, especially in social contexts where these are potentially in conflict. We can safely assume that evolution has predisposed every organism to develop the motivation to look after at least its own short-term interests quite naturally—but not necessarily the interests of the group or species (e.g. Campbell, 1975; Vine, 1982; Wilson, 1978). So the task of morality is to counter or extend self-interest, partly towards longer-term personal prudence, but more distinctively to increase the compass of our social concern. In the words of Warnock (1971, p. 26), it promotes 'the betterment . . . of the human predicament by seeking to countervail "limited sympathies" and their potentially most damaging effects.' Broadly speaking, the empirical evidence appears to support the claim that we need moral codes for social life to be tolerably harmonious and satisfactory—because the diversity of human ideals, goals, and inclinations makes some degree of conflict and competition between individuals, and within and between human groups, 'real, inevitable, and ineradicable' (Mackie, 1977, p. 237).

But this does *not* entail the extreme Hobbesian claim that without moral codes social life would be a perennially ruthless blood-bath. It is likely that to some degree our species does have natural pro-social tendencies to advance the welfare of each other, and that these dispositions are probably 'genetically primed' to be learned rapidly during socialization (e.g. Bar-Tal, 1976; Eibl-Eibesfeldt, 1971; Mussen and Eisenberg-Berg, 1977). Such tendencies will thus partially counteract inborn or learned tendencies towards selfishness and aggressiveness which might otherwise make social cooperation almost impossible. It is essential to recognize the fact that we are and always have been a strongly social species, whose members necessarily depend on each other for personal as well as collective goal-attainment and welfare, and in some contexts for survival itself (e.g. Moscovici, 1977; Stark, 1976). Pure individualism is a mythical view of human nature. So culturally constructed means to regulate conflicts of interest, extend our sympathies, and sustain high levels of pro-social activity are thus essential to protect our humanity itself. (On the other hand, a constructivist view of morality must allow that socially created moral codes may sometimes go beyond merely counteracting selfishness, even coming to prescribe levels of altruism which seriously damage the individual's own welfare and interests if the code's precepts are followed literally. Although most persons are unlikely to follow such a code slavishly, it may still generate either excessive guilt, or moral cynicism, and thereby prove to be as personally and socially maladaptive as a code that is too weak.)

On the present view, moral codes are prompted, adopted, and sustained, either unreflectively or through rational deliberation, because in general they have functional utility in advancing our more far-sighted ideals, concerns, and needs. But they can only serve this function if they are collectively *shared* within a community of interacting persons. A moral code must always attain at least some basic level of consensual acceptance within a group if it is to be adaptively effective. And that consensus must ideally be capable of evolving to modify the code if the socio-ecological conditions which affect a community's lifestyle themselves change. Furthermore, the constructivist must assume that the justification and authority for any morality is entirely human and humane, depending ultimately on the fact that we do share altruistic and compassionate sympathies for others, as well as prudential concern for our own long-term advantage; and that we can at least tacitly agree to promote such interests. The basis of moral obligation is thus naturalistic in a Humean sense; morality is not binding just in case there actually are transcendental ethical realities to be discovered, nor because individual reason alone is sufficient to prescribe ideal modes of conduct (as Kant is often held to have believed). We are obliged by a code and its prescriptions in so far as they are rational extensions of values and sentiments to which we have a *prior* commitment, recognized at least in our more rational and benevolent moments.

But in this case the primary reference of a moral code concerns behaviour between members of a given, socially cohesive community. As anthropologists have often emphasized, morality is primarily an in-group phenomenon (e.g. Edel and Edel, 1968; Ginsberg, 1961; Linton, 1952; von Fürer-Haimendorf, 1967). Indeed, even within a moral community, the scope of some consensual rules may be taken to be limited to particular sub-groupings of agents or patients of actions. There is clearly nothing intrinsic to humanly constructed moral codes which makes them applicable to all persons at all times and in all contexts. Such partiality may even be partly rooted in our inherited biology (Vine, 1981, 1982); but there are also moral philosophical justifications for some limits on the universality of moral obligations (e.g. Brandt, 1979; Mackie, 1977; Melden, 1977).

This view of morality is itself both incomplete and partisan, and would not be accepted by all moral philosophers. But it does not presuppose the total subjectivism and relativism which makes an extreme constructivist view of morals aversive to many. Nor does it prejudge what determines the logical form and precise content of an adequate moral code. The issue of whether any particular form or content of a moral code is objectively superior to all others hinges on the universality of basic human values, interests, sympathies, capacities, and so on. For cultural relativists, like Baumrind (1978), the conflicting interests of different cultures, and classes within cultures, are too divergent to make the notion of even a hypothetically universal moral consensus plausible. But some anthropologists, like Edel and Edel (1968), do find a limited measure of universal consensus in some basic features of different cultures' moral codes—which suggests that a partial moral objectivism might be appropriate for our species. Certainly many moral philosophers would claim that our basic natures are invariant enough to require that some central features should be similar in any community's moral code as a matter of rational necessity (e.g. Melden, 1977; Midgley, 1978; Nagel, 1970; Williams, 1972).

Nevertheless it is surely inappropriate for the ethical theorist to assume a priori that every rationally adequate rule must be universally applicable to every human being; or even that one code is objectively preferable to another just because more or all of its rules prescribe universally impartial treatment of all persons' interests. A special case must be made out, both empirically and logically, to support claims of universal applicability, just as it must to show the objective validity of the substantive content of any rule. In all probability both moves are rationally demonstrable, essentially on grounds of shared humanness being a minimal universal bond, in respect of certain fundamental moral rules that protect basic rights to life and liberty. Probably these should rationally be adopted by everyone and extended to all persons everywhere, although the case for making them absolute and exceptionless remains controversial, depending on which over-arching ethical ideal one adopts as a datum. In any event, for many kinds of moral rules we certainly do not have the required demonstrations of the objectivity and universal applicability of particular formulations. So in general we would be unwise to claim, unless we are prepared to embrace ethical realism, that even those moral rules which attain firm and rational consensus in any one society are *necessarily* appropriate and prescriptively binding for and towards all other societies and their members. In fact an aspect of the moral tolerance which fosters the possibility of progressive moral innovation is surely the capacity to resist the temptation to seek to impose complete moral codes universally.

Also, despite the obvious risks in accepting a measure of moral relativism, and of justifying prejudicial treatment of particular groups or sub-cultures by acknowledging the partiality of moral rules, there are other benefits as well. Not only does this viewpoint counteract the dangerous potential excesses entailed by the reification of particular rules, it also resists the debilitating effects of reasoning that one should be 'an agent of justice all over the world all the time' (Haan, 1978, p. 303). This universalist consideration would surely otherwise make it impossible to live a positively evaluable moral life without virtually submerging pursuit of one's own interests. But in any case, the main purpose of the present discussion has been to show why any psychological attempt to chart the progress of the individual towards moral maturity should avoid resting upon highly contentious objectivist assumptions, and why it must start from a recognition of the major role that social commitments play in explaining how morality in fact functions. I shall now seek to demonstrate how Kohlberg's theory suffers from his neglect of these two issues, leading him to misconstrue the nature and sources of moral maturity.

Kohlberg's Cognitive-Developmental Theory

I shall focus on particular facets of Kohlberg's account of moral development which suggest that many of the theory's defects stem from an implicit commitment to an ethical realism that cannot be reconciled with the Piagetian constructivist principles upon which the theory is more visibly and viably based. For the most part this will involve concentrating on his account of what constitutes the most developed forms of moral maturity, as represented by his claims about 'post-conventional' or 'principled' morality, and in particular its highest Stage 6 form. It is this feature which has already attracted much of the most damaging criticism of the theory (e.g. Codd, 1977; Morelli, 1978; Puka, 1976; Trainer, 1977), including strong attacks on the 'cultural imperialism' which is inherent in seeking to make one particular and ideologically partisan ethical ideal into the universal touchstone of moral maturity (Baumrind, 1978; Simpson, 1974; Sullivan, 1977; cf. Emler, Chapter 3).

Although I shall draw upon many of the objections raised by these critics, they will be recast here in terms of the framework already presented—this in turn will suggest ways in which Kohlberg's theory might effectively be purged of its most objectionable features and begin to be reconstructed, while still building on much of the foundation that he and Piaget have established.

Fundamental to Kohlberg's enterprise is the assumption that the natural course of moral development involves progressively creating for oneself, through an invariant sequence of irreversible stages, an integrated system of cognitive structures which can deal with moral problems in the most rational way of which human beings are capable. Ideally these structures permit one to apply to the moral realm the most refined forms of 'formal operations' abstract reasoning; and to make moral judgments rational and impartial enough to transcend the particular preferences and prejudices likely to be built into the predominant moral code of one's own particular culture. Although moral feelings, and actual moral conduct, may be heavily influenced by culture-specific and idosyncratic factors in development, the postulated stages in the development of moral reasoning are held to follow a universal sequence. Cultural circumstances may inhibit actual attainment of the most refined forms of judgment, but their nature is claimed to be culture-independent.

Kohlberg explicitly adopts the controversial position that the moral domain proper deals neither with personal virtues nor with ultimate values, but essentially with the procedural considerations for fairly resolving conflicts of obligation. On this 'deonotological' view of morality (as being centrally concerned with the nature of rights and duties) all mature moral judgments have an ideal form, irrespective of the content of what they actually prescribe. They pre-empt other judgments, and their form is 'universal, inclusive, consistent, and grounded on objective, impersonal, or ideal grounds' (Kohlberg, 1971, p. 215). Mature judgments reflect the nature of the cognitive structures on which they depend, which must be fully 'equilibrated' in the Piagetian sense (reversible, consistent, generalizable, etc.). Kohlberg seeks to show, drawing heavily on the philosopher Rawls (1971), that abstract reasoning about ideal forms of fairness makes procedural rules of justice, based upon reciprocity and equal consideration of interests, into the cornerstone of matural moral judgment. But Kohlberg also holds that when this level of appreciation is fully attained it must specify a unique content for the central values of any moral code—namely a Kantian respect for the equal dignity and autonomy of *all* individuals, and for their interests and welfare. This requires that everyone, just by virtue of being human, is to be accorded a set of basic rights to life and liberty which pre-empt lesser considerations such as partisan loyalties and even societal laws. Reference to these universal moral principles permits mature moralists to arrive independently at unique solutions to moral dilemmas where the most central moral values are at stake—for example the rejection of capital punishment (Kohlberg and Elfenbein, 1975). They are supreme principles because they alone could yield rational agreement if people were to consider the full range of perspectives relevant to a moral problem.

The rationalist objectivism and individualism implicit in Kohlberg's position is relatively transparent. He believes that reaching Stage 6 moral maturity (in any time, place, and cultural tradition) entails recognizing one unique set of absolute, and universally applicable, impartial principles of justice as rationally compelling. But whereas Piaget (1932) appeared to ground mature respect for justice itself on an assumed prior respect for persons, arising out of actual affiliations and interactions with them, Kohlberg has given a negligible significance to actual social relationships and effective attachments in accounting for advances in moral cognition and commitment to moral rules. The former evidently do no more than provide the raw materials for the rational reflection which stimulates structural advances.

Although Kohlberg admits that sympathetic concern for others is present at each stage, his formalist conception of morality can give it no moral role at all. This curiously impersonal view of the roots of subjectively experienced moral obligation arises from his most central assumptions. His most extended discussion of the rationale for his theory (Kohlberg, 1971) is often confusing, but suggests fairly clearly that his overriding concern is to justify theoretically an objectively supreme morality—one which will preclude relativism by establishing the rational necessity of some particular moral value or basic set of ethical principles. Believing that only procedural rules of universal justice can be demonstrated to have this objective and absolutely prescriptive status, he is led to conceive of the moral domain in terms of justice reasoning, and moral development in terms of advances in cognitive justice structures. He asserts that 'a justice structure organizing patterns of role-taking in moral conflict situations is the common core at every (moral) stage' (p. 214). This suggests that justice conceptions are necessary before affect can be channelled in moral directions at all. Because only principles of distributive justice (equity, or equality of consideration), and commutative justice (reciprocity, or equality in exchange), can resolve conflicting interests and sympathies impartially, they constitute 'what is most distinctively and fundamentally moral' (Kohlberg, 1976, p. 40). So it appears that Kohlberg must hold that a genuinely *moral* respect and concern for persons, the elusive Stage 6 commitment to 'the sacredness of human life as representing a universal human value out of respect for the individual' (Kohlberg, 1971, p. 169) can only emerge out of prior recognition of these abstract justice principles. Thus the only legitimate source of moral obligation to others must be our convictions about justice—instead of our sense of social obligation to other persons itself being what generates and justifies adherence to a moral code embodying principles of justice. The latter form of commitment to a moral code must be morally as well as cognitively deficient. Indeed, Kohlberg (1978) now admits that few people ever actually attain Stage 6 reasoning, and relegates it to the status of a largely hypothetical rational ideal of an admittedly a priori kind. Thus affective concern for others' welfare can scarcely ever qualify as *moral* concern at all in Kohlberg's eyes.

It scarcely needs saying that Kohlberg's theory is based on a view of the nature of morality strongly at variance with that which I have advanced here, stressing the content, social motivation for, and functions of moral codes. He asserts that the higher developmental stages are morally as well as cognitively superior, simply because formal criteria about what makes a judgment distinctively 'moral' are progressively more fully met—with Stage 6 judgments being categorically prescriptive and universalized, fully differentiated from issues of reward and punishment, social expectations and affective ties, utility or adaptiveness, and so on. A broader conception of what morality is completely undermines this claim. And it is surely disingenuous for him to disclaim any specific commitment to 'a theory of the good, a theory of virtue, or rules for praise, blame, and punishment' (Kohlberg, 1971, p. 125). Stage 6 moral principles are seen as the ideal, objectively superior, form of moral assessment; and if so then to espouse them must surely be virtuous. In any case they evidently do embody a conception of morally good conduct, entailing choices which put a strong premium on respect for individual life and liberty, and on totally impartial treatment of everyone's interests. A normative ethic simply cannot be entirely procedural. Thus it will not do for Kohlberg to insist that his criteria for identifying increasing moral maturity are now fully independent of content, relying wholly on the form of moral judgments—especially as he can no longer claim as an empirical fact that Stage 6 reasoners happen to agree on the content of their basic moral code.

Let us grant the highly disputed claims that Kohlberg's measured stages genuinely reflect purely formal features of moral reasoning or judgment; and that Stage 6 principles and judgments would not only be the same for all persons capable of the appropriate moral reflection, but could be shown to be rationally superior for assessing conflicts of interest, irrespective of context and the identities of the relevant parties. That *might* establish the universal prescriptive superiority of such a mode of justice reasoning, and of a moral code embodying these features—but only if further presuppositions are made about the ethical pre-eminence of an obligation to be bound by justice considerations. To make principled justice the core of a substantive ethic, especially one that is held to be universally and objectively binding, involves factual and prescriptive assumptions about what rational beings are capable of believing and willing, and about what things are good for people to do, experience, and become.

Any moral code which is to be rationally defensible must either be grounded upon some naturalistic stance, so that its prescriptions derive partially from a consensual view of what people need or want, or it must depend upon some authoritative non-natural basis for identifying what is right for us. If our essential human needs, social concerns, and wants *are* demonstrably invariant, then the content of a universally obligatory core to human morality might be ultimately derivable from these. But Kohlberg appears to regard such naturalistic factors as morally irrelevant, no doubt because without such certain demonstrations moral partisanship and relativism may be allowed in. And reason alone can only specify means to ends, not prescribe what are fundamentally good ends. Thus the justification for his supposedly objective Stage 6 justice ethic cannot arise from a constructivist moral ontology. So it must instead be presumed to be rooted in the discovery of what is transcendentally prescribed as intrinsically and universally good or right.

Like Kant before him, Kohlberg actually smuggles in an ultimate ethical value of respect for the interests of others under the pretence that it is simply equivalent to the determination of rights and duties by reference to purely procedural rules. To admit that respect for human dignity is not identical to commitment to justice principles, and actually underlies them in motivational terms, would force Kohlberg to acknowledge naturalistic and social sources for moral obligation. To make a unique, objectively binding moral code the product of mature individual reasoning, yet to divorce it from our natural motives and socially constructed realities, must require the postulate of some independent source of obligation to others. Unable to derive it from reason alone, he must simply conjure it up. Implicitly, Kohlberg must hold that the Stage 6 moralist intuits a definitive, prescriptive ethical reality which alone can transcend immature social commitments. It is scarcely surprising that this hypothesized developmental stage has become an embarrassment to the theory.

Thus Kohlberg's unwillingness to ground the justification of morality partly in its functional effectiveness in promoting humanly valued ends, or to derive its prescriptiveness partly from our actual social commitments to each other, forces him towards an unacknowledged ethical realism. Equal respect for all persons' interests, coupled with the ethical pre-emptiveness of procedural justice principles, appear together out of nowhere to be accepted as moral absolutes. At times Kohlberg almost admits the ethical realism underlying this moral objectivism, for instance by citing with approval Socrates' statements that 'virtue is ultimately one . . . regardless of climate or culture . . . the name of this ideal form is justice . . . virtue is knowledge of the good . . . or intuition of the ideal form of the good' (Kohlberg, 1971, p. 232). Without such an intuition he cannot hope to demonstrate against the sceptic why justice principles do indeed constitute the core of a perfect morality. Yet it is an intuition which only the ethical realist can confidently share. Rawls (1971) certainly would not claim to have demonstrated any such moral absolutes of the kind that Kohlberg seeks.

I assume here that Kohlberg's account of the development of the logical forms of pre-principled moral reasoning is, descriptively, likely to be broadly correct (e.g. Broughton, 1978; Gibbs, 1977; Rest, Davison, and Robbins, 1978)—but only as one artificially isolated aspect of moral development as a whole. It also seems plausible to accept that a fully principled morality, embodying fully equilibrated formal operational thought, will be superior to that of lower stages in a strictly cognitive sense, because it is more rationally adequate in being able to analyse complex moral dilemmas more efficiently. Irrespective of whether we can specify one uniquely valid set of moral principles, such a level of reasoning will, as Kohlberg suggests, allow for greater generality and comprehensiveness of moral judgments, for consideration of more relevant factors in making them, for clearer distinction between moral and non-moral considerations, for less arbitrariness or partiality of application of evaluative criteria, and so on.

Thus a cognitively mature morality will indeed be one such that general principles can be applied to adjudicate on conflicts of interests in ways which will be rationally superior to attempts to rely blindly upon specific moral rules. Ideally, a principled morality is organized parsimoniously and coherently, it is impartially detached and universalizable in the sense that anyone could apply it to a given moral problem and reach the same conclusion given appropriately similar conditions. And it is more reflective and potentially self-critical than a pre-principled morality, since principles are the general and abstract grounds on which specific moral rules can be evaluated (Boyd, 1978). It can thus provide a basis for rejecting social conventions, laws, or even complete moral codes, under appropriate circumstances.

What is much more controversial is whether holding a principled morality is always morally superior to holding a pre-principled one. Once Kohlberg's ethical realism and narrowly formalist specification of what 'moral' means are rejected (and especially if conduct itself is taken as its primary referent), then the necessary connection simply vanishes. Certainly there can be alternative principled moralities, and certainly these can conflict with each other (e.g. justice versus utilitarian moralities), or with less systematic, pre-principled moral codes. And even if some form of ethical objectivism can be defended, demonstrating that a particular moral code, or a single overriding principle, or hierarchy of principles, is indeed universally superior to others in ethical terms, this will not in itself suffice to show that the actions or characters of principled moral reasoners are necessarily morally preferable to those of pre-principled thinkers of any lower stage. On balance, in the absence of a convincing defence of the absolute ethical superiority of Kohlberg's particular set of proposed Stage 6 principles, or of convincing empirical evidence that people do reach Stage 6 thought and live by it, it is safer not to accept any of Kohlberg's own claims about the principled level of morality at present, other than its greater 'methodological' rationality or cognitive sophistication.

Moral Development and Moral Commitment

Turning now to the main developmental factors likely to permit and stimulate progress through the successive restructurings of moral thought, I shall first attempt to identify some deficiencies in Kohlberg's account of these determining conditions. Kohlberg (1976) claims that Piagetian 'concrete operational' thought is a necessary but not sufficient condition for attaining the pre-conventional moral level, while Stage 4 conventional moral reasoning requires the most basic 'formal operational' capacities; and principled reasoning requires more advanced formal abilities. Both correlational and intervention studies give general empirical support for at least the first two of these hypotheses (e.g. Faust and Arbuthnot, 1978; Keasey, 1975; Kuhn, Langer, Kohlberg, and Haan, 1977; Smith, 1978)—although Turiel (1978) doubts whether various domains of thinking really are as structurally interdependent as Kohlberg and others assume, i.e. whether the moral stages are unitary.

The other necessary condition of moral advance which Kohlberg identifies is the progressive development of one's role-taking capacity to adopt the perspective of another, for which tentative Piagetian developmental stages have been independently identified (Flavell, 1974; Selman, 1975, 1976). The claim is that higher moral reasoning stages require progressively more elaborate coordination of various viewpoints other than one's own, involving fuller reflective appreciation of the thoughts and feelings of others. Here the published evidence other than Selman's is less substantial as yet (e.g. Moir, 1974; Smith, 1978). Even the detailed theorizing does not really extend into the level of principled moral reasoning, but data appear so far to be at least consistent with Kohlberg's relevant postulates.

It is probably fair to conclude that both general cognitive and role-taking structural advances *are* necessary conditions for the development of moral reasoning, but that not enough is known to specify yet the precise features of either needed for constructing a principled morality. Furthermore, it has certainly not been established that these two necessary factors are also jointly sufficient to promote moral development, even within the strictly hypothetical realm of moral reasoning. (Nor does Kohlberg's recent recognition that 'ego-strength' plays a further part make his account of what promotes moral development more convincing.) I have already suggested that such factors cannot possibly suffice if the stages of moral reasoning are to involve the experience of obligation and a motivational commitment to *acting upon* one's moral judgments; and that this identifies a major omission from Kohlberg's account of moral development. This defect is partially masked by his confounding, as do many other writers, the terms 'empathy' and 'sympathy'; so this problem merits further consideration here.

Kohlberg states that role-taking 'goes on in *all* social interactions and communication stituations, not merely in ones that arouse emotions of sympathy or empathy' (Kohlberg, 1976, p. 49). This reveals that he is prone to equate empathy and sympathy, and to see them as emotions which may be evoked when taking another's viewpoint. He thus glosses over a very significant distinction, namely that between *understanding* that someone has particular feelings or motives and knowing what these feel like, versus actually *sharing* them—feeling them vicariously on behalf of the other, because one has affectively and wholeheartedly (not just cognitively) put oneself in their position. I shall refer to the former process as 'empathy' and to the latter as 'sympathy' following standard English usage.

As studied by Selman, social role-taking stages predominantly concern the development of empathic capacities, and so refer to understanding of another's perceptions, motives, feelings and so on. Yet when Selman talks of 'empathy' or 'reflective empathy', it is clear that he sometimes does mean affective 'sympathy'. For example he suggests that 'we cannot guarantee that a child with a high level of perspective-taking will apply his understanding in an empathic way' (Selman, 1975, p. 43). He does claim that affective sympathy depends not merely on understanding the differing perspectives of others, but also on one's 'conception of persons'—which seems to refer to a grasp of relations between feelings, motives, and behaviour; but this still remains essentially cognitive. Although he explicitly recognizes that actual sympathetic sharing of feelings can arise early in infancy, Selman's tendency to confuse sympathy with empathy prevents him from seeing that his analyses tell us nothing about the former. Yet surely it is *sympathy* which is essential for the development of the moral commitments which Selman and Kohlberg wish to explain. Empathy alone might give moral understanding of a sophisticated kind; but being able to verbalize in accordance with some moral code, even at the principled level, is different from actually holding it. And it cannot be equated with true moral maturity, since it need never lead to relevant actions.

Kohlberg (1976, p. 33) has now sought to identify in his own system 'a more general structural construct which underlies *both* role taking and moral judgement', the 'sociomoral perspective'. This 'refers to the point of view the individual takes in defining both social facts and sociomoral values or oughts', and parallels the moral reasoning stages themselves. But still Kohlberg offers no real analysis of how sympathetic concern for others enters into this perspective; thus his theory still omits the crucial cognitive-affective and social determinants which would link a detached cognitive understanding of conflicts of interest to any truly 'sociomoral' motivational basis for pro-social action. Again, this is no doubt explicable by his determination to avoid any factors which might permit the possibility of moral relativism.

A genuinely constructivist view of morality must risk this, because it acknowledges the contingent and culturally variable nature of some of the human values and sympathies upon which our reason must build. Thoroughgoing social constructivism must start from the ethical assumption that moral obligations and specific codes are not forced upon us, at least by gods or by logic alone, but are humanly created out of the raw materials of our natures, our perceived social realities, and our relationships with the world we live in. Morality is centrally motivated by social sympathies; and in the last resort the legitimation for any moral code must be some actual form of sharing of values, not only in abstract understanding, but also in active commitment to the interests of others. Commitment which yields a sense of genuine moral obligation must surely have its roots in our capacity for sympathetic concern, and in our recognition of implicitly contractual involvement in each other's projects and lives (Melden, 1977)—although admittedly there are problems in contractarian ethical theories which still need to be resolved (Dworkin, 1978). Progressive extension of such concern, and a more profound recognition of human interdependency serving to increase the size of one's subjective moral community, may be major features of moral developmental stage sequences (Vine, 1981)—ones which Kohlberg is unable to acknowledge.

More systematic and empirically based attempts to integrate the development of altruistic sympathies and social attachments (Hoffman, 1975, 1976) with that of formal moral reasoning will surely be one fruitful area of future research on moral development, although more attention to the typical developmental sequences for sympathy itself will first be needed. In fact the current trend of cognitive-developmental research does appear to involve a move away from the earlier assumption that moral development is governed by holistic advances in a single monolithic structural cluster, although there are disputes about how early the various systems become cognitively differentiated (Turiel, 1978). Apart from the partial separation of role-taking stages from moral stages, which Kohlberg himself has acknowledged, other research has begun to suggest distinct developmental stage sequences for various features of moral and socio-political understanding (cf. Weinreich-Haste, Chapter 5). Thus Damon (1977) has tentatively identified stage sequences for conceptions of justice, for respect and friendship for peers, for conceptions of and attitudes to authority, and for understanding general social rules. Turiel has also studied shifts in reasoning about social conventions and regulations (Nucci and Turiel, 1978; Turiel, 1975, 1978). Finally, Haan (1978) has distinguished separate stages for moral thinking in the domain of interpersonal relationships rather than about impersonal issues concerning social institutions. There are also related suggestions of developmental sequences for political (Tomlinson, 1975) and even religious (Kohlberg, 1974) areas of understanding and evaluation.

No attempt can be made here to analyse the nature of these various features and sequences, nor to consider the structure of their interrelationships. What is clear, however, is that together they suggest a much more complex picture of moral development (in the broad sense) than Kohlberg's unitary view indicates. Haan's study is particularly suggestive, for if mature moral thought regarding interpersonal loyalties and commitments must be distinguished theoretically from mature reasoning about social institutions, then the case for moral rules being necessarily impersonal and impartial is arguably much greater in the latter case. And her more affective focus may give clues to how moral behaviour and thought might sometimes begin to regress when social conditions make the maintenance of either interpersonal or institutional sympathies more difficult. Kohlberg's rationalism simply rules out the possibility of cognitive-affective regression.

This last point emphasizes again how seriously Kohlberg has neglected the influence of actual social experiences in the acquisition or maintenance of firm moral or pro-social commitments. If the essence of morality and its psychological representation is actually rooted in the essential intersubjectivity of persons, then moral development theory must take more direct account of early social experience and its cultural setting. The ways in which this encourages, yet also constrains, our progressive extension of the audience for our primary social sympathies must be considered, since these will limit the extent to which factors connected with cognitive equilibration can suffice to promote commitment to a principled morality. Sympathetic (rather than simply empathic) role-taking must depend heavily, as Rawls (1971) recognizes, on the actual forms of social life that a social structure embodies. Education in role-taking can have limited effect in the absence of lasting experience of participation in flexible social relationships, involving self-chosen, reciprocal, and long-term commitments to others, which alone can make hypothetically ideal moral perspectives concretely realizable and motivationally binding upon us.

This suggests that moral maturity must be culturally relative in a more profound sense than Kohlberg has recognized. If the conception of an optimal ethic which can be envisaged within a society is itself necessarily limited by social structural constraints on relationships, and by other aspects of the forms of cultural adaptation which that society has realized, it becomes dangerous and even unfair to judge the moral maturity of a society's members by a standard developed in another culture. It may sometimes be possible to judge their typical forms of moral reasoning as less cognitively advanced; but to judge that another culture's conceptions of the good life are ethically inferior, or to evaluate their conduct as less morally praiseworthy even when they adhere to their own ideal codes as closely as we do to ours, may rarely be justifiable in rational terms. A moderate 'realistic relativism', which takes account of both universal and variable naturalistic features of human social life (Brandt, 1979) may permit us to establish some minimal rationality objective core for an ideal humanly constructed morality—but even then not necessarily to judge others by this code.

A psychological theory of development must seek to avoid defining moral maturity in ways which preclude individuals in other social classes, cultures, or historical epochs from attaining the moral status which we must regard as evaluatively superior. This does not mean that we should necessarily condone conduct which we find inhumane, or refrain from seeking to persuade others to change their code (but only by means that do not in turn morally compromise ourselves in respect of our own code). As yet we are so lacking in an adequate account of principled morality and its sources that we can say very little about moral maturity with any confidence. For the present at least we must seek to understand ethical diversity rather than proscribe it. Pre-emptive and premature theories of moral maturity threaten to stifle the open advocacy and argument which is one significant part of what morality is necessarily about, and which is itself a major source of social evolutionary as well as developmental moral advance.

The unjustified and unrecognized assumption of ethical realism actually provides, in the name of recognizing objective truths about morality, or even under the laudable guise of asserting the universal dignity of individual persons, an unintended (but nonetheless culpable) base from which the more obnoxious forms of moral partiality can even appear to derive spurious suport (Mackie, 1977). For we have ample evidence that the moral crusader, armed with certainty about what codes and principles ought to be accepted by others, is often prepared in practice to seek to impose those standards universally. Sexism, racism, colonialism, and the condescensions of paternalism have at times all been spuriously justified by such assumptions of moral superiority on the part of groups with the power to exploit other groups (cf. Breakwell, Chapter 13).

The abuses often perpetrated in the name of treating each person as an 'end-in-oneself', a socially detached soul awaiting correction and salvation, might lead a social constructivist to propose instead that we should consider persons as 'ends-in-each-other'. Such an ethic of charity or love (Puka, 1976) might be no more 'correct' in absolute terms, but it would remind us that tolerance and caring may have at least as good claims as justice to being major moral virtues—especially tolerance for the autonomy of other communities when they have constructed moral codes for their own collective purposes rather than ours. The moderate moral relativist can at least insist that no-one can be justified in acting on the assumptions of moral absolutism, or in constructing a priori theories which might appear to justify such acts.

References

Bar-Tal, D. (1976). *Prosocial Behaviour, Theory and Research*, Hemisphere Publishing Co., Washington.

Baumrind, D. (1978). A dialectical materialist's perspective on knowing social reality. In W. Damon (Ed.), *Moral Development*, Jossey-Bass, San Francisco. pp. 61–82.

Berger, P., and Luckmann, T. (1967). *The Social Construction of Reality*. Allen Lane, The Penguin Press, London.

Berger, P., and Pullberg, S. (1965). Reification and the sociological critique of consciousness, *History and Theory*, **4**, pp. 196–211.

Boyce, W. D., and Jensen, L. C. (1978). *Moral Reasoning, A Psychological-Philosophical Integration*, University of Nebraska Press, Lincoln.

Boyd, D. R. (1978). An interpretation of principled morality. *Journal of Moral Education*, **8**, 110–123.

Brandt, R. B. (1976). The psychology of benevolence and its implications for philosophy. *Journal of Philosophy*, **73**, 429–452.

Brandt, R. B. (1979). *A Theory of the Good and the Right*, Clarendon Press, Oxford.

Broughton, J. (1978). The cognitive-developmental approach to morality: a reply to Kurtines and Greif. *Journal of Moral Education*, **7**, 81–96.

Campbell, D. T. (1975). On the conflicts between biological and social evolution and between psychology and moral tradition. *American Psychologist*, **30**, 1103–1126.

Cattell, R. B. (1972). *Beyondism, A New Morality from Science*, Pergamon Press, Oxford.

Codd, J. A. (1977). Some conceptual problems in the cognitive-developmental approach to morality. *Journal of Moral Education*, **6**, 147–157.

Damon, W. (1977). *The Social World of the Child*, Jossey-Bass, San Francisco.

Dworkin, G. (1978). Moral Autonomy. In H. T. Engelhardt, Jr, and D. Callaghan (Eds), *Morals, Science and Sociality*, Hastings Center, New York.

Edel, M., and Edel, A. (1968). *Anthropology and Ethics: The Quest for Moral Understanding*, Rev. edition, Case Western Reserve University Press, Cleveland.

Eibl-Eibesfeldt, I. (1971). *Love and Hate, On the Natural History of Basic Behaviour Patterns*, Methuen, London.

Faust, D., and Arbuthnot, J. (1978). Relationship between moral and Piagetian reasoning and the effectiveness of moral education. *Developmental Psychology*, **14**, 435–436.

Flavell, J. H. (1974). The development of inferences about others. In T. Mischel (Ed.), *Understanding Other Persons*, Basil Blackwell, Oxford. pp. 66–116.

Flew, A. G. N. (1967). *Evolutionary Ethics*, Macmillan, London.

Gibbs, J. C. (1977). Kohlberg's stages of moral judgement—a constructive critique. *Harvard Educational Review*, **47**, 43–61.

Ginsberg, M. (1961). *Evolution and Progress*, Heinemann, London.

Haan, N. (1978). Two moralities in action: relationships to thought, ego regulation, and development. *Journal of Personality and Social Psychology*, **36**, 286–305.

Hampshire, S. (1978). Morality and pessimism. In S. Hampshire (Ed.), *Public and Private Morality*, Cambridge University Press, Cambridge. pp. 1–22.

Harré, R., and Secord, P. F. (1972). *The Explanation of Social Behaviour*, Basil Blackwell, Oxford.

Hoffman, M. L. (1975). Developmental synthesis of affect and cognition and its implications for altruistic motivation. *Developmental Psychology*, **11**, 607–622.

Hoffman, M. L. (1976). Empathy, role-taking, guilt, and development of altruistic sympathies. In T. Lickona (Ed.), *Moral Development and Behaviour: Theory, Research, and Social Issues*, Holt, Rinehart, and Winston, New York. pp. 124–143.

Keasey, C. B. (1975). Implicators of cognitive development for moral reasoning. In D. J. De Palma and J. M. Foley (Eds), *Moral Development: Current Theory and Research*, Lawrence Elbaum Associates, Hillsdale, New Jersey. pp. 39–56.

Kelly, G. A. (1955). *The Psychology of Personal Constructs*, W. W. Norton, New York.
Kelvin, P, (1969). *The Bases of Social Behaviour*, Holt, Rinehart, and Winston, London.
Kitwood, T. (1977). What does 'having values' mean? *Journal of Moral Education*, **6**, 81–89.
Kohlberg, L. (1971) From is to ought: how to commit the naturalistic fallacy and get away with it in the study of moral development. In T. Mischel (Ed.), *Cognitive Development and Epistemology*, Academic Press, New York. pp. 151–235.
Kohlberg, L. (1973). The claim to moral adequacy of a highest stage of moral judgement. *Journal of Philosophy*, **70**, 630–646.
Kohlberg, L. (1974). Education, moral development and faith. *Journal of Moral Education*, **4**, 5–16.
Kohlberg, L. (1976). Moral stages and moralization: the cognitive-developmental approach. In T. Lickona (Ed.), *Moral Development and Behaviour: Theory, Research and Social Issues*, Holt, Rinehart, and Winston, New York.
Kohlberg, L. (1978). Revisions in the theory and practice of moral development. In W. Damon (Ed.), *Moral Development*, Jossey-Bass, San Francisco. pp. 83–88.
Kohlberg, L., and Elfenbein, D. (1975). The development of moral judgements concerning capital punishment. *American Journal of Orthopsychiatry*, **45**, 614–640.
Kuhn, D., Langer, J., Kohlberg, L., and Haan, H. (1977). The development of formal operations in logical and moral judgement. *Genetic Psychology Monographs*, **95**, 97–188.
Lickona, T. (1976). Critical issues in the study of moral development and behaviour. In T. Lickona (Ed.), *Moral Development and Behaviour: Theory, Research and Social Issues*, Holt, Rinehart, and Winston, New York. pp. 3–27.
Linton, R. (1952). Universal ethical principles: an anthropological view. In R. N. Anshen (Ed.), *Moral Principles of Action, Man's Ethical Imperative*, Harper Bros, New York. pp. 645–660.
Lock, A. (Ed.) (1978). *Action, Gesture and Symbol, The Emergence of Language*. Academic Press, London.
Lorenz, K. (1974). *Civilized Man's Eight Deadly Sins*, Methuen, London.
Lorenz, K. (1977). *Behind the Mirror, A Search for the Natural History of Human Knowledge,* Methuen, London.
Mackie, J. L. (1977). *Ethics: Inventing Right and Wrong*, Penguin Books, Harmondsworth, Middlesex.
Margolis, J. (1971). *Values and Conduct*, Clarendon Press, Oxford.
Melden, A. I. (1977). *Rights and Persons*, Basil Blackwell, Oxford.
Midgley, M. (1978). *Beast and Man, The Roots of Human Nature*, Harvester Press, Hassocks, Sussex.
Moir, D. G. (1974). Egocentrism and the emergence of conventional morality in pre-adolescent girls. *Child Development*, **45**, 299–304.
Morelli, E. A. (1978). The sixth stage of moral development. *Journal of Moral Education*, **7**, 97–108.
Moscovici, S. (1977). *Society Against Nature: The Emergence of Human Societies*, Harvester Press, Brighton, Sussex.
Mussen, P. H., and Eisenberg-Berg, N. (1977). *Roots of Caring, Sharing and Helping: The Development of Prosocial Behaviour in Children*, W. H. Freeman, San Francisco.
Nagel, T. (1970). *The Possibility of Altruism*, Clarendon Press, Oxford.
Neisser, U. (1976). *Cognition and Reality, Principles and Implications of Cognitive Psychology*, W. H. Freeman, San Francisco.
Nucci, L. P., and Turiel, E. (1978). Social interactions and the development of social concepts in pre-school children. *Child Development*, **59**, 400–407.
Pahel, K. (1976). Moral motivation. *Journal of Moral Education*, **5**, 223–230.

Piaget, J. (1932). *The Moral Judgement of the Child*, Routledge and Kegan Paul, London; 1977 edn, Penguin Books, Harmondsworth, London.
Piaget, J. (1972a). *The Principles of Genetic Epistemology*, Routledge and Kegan Paul, London.
Piaget, J. (1972b). *Psychology and Epistemology, Towards a Theory of Knowledge*, Penguin Books, Harmondsworth, Middlesex.
Puka, B. (1976). Moral education and its cure. In J. R. Meyer (Ed.), *Reflections on Values Education*, Wilfred Laurier University Press, Ontario. pp. 47–87.
Rawls, J. (1971). *A Theory of Justice*, Harvard University Press, Cambridge, Mass.; 1972 edn., Oxford University Press, London.
Rest, J. R., Davison, M. L., and Robbins, S. (1978). Age trends in judging moral issues: a review of cross-sectional, longitudinal, and sequential studies of the Defining Issues Test. *Child Development*, **49**, 263–279.
Richards, M. P. M. (Ed.) (1974). *The Integration of a Child into a Social World*, Cambridge University Press, Cambridge.
Selman, R. L. (1975). Level of social perspective taking and the development of empathy in children: speculations from a social-cognitive viewpoint. *Journal of Moral Education*, **5**, 35–43.
Selman, R. L. (1976). Social-cognitive understanding, a guide to educational and clinical practice. In T. Lickona (Ed.), *Moral Development and Behaviour: Theory, Research and Social Issues*, Holt, Rinehart, and Winston, New York. pp. 299–316.
Simpson, E. L. (1974). Moral development research: a case study of scientific bias. *Human Development*, **17**, 81–106.
Smith, M. E. (1978). Moral reasoning, its relation to logical thinking and role-taking. *Journal of Moral Education*, **8**, 41–49.
Stark, W. (1976). *The Social Bond: An Investigation into the Bases of Law-Abidingness, Vol. 1. Antecedents of the Social Bond: The Phylogeny of Sociality*, Fordham University Press, New York.
Sullivan, E. V. (1977). A study of Kohlberg's structural theory of moral development: a critique of liberal social science ideology. *Human Development*, **20**, 352–376.
Tomlinson, P. (1975). Political education: cognitive-developmental perspectives from moral education. *Oxford Review of Educaton*, **1**, 241–267.
Trainer, F. E. (1977). A critical analysis of Kohlberg's contribution to the study of moral thought. *Journal for the Theory of Social Behaviour*, **7**, 41–64.
Turiel, E. (1975). The development of social concepts: mores, customs, and conventions. In D. J. De Palma and J. M. Foley (Eds), *Moral Development: Current Theory & Research*, Lawrence Erlbaum Associates, Hillsdale, New Jersey. pp. 7–37.
Turiel, E. (1978). The development of Concepts of Social structure: Social convention. In J. Glick and K. A. Clarke-Stewart (Eds), *The Development of Social Understanding*, Gardner Press, New York. pp. 25–107.
Vine, I. (1981). In defence of 'speciesist' ethics. Unpublished ms.
Vine, I. (1982). Sociobiology and Social psychology—rivalry or symbiosis? The explanation of altruism. *British Journal of Social Psychology* (in press).
Von Fürer-Haimendorf, C. (1967). *Morals and Merit, A Study of Values and Social Controls in South Asian Societies*. Weidenfeld and Nicolson, London.
Voyat, G. (1978). Cognitive and social development: a new perspective. In J. Glick and K. A. Clarke-Stewart (Eds), *The Development of Social Understanding*, Gardner Press, New York. pp. 11–24.
Warnock, G. J. (1971). *The Object of Morality*, Methuen, London.
Williams, B. (1972). *Morality: An Introduction to Ethics*, Cambridge University Press, London.
Wilson, E. O. (1978). *On Human Nature*, Harvard University Press, Cambridge, Massachusetts.

Morality in the Making
Edited by H. Weinreich-Haste and D. Locke
© 1983, John Wiley & Sons, Ltd.

CHAPTER 3

Morality and Politics: The Ideological Dimension in the Theory of Moral Development

NICHOLAS EMLER

Introduction

This chapter will primarily be concerned with the ideological orientations that are represented in Kohlberg's theory of moral development. The pursuit of this objective, however, raises other more general issues. It seems to have become popular for social scientists to use the charge of ideological bias as a stick with which to beat their intellectual opponents. The charge may often be merited but as a colleague reasonably observed, once you have shown the bias to exist, 'so what?' Is it after all any more than a truism to say that any theory of human nature is shaped by historical and cultural influences, that it reflects and recommends particular human values? It would be a strange theory of which this was not true.

I hope to show that there is something of significance to be learned from consideration of a theory's ideological orientation, in this case about the more important assumptions underlying much work in social and developmental psychology, and about the connection between moral and political attitudes. Apart from enriching our understanding of a field of research and its implications it may also help us to appreciate the limits of the questions that have been asked.

The discussion is organized around three main ideological themes: rationalism, individualism, and liberalism. It cannot be emphasized too strongly that these themes are in no sense unique to Kohlberg's theory, and on one level the theory serves here to exemplify the manner of operation of these themes within a wider area of scholarship. I shall begin by identifying some of the major terms.

Ideology

I take an ideology to be a set of beliefs, characteristic of a social group, which 'explains' its culture, its position and relation to other groups, and which rationalizes its values, priorities, and social arrangements. These beliefs may, according to some external criterion, be true or false, benevolent or malevolent, emancipatory or manipulative. They may invert the truth, conceal it, provide a partial and selective representation of it, or simply direct attention to the irrelevant. But what makes a set of beliefs an ideology is its function—promoting a particular way of life or set of social arrangements or political programme.

I am inclined towards the view of ideology to be found in Marxist social theory. In this view, ideology, like social organization, is shaped by the material conditions of a group's existence, these conditions including the ecology, economy, and accumulated technological resources of the culture. There is also in this view an implication that ideology involves a degree of false consciousness. However, the lesson of history appears to be that consciousness is always partial if not false, and social theories, even though they differ from lay prejudices in several important respects, share this quality of partiality.

Individualism

Individualism is taken to be a particular way of interpreting the relationship between an individual and his or her social group, collective, or culture. There are several forms of individualism but all share the same core assumptions. These include the notion that society is no more than an aggregate of discrete individuals, each pursuing his own goals and interests. Social living usually happens to be more advantageous than solitary living and, when it is, individuals join together in a communal group. But the collective is formed only after a kind of cost/benefit analysis has taken place, and if at a later date the results should be reversed then it is implied that the group will be dissolved.

A related aspect of individualism is the idea that the process of being socialized into a group fundamentally transforms a person's original nature. There is presumed to be a deep incompatibility between the needs of individuals and the needs of groups, and the kinds of sacrifice required by the demands of group membership forever alter and restructure the soul of the socialized person. It is also often implied that the influence of the group on the individual is such as to undermine his rationality and the objectivity of his perceptions.

There are of course defensible alternatives to this view of the relationship between humans and their culture. One such, which is more characteristic of sociological than psychological theory, might be called communalism. It is the view that people only become human when they are integrated into a social group, that group living promotes, facilitates, and encourages individual development and that persons who live outside human society are in fundamental ways less than human. In other words, communal living and membership of social units are natural states of affairs rather than artificial devices alien to man's natural tendencies. Indeed, these constitute essential features of the way in which humans as a species have adapted to their environment (cf. Moscovici, 1976, Humphrey, 1976).

Rationalism

Rationalism constitutes a form of intellectual individualism. It refers to a set of beliefs about how the mind works and how knowledge is acquired. The most distinctive features of rationalism today are a French creation, the legacy of Descartes and his successors. In the Cartesian 'cogito' we have the claim that the starting point for all knowledge is the individual's experience of his own existence. This laid a basis for the protest of the individual thinker against interference by Church and State in matters of intellectual judgment. What was true and good was no longer to be determined by collective wisdom or ecclesiastical authority, but by solitary thought.

Rationalism represents a supreme confidence in the power of reason, and correspondingly it accords a minor place to emotion or desire, the unconscious or socially derived prejudices in human thinking. Cognitive activity is simultaneously the highest, most distinctive, and most fundamental human activity. Knowledge is acquired by the direct confrontation of thought with experience, but thought is not necessarily disciplined by experience because reason is sufficient in itself to produce valid knowledge.

Three consequences fall out of this doctrine of the self-sufficiency of reason. First, the role of experience in the development of knowledge is minimized, an attitude exemplified by Einstein's sublime indifference to any experimental verification of his theory. Second, science is seen as somehow independent of its sociocultural origins. This is an interesting distortion because the institution of science emerged partly in response to the manifest limitations of intellectual individualism. Intellectual judgment in scientific work was saved from a complete and arbitrary relativism by the social organization of this activity. Not only does rationalism under-emphasize the social origins of scientific ideas, it also ignores the extent to which scientific knowledge, like any other knowledge, represents the fruits of collective activity (cf. Emler and Heather, 1980). Instead of acknowledging science as a cultural invention, it is seen as an individual activity the propensity for which is a natural endowment. Science is taken to be the embodiment of a universalizable set of standards that owe nothing to history or social organization.

Third and finally, rationalism leads to the apotheosis of mathematics. Mathematical reasoning is the highest exercise of intelligence and mathematical proof the surest form of knowledge. As Russell (1946) put it, 'The perfect model of truth is the multiplication table, which is precise and certain and free from all temporal dross' (p. 775). Wisdom, scope, experience, and judgment, by a peculiar inversion of priorities, become in principle less admirable than sheer logic in the storehouse of human talents.

There are alternatives to rationalism as an epistemology and a theory of cognition. The empirical sciences provides an important example. The tradition of empiricism, exemplified in recent times by Hume and William James, holds that knowledge begins in experience and must ultimately be verified by experience. Implicit in this empirical tradition is a profound scepticism regarding the degree to which human actions are or even can be governed by reason; as Hume noted, 'Reason is, and ought only to be the slave of the passions, and can never pretend to any other office than to serve and obey them.'

Hume and James were philosophical psychologists who arrived at their views of the nature of reason and the origins of knowledge, ironically enough, through a form of introspection. Using an entirely different methodology, interviews with the mentally disturbed, Sigmund Freud and Carl Jung (inspired perhaps by the writings of Schopenhauer and Nietzsche) came to rather similar conclusions concerning the role of reason in the conduct of human affairs. In the tradition of Freud and Jung, reason is an illusion, and rationality is a facade, an act one mounts in order to disguise one's true (and usually publicly inadmissible) intentions which are themselves based on instincts. Moreover, to the degree that one attempts to operate exclusively according to the canons of reason, one will only exacerbate the neurosis that produced this compulsion in the first place.

Finally, classical sociological theory, based on the study of comparative social history, reaches an even more extreme view regarding the limits of human reason. For Durkheim (1938) man is even more a slave to forces outside his awareness than Freud ever dreamed. Cartesian rationality is an institutionalized thought form, a way of thinking and speaking that is characteristic of one particular culture and social class and one particular point in history with no unique or compelling claims on our credibility. We might also note that, in contrast with the rationalist claim that logic and mathematics represent the highest forms of human intelligence, the sociologist George Herbert Mead argued the title belongs to the capacity to analyse human relationships.

Liberalism

As used here the term 'liberalism' is closely connected to rationalism and individualism. There are also of course important differences, particularly between liberalism and rationalism, hence the desirability of considering each separately. Liberalism here refers to a political perspective that has at least the following elements. First is the belief that there is no innate human nature; human nature is plastic and malleable, and personality is essentially a reflection of a social environment. Second, innate differences between people are denied, specifically differences in talents or capabilities that might produce differential status or achievement. Such differences as exist are assumed to arise through education. These various elements combine to justify an emphasis on equality of opportunity (as distinct from equality of outcomes). A further and pervasive theme in liberal political philosophy is individualism. Government is a remedy for some of the inconveniences of the state of nature, but is not a perfect one. Thus individuals are to be protected from the whims of the state through the social contract from which government is ideally to arise, a contract between free individuals and those who are to govern. The terms of this contract are to be such as to protect the natural rights of individuals, particularly their rights to private property. If governments fail to meet their side of the contract they can be justly resisted; if their performance does not please the majority of individuals, they can be voted out of office.

The liberal is also inclined towards ethical individualism. Although there are taken to be certain inalienable individual rights, there is also to be tolerance for differences in belief. This tolerance may at first have sprung from an economic motive. Liberalism, has historically been allied to the pursuit of commerce and in this, intolerance, particularly of a religious kind, was an inconvenience. A further element in liberalism is its optimism about mankind. People are held to be reasoning and reasonable creatures and this, combined with assumption of the plasticity of human nature, is taken to mean that mankind is ultimately perfectable, and to justify faith in progress. Differences in status can, and therefore should, be reduced or eliminated by providing the less advantaged with the tools and opportunities for social progress. Finally, then, liberalism has come to entail a commitment to active social engineering as a way of achieving progress.

One obvious alternative to liberalism is a conservative view composed of corresponding alternative elements; for example, that there is an original or innate human nature, that differences in native endowments lead to differential status, that people are not basically reasonable but often act in self-defeating ways, that social progress may be an illusion, and that social engineering is bought at the cost of ethnic and personal identity, that there is an inevitable tradeoff between freedom and happiness, and that civilization may only be preserved through a degree of social injustice.

Other alternatives lie at the opposite extreme as for instance those political philosophies which place social justice above all other considerations including individual rights, which advocate instead some form of collectivism and subordination of individual interest to state authority, and finally which reject the piecemeal social reform of liberalism in favour of wholesale revolutionary change.

Ideology in Contemporary Social Psychology

In contemporary social psychology individualism remains probably the most prominent of the three ideological themes I have outlined, but individualism in this context has reflected a set of methodological strategies as well as a collection of values. Thus the unit of analysis is the monad, the isolated individual and his or her cognitive and perceptual processes, in social as much as in other branches of psychology. Psychological models of human functioning are based on an unmoderated form of intellectual individualism according to which it is the individual who acts, thinks, and chooses, who invents, solves problems, and discovers truth. Therefore it is the individual that must be studied.

In this respect individualism has come to serve the ends of social control rather than the liberal goals of social reform. Critics who have commented on a preoccupation with methods and techniques in social psychology at the expense of theories and ideas (e.g. Moscovici, 1972) may be reacting to a psychology shaped to administrative and bureaucratic uses, to goals of prediction and control. Much of psychology in the psychometric tradition is oriented in this direction, as are theories of development as behaviour modification. But however efficacious these psychologies are as technologies they potentially serve a significant ideological function. They underwrite accounts of social problems which locate the malfunction in specific persons rather than the social systems to which they belong. The implication of such accounts is that remedies lie in the 'readjustment' of individuals rather than reconsideration of the priorities of social institutions.

Despite the influence of administrative and bureaucratic values on social science, social psychology has largely retained a commitment to individualistic values that are directly opposed to these (Hogan and Emler, 1978). Liberalism, rationalism, and individualism are themes common to much of the modern work in social psychology, whether it be person perception, attitude change, social influence, communication, or interpersonal attraction that is the object of study. Theories of moral development are of particular interest, however, because they are concerned more specifically with the beliefs and values that characterize these ideological themes.

Kohlberg's Theory and its Ideological Orientation

The details of Kohlberg's theory of moral development are dealt with elsewhere in this volume (see Weinreich-Haste, Chapter 1) and require no detailed exposition here. But to orient the discussion that follows it will be helpful to outline briefly the last three of the six stages of development that Kohlberg describes. It is the claims made for these that are most critical for the issues raised in this chapter.

Kohlberg's fourth stage is a sophisticated form of conventional morality. Its orientation is to the social order as it exists, to fulfilling the duties entailed by the individual's role in this order, and to defending the social system against its enemies—the lawless, dissidents, and hostile foreign interests. Beyond this stage, morality becomes detached from what is merely conventional. It becomes instead orientated to criteria for the right and the good which have an objective and pan-cultural validity. Moral thinking at this level is described as

'post-conventional' or 'principled'. Stage five is concerned with rational procedures for making, as opposed to simply maintaining, laws. It embodies a social-
contract view of the relation between individual and society, and appeals to
utilitarian considerations to justify rules. The sixth stage is the recognition that
there are non-relative and universalizable moral principles beyond mere utility,
these including respect for the dignity of individuals as ends, and justice as
impartial and equal respect for each individual's rights and claims.

Kohlberg's theory offers a novel solution to the problem of moral or political
bias in social science. Until recently the most respectable response to this problem was to demand a scrupulous neutrality from the scientist, to insist that the
facts be allowed to speak for themselves, and to be ever vigilant against any
taint of bias. A more recent response has been to recognize the inevitability of
bias and even welcome it, to choose sides on the basis of one's personal tastes,
and make one's work serve one's prejudices. Kohlberg's solution is to seek to
establish which values are objectively more adequate than others. This has the
merit of avoiding the meaningless and often phoney neutrality of the first solution and the apparently arbitrary choice of the second. Kohlberg has sought, in
his own words to 'commit the naturalistic fallacy and get away with it' (cf.
Kohlberg, 1971b). This is an important innovation and important therefore to
ask whether he has been successful.

Kohlberg's theory of moral development advocates the validity of the moral
perspective to be found at the principled level and in particular at the sixth
stage. Inspection of the theory reveals that overall it underwrites the beliefs and
values that are characteristic of individualism, rationalism, and liberalism. I
shall argue that this orientation is not entirely a conclusion urged by a pattern of
empirical findings. Instead it is built into the very assumptions and methods on
which the theory is built.

Individualism in Kohlberg's Theory

The manner in which research is presented to subjects is often revealing of the
investigator's values. In the study of moral attitudes it is not uncommon to find
interviews or questionnaires introduced with a statement to the effect that there
are no right or wrong answers to the questions that follow and that everyone has
their own opinion. We tend not to be as surprised at this as we might be if, for
instance, such remarks were made at the beginning of an intelligence test, but
perhaps we should at least ponder for a moment what they imply. They carry
the message that the investigator accepts the validity of a fairly extreme form of
ethical individualism and relativism. They may suggest to the subject that this is
a position he also should accept and answer accordingly. More generally, they
raise the possibility that the investigator's theory of moral development has
been so framed as to exclude any aspects of development except those which
correspond to this ethical orientation. A review of theories of moral development reveals that their individualistic assumptions in fact run considerably
deeper.

Kohlberg's theory of moral development shares with most others the assumption that the natural direction of moral development is towards internalized moral controls; a morally mature individual is a morally autonomous individual. However, Kohlberg takes and develops this assumption of moral self-sufficiency further than other theorists in several respects. In most accounts of moral development it is at least accepted that what is internal has been internalized for it was first external in the form of cultural norms. Kohlberg's moral hero moves beyond any such dependence on cultural definitions of morality.

From the earliest stages the individual independently constructs a moral perspective. Even when he accepts conventional virtues and standards, he does so autonomously—he makes them his own, experiencing their claim on his commitment as an internal compulsion.

This theoretical emphasis follows in part from Kohlberg's methodological orientation. It has always been characteristic of psychology to take the individual as the self-contained unit of analysis but in the study of moral development this has generally been mitigated by consideration of the social context of development. Research in the naturalistic tradition, for instance, has dealt with the interplay between parental behaviour and the child's moral characteristics (e.g. Hoffman and Saltzstein, 1967). Social learning theorists have concerned themselves with effects of contingencies in the social environment on individual's moral habits (e.g. Aronfreed, 1976; Bandura, 1971). Even Piaget (1932) saw moral consciousness as the reflection of forms of social relationship.

In Kohlberg's approach the unit of analysis is more completely the individual. The closest Kohlberg comes to any consideration of the relation between individual development and the social environment is in his reference to the importance of role-taking opportunities (e.g. Kohlberg, 1969, 1971a). However, this issue has only ever been considered in terms of the relation between one set of internal processes and another. One set of competencies, role-taking skills, is shown to underlie another, moral reasoning skills (e.g. Moir, 1974; Selman, 1971). Likewise, proposals about links between cognitive and moral development retain the individual as the exlusive and sole focus of analysis.

There is, of course, evidence which clearly indicates a connection between environmental conditions and individual development (e.g. Gorsuch and Barnes, 1973; White, 1975), but the theory allows only that such conditions can facilitate or inhibit the individuals's intrinsic developmental tendencies; they cannot and do not impart to development any specific directional bias.[1]

It is the hypothesis of further levels of moral development, beyond a conventional orientation, that is the most distinctly individualistic feature of Kohlberg's theory. According to Kohlberg, his research proves that individuals can ultimately discover for themselves the basis for a morality which owes nothing to culture or historical heritage, which is instead purely the spontane-

---

[1] Kohlberg's recent interest in just communities represents a new and significant departure from the individualism of his former position (e.g. Kohlberg, Scharf, and Hickey 1973). So far, however, it has led to no significant modifications to the individualism initially built into the theory.

ous product of individual thought. Kohlberg takes issue with two claims made by social philosophers, 'all norms and values are relative so that there is no ground for morality better than our culture's, and . . . moral norms ungrounded in collective belief are unsatisfying to their propounders as well as to others' (Kohlberg, 1971b, pp. 199–200). His research provides a defence of ethical individualism by showing that a significant minority of persons do arrive at moral principles that are independent of cultural context and yet have compelling validity for the individual and, further, that members of this minority are developmentally more mature than others because they arrive at their position through a rejection of the adequacy of conventional definitions. This is a form of Cartesian rationalism, the idea that truth can be apprehended directly through the private exercise of individual reason. What is critical for Kohlberg's position is whether in fact post-conventional perspectives do represent developmentally more advanced stages than others, and whether they are spontaneous intellectual emergents. These claims will be critically examined later in the chapter.

It is also characteristic of Kohlberg's theory that it gives little attention to moral action as distinct from moral reasoning. It appears to be assumed that for all practical purposes one need look no further than the individual's capacities for moral reasoning in order to account for moral action. Here again we encounter a form of individualism in which it is assumed that individuals act autonomously and independently rather than contingently and interdependently; they do not co-operate or inter-act. There are therefore, no new and significant conditions entailed in social action that are not already present in individual thought, and so no need to study action as such. Whereas for Piaget thought was in a sense the internalization of action, for Kohlberg action appears only to be the externalization of thought.

I have suggested that Kohlberg's theory is based on the view that each person privately and independently constructs his or her own moral theory. Later we shall see that these moral theories, in their most developed forms, also incorporate values that are individualistic. But first let us consider the psychological process that is supposed to lie at the heart of moral development—reasoning.

Rationalism in Kohlberg's Theory

The rationalism of Kohlberg's theory is its most transparent, even self-proclaimed, feature. Moral development is seen as essentially a cognitive process with cognitive products. Development consists of the successive emergence of increasingly complex and adequate forms of moral reasoning. Moral action is compelled by moral thought and thought generates decisions or conclusions that are morally compelling because they are *logically* compelling. The dynamics of development are to be found within the organization of moral reasoning itself. Failure to reach logically satisfying or cognitively balanced solutions to moral problems generates a pressure towards the transformation of thought into patterns which can produce such solutions. Under pressures which arise therefore from the inherent contradiction in existing patterns of thought, new patterns or 'structures' spontaneously arise. Their form is always an elaboration of the previous pattern. Both the logic and the dynamics of change are thus located within the individual; development is self-generated (see also Vine, Chapter 2).

The enthusiasm for cognitive models of psychological functioning is by no means peculiar to Kohlberg; it is endemic in contemporary social psychology (Hogan and Emler, 1978). Witness, for instance, the domination of attitude theory by models of cognitive consistency or the person perception literature by attribution theory. Kohlberg's theory of moral development appears to be modelled on Piaget's theory of intellectual development, specifically Piaget's structural theory (Turner, 1973), rather than the functional theory of his early work. For Piaget in this later mood, the fundamental elements of thought are logico-mathematical concepts (e.g. Piaget, 1951). Reasoning in its purest form is equated with logic, and its highest expression is abstract and purely formal reasoning.

This form of thought is revealed to be of a type that conforms to the canons of a particular philosophy of inquiry; it is hypothetico-deductive. Piaget's account of the 'highest' stage of intellectual development reflects several aspects of the more prestigious and 'scientific' sciences (e.g. Inhelder and Piaget, 1958). For instance, this stage involves the ability to discover a set of laws which generate non-contradictory predictions, the ability to separate and eliminate the effects of variables by manipulating each in turn while holding others constant (Newtonian mechanics comes naturally to the individual apparently, but not Open Systems Theory), the ability to set up and test hypotheses that are comprehensive and mutually exclusive, to grasp relations of correlation and proportionality, and to understand the roles of chance and probability. Piaget also emphasizes concepts of time, space, substance, number, and causality as the natural categories of knowledge. While thought is described in terms of logico-mathematical structures, the problems it solves are those posed by the natural or material environment. The social environment, if considered at all, is but a special case which can be subsumed under the same general model.

Finally, in a manner which echoes the commitments of logical positivism, Piaget's description of intellectual development denies, discounts or ignores the relevance of personal motivation and interest, restricting itself to what is accepted as pure intellect abstracted from both the identity of the thinker and the circumstances of his historical and cultural situation. Piaget would have it that thought is inherently inclined to become increasingly objective and detached from the idiosyncracies of personal experience.

The Piagetian parallels in Kohlberg's theory are both general and specific. Kohlberg adopts the Piagetian principle of developmental progression— 'equilibration'. He also shares Piaget's stress on logic as the foundation of thought, and the idea that formal, abstract, and 'decentred' modes of thinking define the natural endpoints of development. Kohlberg, however, shifts the stress further in a rationalist direction. Piaget insists that cognitive processes are systems of action; to know something is to act upon it. Piaget's model of the relation between subject and object thus has a dialectical quality, even though Piaget assumed that development produces systems of action increasingly freed from concrete contexts of application. Kohlberg instead deals almost exclusively with reasoning as such.

Specific parallels are drawn between stages in the development of logical operations and stages of moral 'operations'. The higher moral stages, for instance, are defined by the capacity for abstract and hypothetical speculation. The post-conventional stages are distinguished from others by the ability to consider meta-ethical issues as, for instance, the adequacy of moral principles per se considered in the abstract (Kohlberg, 1973).

The interpretation of moral development as the development of reasoning is supported in various ways by Kohlberg's research strategy. First, in order to study the moral orientations of his subjects, Kohlberg poses *moral dilemmas*, problems in which one moral principle appears to be pitted against another. Alston (1971) agrees that this is sensible; if you want to study people's reasoning you must give them problems to reason about. Ideally, these problems should be challenging and unfamiliar, for otherwise your subjects may fall back on established remedies; they might offer a solution without truly reasoning about the problem at all. Alston's point is that insofar as Kohlberg's dilemmas successfully forestall such strategies they may provide an underestimate of the significance in everyday practical moral problem solving of reliance on practised solutions, tried and familiar routines, and common cultural remedies.

Kohlberg is quite clear that his dilemmas are intended to represent *moral* conflicts, which is to say conflicts between one moral principle and another rather than between a moral principle and a personal desire or pragmatic consideration. The intention is that the reasoning be focused on a choice between two different moral principles and thus reveal the reasoners' criteria for such choice. Regardless of how well this procedure works one could still argue it is irrelevant if one believes that social systems have evolved in such a way as to reduce the routine occurrence of conflicts between principles. The use of such conflicts also introduces a selection bias as the researcher must decide, a priori, what constitute moral as opposed to other kinds of principle, and then choose which of these principles should be opposed to one another.

Constructing the dilemmas appropriately is probably not enough to ensure that data of the required kind will be obtained. The dilemmas are presented in an interview, and it is probable that the interviewer must do more than simply present the stimuli. The interviewer must also negotiate with the subject about the kind of responses that are acceptable. The subject must be persuaded that the situation is one in which he or she should display reason. This element of negotiation is generally ignored but it is precisely what Kohlberg's moral judgment interview involves, a set of implicit and explicit messages to the subject which operate to manipulate the subjects' self-presentation. This may be why the interview is more successful than other forms of assessment in producing more 'complete', 'adequate', or 'uncontaminated' data. The series of probes and the flexible questioning procedure employed by an interviewer who has an idea of what appropriate data should look like all conspire to induce the subject to offer 'reasons' for answers. If that is not sufficient, responses which are not seen to be 'reasons' for the purposes of the theory are simply ignored in the coding process.

The subject's performance in the interview as a person who 'reasons' about moral issues is facilitated in another way. The dilemmas are hypothetical. The subject is therefore abstracted from a context of concrete choice with real consequences, and he is free to speculate without the hindrance of normal decision-making pressures. Consequently, the subject is also encouraged to consider the dilemmas hypothetically, that is, from the perspective of a disinterested third party who is uninvolved and whose passions are unengaged. To the degree that this methodology is assumed to model reality, we are asked to accept the fiction that man thinks, then decides, then acts.

Finally, the dilemmas, for all their challenge, are oversimplifications. The complexities of real-life problems are effectively excluded. The subject does not have to confront the subtle ambiguities of particular human natures, his never complete knowledge of them or the situation, the contradictions and confusions in his own self-knowledge, ambivalences of feeling and the never-static nature of interpersonal problems, for others also do not stop acting and reacting. Can the style of a person's problem-solving elicited in response to hypothetical dilemmas, simplified and frozen at a moment in time, really correspond to that person's style in life?

A rationalist emphasis is not only reflected in the general form of the theory. It is also to be found in the descriptions of the post-conventional level of moral thought. Indeed, it is the implication that the natural trend of development is increasingly rationalist that justifies this emphasis in the theory as a whole.

At stage five, rational considerations are prominent, as for instance in the preoccupation with a rational procedure for agreeing upon legal reforms, and rational criteria for choosing between alternative laws and rules. The trend is completed in the sixth stage which embodies in a more complete form the doctrine of the self-sufficiency of reason. It differs from all other stages in its orientation to moral absolutism and a priorism, and the total emancipation of moral principles from any specific cultural setting. The moral philosophy of this stage is in the tradition of abstract formalism with clear acknowledged links to Kant, Hare, and Rawls. It is, in psychological terms, the final and complete triumph of reason over moral uncertainty.

There is another distinct feature of the sixth stage. It identifies morality with justice, as does Kohlberg himself (e.g. Kohlberg, 1976, p. 40). All moral concerns, Kohlberg would have it, reduce to questions of justice and each stage of reasoning is at its core an interpretation of justice. Development is a response to the limitations of the interpretation provided by each stage. Stage six transcends all others because it does not confound justice with other considerations and because it banishes all indeterminacy.

For Kohlberg and the perspective of stage six, justice is interpreted in rationalist terms. This interpretation is opposed to ambiguity. It presupposes there are no irreducible conflicts of interest in life, only failures of reason. This is the justice of a cool, dispassionate, detached perspective. It denies the moral legitimacy of an emotional dimension. It is instead the perspective of 'one whose blood is very snow broth, that never feels the wanton stings and motions of the sense'.

Of the possible objections to rationalism, I want to emphasize here the autonomy of consciousness that it presupposes. The anthropologist Robin Horton proposes that there is a key difference between the styles of thought typical of Western science and those characteristic of traditional societies such as are to be found among indigenous African cultures. In the latter, 'there is no developed awareness of alternatives to the established body of theoretical tenets; whereas in scientifically oriented cultures such an awareness is highly developed' (Horton, 1971, p. 230). This difference is the clue to a whole constellation of attitudes which distinguish the two cultures. There is also an almost point-for-point correspondence between these distinctions and those that mark off post-conventional thought from the other stages. Both post-conventional and scientific thought are reflective rather than unreflective (Horton, 1971, p. 237). That is, both are concerned with general norms for choosing between alternative propositions, in one case moral, in the other factual. Both favour the 'segregation of motives' as opposed to 'mixed motives' (Horton, 1971, pp. 237–238). In Kohlberg's theory, moral development is the gradual purification of the justice concept through its segregation from 'non-moral considerations'. In both there is a destructive rather than protective attitude towards established theory. In post-conventional morality, established conventions, tradition, and laws must be tested against rational considerations or higher order principles. There are also certain qualities of traditional thought which create moral domains quite different to those identified in post-conventional thinking. For instance, a protective attitude towards the category system (Horton, 1971, pp. 251–252) creates categories of offence which arise from its violation—what we call taboos.

These observations lead me to two general points. First, whatever the virtues of rationalist and scientific attitudes—and it need not be denied that such virtues exist—these attitudes are characteristic of particular social systems and arise from conditions that are peculiar to these systems. The idea of a rational, autonomous conscience, untouched by history and circumstance, personal biography and social structure, or even by the natural history of the species, has the ontological status of the tooth fairy and the Easter bunny. Second, the tendencies described by Kohlberg's stage sequence, if they are peculiar to a particular kind of culture and its associated intellectual values, may not translate adequately to others.

Liberalism in Kohlberg's Theory

Liberalism is opposed to all forms of authority which appeal to tradition or power, and in this sense most theories of moral development are inclined to Liberalism. They assume that each individual should have the right to manage his own affairs and be responsible for his own conduct. However, they confront a serious difficulty. Having championed the autonomous conscience it was necessary to establish autonomy as the proper condition of mankind in society. Freud was pessimistic, believing an element of authoritarian constraint to be the inevitable price of civilized existence. Piaget was prepared to embrace the liberal ideology of progress and assume that the more rational solution of co-operation between autonomous equals would prevail against constraint.

The difficulty was that constraint seemed the prevalent condition of adult social relations and the historical trend if anything was towards even wider submission to a superordinate external authority, the state. Kohlberg's solution was to show that the formal authority of the state is different in kind from the authority attributed to more powerful individuals. Each reflects a distinct stage of moral thought, the first corresponding to Kohlberg's stage four, the second to stage one. What had previously been thought of as the autonomous liberal conscience turned out only to be a moral emancipation from the constraint of power relations, not a genuine emanicipation from the authority of tradition and the collective. This latter was to be found in Kohlberg's post-conventional stages. Stages four, five, and six, therefore, take the theory directly into the arena of political authority. Each of these stages represents a distinct position regarding the basis for and limits of political legitimacy, though stages five and six tend both to converge on a liberal position.

Several aspects of the fifth stage are consistent with a liberal position, though it could be argued they are also consistent with quite different political philosophies. The relativism of stage five parallels the religious tolerance of classical liberalism; like liberalism it is internationalist rather than nationalistic. As in liberalism also it sets reason above tradition and is oriented toward progress and social reform. The single most compelling parallel with liberal philosophy, however, is in the idea of a social contract. Kohlberg describes the social perspective of post-conventional thought as a 'prior-to-society' perspective (e.g. Kohlberg, 1976, p. 33), or in the terms of Hobbes, Locke, and others, the perspective of men in a 'state of nature'. From this perspective the stage five thinker seeks a rational basis for a set of laws that will, above all else, protect individual rights, rights which are assumed to exist apart from and prior to the law. Paramount among these are an individual's rights to life and liberty. To meet needs of personal security, the stage five thinker conceives of a social contract specifying the terms under which each individual agrees to participate in the collective. He must give his free consent to the laws by which he is to be bound while the laws themselves must serve to protect the rights of individuals.

Kohlberg claims that this stage five solution will, none the less, not be completely satisfactory to a rational individual. It will not, for instance, tell him what to do in situations where legal definitions are questionable or non-existent or in situations which demand civil disobedience because laws which are constitutionally legitimate prescribe unjust behaviour (e.g. Kohlberg, 1971b). This leads Kohlberg to propose a further stage which is capable of giving a social contract a more satisfactory moral basis by providing firm moral principles which are both rational and non-relative. Stage six is intended, therefore, to provide a more adequate solution to the problem of securing individual rights.

We also find that liberal preoccupations are built into the research process itself. The moral dilemmas, employed to elicit styles of moral thought, make core issues out of liberal values such as civil rights and freedoms, property, the value of human life and individual conscience, and each dilemma betrays the central liberal concern—the conflict between individual conscience and authority. The moral dilemmas focus on such issues as the limits of the law's legitimacy, justifications for civil disobedience, the protection of individual rights and freedom of conscience in the face of legal requirements, due process, or the authority of the parent or the state.

One of the more conspicuous obsessions of classical liberalism concerned the right of individuals to hold and protect their private property, particularly property secured through the individual's own labour. Although this emphasis is now seen as somewhat anachronistic it is interesting that in two of the most widely used of Kohlberg's moral dilemmas, such property is a central issue. And it would appear that only the right to life can take precedence over this right.

Finally, if we are correct in identifying post-conventional reasoning with liberalism there should be some relation between the stage of moral thought a person uses and the political leanings that he shows. The various revisions to Kohlberg's stage scoring system that have been made over the years have altered estimates of the distribution of these stages among the adult population. However, most adult moral reasoning should fall within the range from stage three to stage six. According to the foregoing, those with liberal leanings or moderately to the left are more likely to reason at the post-conventional level. Conservatives are more likely to reason in conventional terms. Those of more markedly radical political persuasion are also more likely to show a post-conventional stance, if only because the conservatism of stage four is even less congenial to them than the liberalism of five and six.

Available evidence is of uneven quality, owing to variations in measures of both moral reasoning and political orientation. Thus Fishkin, Keniston, and MacKinnon (1973) used written responses to five moral dilemmas as the basis for their measure of moral reasoning while political orientation was assessed by liking or disliking for thirty-one political slogans. They found that a radical versus conservative orientation correlated $+.33$ with stage six reasoning and $+.26$ with stage five, while the correlation with stage four was $-.68$. A conservative orientation, on the other hand, showed the reverse pattern of correlations. Others, though with variations in method, have found similar relationships (e.g. Alker and Poppen, 1973; Candee, 1976; Fontana and Noel,

1973; Emler, Herron, and Malone, 1979; Sullivan and Quarter, 1972; Rest, 1975a).

The Political Orientation of Kohlberg's Theory: A Critical Appraisal

It is one of Kohlberg's most important claims that the stages identified in his theory reflect structure, not content. The theory deals with changes in the structural complexity and adequacy of moral reasoning and says nothing about the content of moral ideas, so the argument runs. And if accepted it must lead one to interpret correlations betweeen stages of moral reasoning and political orientation as relationships between a structural variable and a content variable. However, as the theory also holds that the content of one's opinions does not determine the structure of one's reasoning, content in such relationships must be the dependent variable. To put it another way, if one's moral reasoning is sufficiently mature, one's politics are more likely to be liberal while those whose reasoning is less well developed will be conservative in outlook.

Before we admit that Kohlberg has succeeded in his epistemological ambition of showing that certain values are objectively more adequate than others, certain objections must be considered. First, the above conclusions assume that the theory sustains a clear distinction between content and structure. I have already argued that it does not, and cannot while values are built into the very assumptions and procedures on which the theory rests.

A second, but not particularly fatal, objection is that there is no clear and objective distinction between the domains of morality and politics. Opinions in both areas rest ultimately on choices about human values. If there is a difference it is only that morality is the more inclusive category. The overlap is apparent if one examines tests of political and moral opinions. Are the questions about justice, punishment, crime, civic responsibility, and property rights in Kohlberg's dilemmas moral questions or political? Clearly they are both. Other measures of moral orientation such as Rest's DIT (Rest, 1975a), Hogan's SEA (Hogan, 1970), Tomkins' Humanitarianism scale (Tomkins, 1965), or Christie's MACH scales (Christie and Geis, 1968), contain the same ambiguities. Correspondingly, measures of political orientation sample what could, with equal felicity, be called moral attitudes. Scales devised to assess the Radicalism–Conservatism dimension always seem to include items on such matters as punishment, religious observance, and standards of sexual conduct. In a similar fashion, scholarly works on moral or political philosophy are seldom in any obvious way exclusively about one rather than the other, as witness Aristotle's *Nicomachean Ethics*, Nietzsche's *On the Genealogy of Morals*, Locke's *Treatise on Government*, Rawls' *A Theory of Justice*. It should, therefore, come as no surprise to learn that moral and political opinions are related since they are by and large one and the same thing.

Though perhaps obvious, this point has sometimes been missed and in consequence has reinforced what I see as certain errors in interpretation. The point is well illustrated by a recent study (Candee, 1976). Candee found that three variables, moral reasoning as assessed by the Kohlberg procedure, an index of concern with rights as opposed to other considerations, and self-rating of political ideology on a nine-point radical–conservative scale were positively inter-correlated. Candee concluded that the 'persons at each higher stage of moral structure more often made decisions in moral dilemmas that were consistent with human rights and less often chose alternatives which were designed to maintain conventions or institutions' (Candee, 1976, p. 1299), and later that such a pattern 'suggests the psychological validity of the philosophic claim that such answers are in a logical or objective sense right' (p. 1300). The first conclusion is by definition true since one way of classifying reasoning at the higher stages is in terms of reference to rights. The suggested distinction between structure and choices in Candee's conclusion, however, does not exist. His second conclusion is only legitimate if there is some other way of demonstrating that the higher stages are indeed 'higher'.

This is the point on which all else hinges. That stages four, five, and six do form a developmental sequence rests on two things, the argument that this sequence is logically necessary, representing an order of increasing adequacy, and evidence that developmental change occurs in this order.

The Higher Types of Moral Reasoning as Sequential Developmental Stages

There are two possible interpretations for the relations found between moral reasoning and political orientation. One, the implication of Kohlberg's theory, is that the perspective of the liberal or radical is based on reasoning and values more adequate than those of the conservative. The other is that Kohlberg's stages four, five, and six simply represent preferences for different politico-moral values. The soundness of the case supporting the first interpretation is therefore critical to the support Kohlberg's theory can give to liberal ideology.

To demonstrate the adequacy of stage six over stage five, Kohlberg points to certain limitations of stage five. Inspection of these limitations—lack of guidance where legal definitions are absent, questionable, or unjust—reveals that they are not internal contradictions in stage five thinking at all. They are simply the differences between five and six that stage six defines as important. On the basis of an intensive study of the kind of meta-ethical thinking Kohlberg associates with stages five and six, Fishkin (1975) concluded that *seven* distinct meta-ethical positions can be defined in terms of rejection or acceptance of each of a set of premises. The position corresponding to stage six is logically distinct from that corresponding to five but is not structurally more complex or objectively more adequate. All that distinguishes these stages is a choice of basic assumptions.

Evidence that six is a later stage of development than five is non-existent. After revisions to his coding system, Kohlberg concluded that no subject in his original longitudinal study had been or become predominantly stage six, and concluded '. . . no real data exists on movement to this highest moral stage' (Kohlberg, 1973, p. 197). On what basis it can still be insisted that this is the highest stage, therefore, is obscure. Fishkin's longitudinal data—covering a two-year period—suggest that, if anything, the chronological trend is from six to five.

This leaves the distinction between stage four and 'post-conventional' reasoning. Kohlberg (1971b) offers two limitations of stage four thought. First, it defines no clear obligations to persons outside the system or to those who do not recognize its rules. Second it provides no rational guides to social change or the creation of laws ex nihilo.

As to the first point, there is an *orientation* to persons outside the system which is consistent with both stage four and traditional conservative perspectives. Anthropologists and social psychologists have called it ethnocentrism. It is hardly an uncommon condition for a group to discover that there are other social orders with different values. It is not surprising, therefore, that in most societies there are well developed styles of response to this problem. The ethnocentric response is that other social orders and value systems are morally inferior to those of one's own group. According to some theories of intergroup relations, such a response is highly functional (cf. Levine and Campbell, 1972). That a moral orientation should define moral obligations to those outside one's own social order is only the moral assumption of the anti-ethnocentric. This point has more to do with the perceived limits of the moral community than with the adequacy of moral reasoning as such (but see also Vine, Chapter 2).

People who do not recognize or accept the rules are identified in both stage four and conservative philosophies as law-breakers or enemies of the social system who must be punished, constrained, or ejected. Such a view is only morally inappropriate to one who believes there are defensible alternatives or moral objections to the existing order.

The second objection, that there must be some rational basis for making social changes and that this is not supplied by stage four, is a normative requirement of rationalism, not a practical requirement for change to occur. History tells us that social changes occur whether or not there is explicit planning, that the contingencies of such change are often poorly understood even by the people who try to produce them, and that rationally guided change may be practically impossible. If social change is to be so guided then its guides must understand the functioning of existing social arrangements. But such insight is likely to be rare if it exists at all, for the same reasons that rational control of change is difficult. Individuals have information-processing limits, as well as limited informational resources to draw upon. By any standards, social systems are extremely complex phenomena and the data on any one that is available to an individual, even were he able to absorb it all, will always be partial and incomplete. Simon (1957), developing a similar point in his concept of 'bounded rationality', pointed out that even though individuals may intend to act rationally, they can only ever do so in a limited fashion. On the other hand, social systems can be and often are functional without those who submit to their requirements understanding why or needing to.

Social change is a fact rather than a moral necessity, and it is morally desirable, as I have suggested, primarily from the point of view of liberalism. From the conservative point of view it is often considered morally undesirable. The conservative might, with justification, take a jaundiced view of the liberal's enthusiasm for rationally guided change because the conservative realizes the liberal understands less than he thinks about the processes he is trying to change and so does more harm than good.

It should not be assumed that either the stage four or the conservative thinker necessarily lacks articulate criteria for modifying the law. Their criteria are simply different from those of the stage five and liberal individual. While the latter tend to favour changes that protect or extend individual rights and equality, the former might, for instance, prefer changes which strengthen collective security.

Finally, the creation of laws ex nihilo is only a problem for those who believe in a state of nature prior to society. The state of nature is at best a useful legal fiction, and in practice no one has the option of revoking their social contract and returning to this state.

The evidence for an invariant sequence of development from four to five (or six) is of three kinds: longitudinal, correlational, and experimental. Kohlberg's is the only substantial longitudinal study that potentially covers this change, and various 'inconsistencies' in the developmental pattern (regressions) (e.g. Kohlberg and Kramer, 1969) have led to significant revisions in the coding system. Kohlberg (1976) has recently said that the post-conventional level is only reached after the age of twenty and then by only a few individuals. Unfortunately, the relevant data still await final publication. Holstein (1976) found that over a two-year period there was some tendency toward change from stage five to four amongst the members of an adult sample. Two studies of adult moral reasoning that have included data on the relationship to age (Weisbroth, 1970; Fontana and Noel, 1973) reported a zero correlation between moral stage and age.

Another correlational strategy is to show that the difference between four and five is related to some other difference known to be developmental. Thus, Kuhn, Langer, Kohlberg, and Haan (1977) sought to show that the development of post-conventional or principled reasoning is based on the development of formally operational thought. An earlier attempt by Tomlinson-Keasey and Keasey (1974) was frustrated by the very small number of subjects found at the post-conventional level (5). However, those reasoning at the conventional level were disproportionately beyond the stage of concrete operations. In the event, Kuhn et al. (1977) apparently encountered similar problems. Only one of their tables (15, p. 155) reports separate data for post-conventional subjects (as opposed to those who showed some mixture of conventional and post-conventional thought). That these subjects had reached formal operations is not particularly informative given that there were only two of them (out of 230). The corresponding possibility, that stage four subjects are less likely to have achieved formal operations than those who show some evidence of advance on stage four, receives no support from the data.

Several experimental investigations have been directed at inducing developmental change and are claimed to support the hypothesized developmental sequence insofar as it proves easiest to induce change in a direction that accords with this sequence. Unfortunately in no such study has any such change been successfully induced from stage four to five and in most the samples have been below the age range within which this change is normally assumed to be possible.

One further form of evidence that could support the sequentiality of stages four and five comes from evidence for comprehension of arguments typical of each stage. It is consistent with Kohlberg's theory that an individual who reasons at stage five will also correctly understand the reasoning characteristic of stage four, though he will have rejected its moral validity. The reverse will not be true; the stage four individual will not be able to comprehend reasoning that is at the stage five level. In a study by Rest (1973), the data reported indicate that four out of twelve individuals classified as stage four could comprehend stage five or six reasoning, and three out of six individuals classified as stage five could comprehend stage five or six reasoning; not a conclusive difference.

A variant of the comprehension task as a test of sequentiality is to ask subjects to try and 'fake' a stage of reasoning higher than their own. It should be impossible to do this effectively if the sequence hypothesized is correct. On the other hand, if stages four, five, and six are not sequential and if, furthermore, they reflect, as suggested, political perspectives, it should be no more difficult for a conservative to predict the moral perspective of a radical than for a radical to predict that of a conservative.

Kohlberg's measure of moral reasoning would, unfortunately, not lend itself readily to the experimental verification of this hypothesis. However, the scale developed by Rest (e.g. Rest, 1975a, b, 1976) is more amenable to an investigation of this sort. Rest reports a correlation of +.68 between his Defining Issues Test of moral reasoning and Kohlberg's Moral Judgment Interview. Yussen (1976) was successful in eliciting from subjects higher scores on the DIT when instructed to give the responses they imagined a moral philosopher would give than when giving their own spontaneous responses. Scores on another measure of moral orientation, Hogan's *Survey of Ethical Attitudes* (Hogan, 1970) have been shown to vary as a function of instructions to 'fake liberal' or 'fake conservative' (Meehan, Woll, and Abbott, 1979). Hogan (Johnson and Hogan, 1979) claims such an effect is to be expected for two reasons. All measures of moral perspectives are also measures of political perspective, and responses to all such measures are forms of self presentation.

That similar effects could be found with Rest's DIT has been the basis for two studies in which the author has recently been involved (Emler, Herron, and Malone, 1979). In the preliminary study we found that conservative students obtained lower scores on post-conventional reasoning (in Rest's terms, P Scores) than liberal, socialist, and communist students ($p < .005$) but higher stage four scores ($p < .00025$). In the second study, students were asked to complete Rest's questionnaire twice, once giving their own views and once completing it as they imagined an extreme radical or an extreme conservative would respond. Data analysis is not yet complete but a preliminary analysis based on a part of the data reveals that left wing students obtained significantly higher scores for post-conventional reasoning than students who decribed themselves as right wing or moderate. Right wing and moderate students obtained higher stage four scores than left wing students. The significant question was whether the right wing and moderate students could alter their pattern of responses in the direction of the left wing pattern when asked to predict the responses of an extreme radical. It appeared that they could (see Table 1).

Table 1

Post-conventional scores	Mean $P\%$	
Radical as predicted by RW	52.75	(RW as self = 31.06)
Radical as predicted by MOD	46.96	(MOD as self = 31.66)
LW as self	50.83	

Stage 4 scores	Mean %	
Radical as predicted by RW	11.81	(RW as self = 43.18)
Radical as predicted by MOD	13.30	(MOD as self = 30.1)
LW as self	16.06	

These findings are consistent with our contention that responses by adults to measures of moral perspective reflect their political perspectives rather than their reasoning abilities.

Alternative Ideologies

It is the fate of popular and successful theories to attract critics, and it often seems that what the critics see in a theory has more to do with their own ideological leanings than what is manifestly the bias of the theory they attack. Critics have attacked Kohlberg for giving succour to whatever political or intellectual philosophy they happen to oppose. To the Marxist perspective of Sullivan (1977) and Baumrind (1978) the theory is establishment liberal. To Rothman and Lichter (1978), apparently pro-establishment, it is left wing or radical. To Simpson's (1974) pan-cultural sympathies, the theory supports American cultural imperialism. To Gilligan's (1977) feminist orientation it is chauvinist and androcentric. To Haan's (1978) interpersonal bias, the theory is overly impersonal. And so on.

Is there then any more sound justification for the ideological bias of this chapter? Not really. The only claim, possibly, that can be made for any such critique is that it draws attention to alternative interpretations or to other issues that are, by virtue of adopting one ideological orientation, relatively ignored. Many of the researchers and reviewers who refer to Kohlberg's theory appear to accept that the stage sequence it proposes is well established on both logical and empirical grounds and thus beyond challenge. This claim turns out to have little foundation when applied specifically to stages four, five, and six. There is a danger in our traditional academic hostility toward conservatism that we are perhaps too ready to see this political orientation as intellectually and morally inferior, and to interpret our data accordingly.

Also we should not forget that not all social theorists have accepted the liberal-consensus view of political authority implied in Kohlberg's theory. Weber, for instance, believed that political authority stems from the capacity to coerce obedience. Others have argued that centralized state authority emerged under conditions in which it became possible to secure the compliance, willing or not, of the large mass of the population (e.g. Harris, 1977). It is often suggested that the ideological consequences of social theories lie in their tendency to ascribe an imperative character to conditions that are in reality mutable. Such a case is provided by theories that account for conventional sex roles in terms of biological requirements. But a perhaps more subtle and significant distortion of reality is achieved by those theories which minimize or obscure the constraint that underlies social arrangements, suggesting instead that these arrangements are the products of voluntary—and therefore reversible—individual choice. Goffman (1975) for one has observed that we have pushed to unreasonable limits W. I. Thomas's famous dictum: 'If men define situations as real they are real in their consequences.' Kohlberg's theory of moral development is no different from most in emphasizing rules, rights, and principles, to the exclusion of power and the practicalities of its use.

Individualism and Rationalism also exclude certain realities of human social existence, as this chapter has suggested. One further example is the preoccupation with morality as self control which does not allow us to consider that dependence may also be a facet of moral maturity. Slater (1971) has suggested that individuals are not naturally self-sufficient and have a deep need to share the responsibility for their actions with others and at times to depend on others to control and direct their behaviour.

Finally, there is a selective emphasis on particular resources in Kohlberg's theory and in his moral dilemmas that is characteristic of the themes I have considered, Individualism, Rationalism, and Liberalism.

'Looking at the resources at stake in Kohlberg's dilemmas, we find they are confined to property, liberty, life and rights. Thus most important of all, the theory ignores the fact that people need each other, and the most significant resources they exchange are care, love, attachment, belonging and emotional security, and the costs are personal hurt and pain, loneliness and rejection. The dilemmas and the categories provided in which to fit responses simply cannot encompass the kinds of moral concerns these conditions raise, yet these conditions form the common matters of our everyday lives. And for all their common and recurrent nature, they are also among the most demanding, complex and intractable, the most distressing and inescapable problems we face.' (Hogan and Emler, 1978)

References

Alker, H. A., and Poppen, P. J. (1973). Personality and ideology in university students. *Journal of Personality*, **41**, 652–671.

Alston, W. P. (1971). Comments on Kohlberg's 'from is to ought'. In T. Mischel (Ed.), *Cognitive development and epistemology*. Academic Press, New York.

Aronfreed, J. (1976). Moral development from the standpoint of a general psychological theory. In T. Lickona (Ed.), *Moral development and behaviour: Theory, research, and social issues*, Holt, Rinehart, and Winston, New York.

Bandura, A. (1971). *Social learning theory*, General Learning Press, Morristown, N.J.

Baumrind, D. (1978). A dialectical materialist's perspective on knowing social reality. In W. Damon (Ed.), *Moral development*, Jossey Bass, San Francisco.

Candee, D. (1976). Structure and choice in moral reasoning. *Journal of Personality and Social Psychology*, **34**, 1293–1301.

Christie, R. and Geis, F. (1968). *Studies in machiavellianism*, Academic Press, New York.

Durkheim, E. (1938). *The rules of sociological method*, University of Chicago Press, Chicago.

Emler, N. P., and Heather, N. (1980). Intelligence: An ideological bias of conventional psychology. In P. Salmon (Ed.), *Coming to know*, Routledge and Kegan Paul, London.

Emler, N. P., Herron, G., and Malone, B. (1979). Relations between moral attitudes and political orientation. Unpublished manuscript, University of Dundee.

Fishkin, J. (1975). Meta-ethical reasoning. Unpublished Doctoral Dissertation, Yale University.

Fishkin, J., Keniston, K., and MacKinnon, C. (1973). Moral reasoning and political ideology. *Journal of Personality and Social Psychology*, **27**, 109–119.

Fontana, A. F., and Noel, B. (1973). Moral reasoning in the university. *Journal of Personality and Social Psychology*, **27**, 419–429.

Gilligan, C. (1977). In a different voice: Women's conceptions of self and of morality. *Harvard Educational Review*, **47**, 481–517.

Goffman, E. (1975). *Frame analysis*, Harper and Row, New York.

Gorsuch, R. L., and Barnes, M. L. (1973). Stages of ethical reasoning and moral norms of Carib youths. *Journal of Cross Cultural Psychology*, **4**, 283–301.

Haan, N. (1978). Two moralities in action contexts: Relationships to thought, ego regulation, and development. *Journal of Personality and Social Psychology*, **36**, 286–305.

Harris, M. (1977). *Cannibals and kings: The origins of cultures*, Random House, New York.

Hoffman, M. L., and Saltzstein, H. D. (1967). Parental discipline and the child's moral development. *Journal of Personality and Social Psychology*, **5**, 45–57.

Hogan, R. (1970). A dimension of moral judgment. *Journal of Consulting and Clinical Psychology*, **35**, 205–212.

Hogan, R., and Emler, N. P. (1978). The biases in contemporary social psychology. *Social Research*, **45**, 478–534.

Holstein, C. G. (1976). Irreversibility, stepwise sequence in the development of moral judgment: A longitudinal study. *Child Development*, **47**, 51–61.

Horton, R. (1971). African traditional thought and Western science. In M. F. D. Young (Ed.), *Knowledge and Control*, Collier-Macmillan, London. (Originally published in *Africa*, Vol. 37, 1967.)

Humphrey, N. K. (1976). The social function of intellect. In P. P. G. Bateson and R. A. Hinde (Eds), *Growing points in ethology*, Cambridge University Press, Cambridge.

Inhelder, B., and Piaget, J. (1958). *The growth of logical thinking from childhood to adolescence*, Routledge and Kegan Paul, London.

Johnson, J., and Hogan, R. (1979). Moral judgements and self-presentations. Unpublished manuscript, Johns Hopkins University.

Kohlberg, L. (1969). Stage and sequence: The cognitive developmental approach to socialization. In D. Goslin (Ed.), *Handbook of socialization theory and research*, Rand McNally, Chicago.

Kohlberg, L. (1971a). Stages of moral development as a basis for moral education. In C. M. Beck, B. S. Crittenden, and E. V. Sullivan (Eds), *Moral education: Interdisciplinary approaches*, Toronto University Press, Toronto.

Kohlberg, L. (1971b). From is to ought: How to commit the naturalistic fallacy and get away with it in the study of moral development. In T. Mischel (Ed.), *Cognitive development and epistemology*, Academic Press, New York.

Kohlberg, L. (1973). Continuities in childhood and adult moral development revisited. In P. B. Baltes and K. W. Schaie (Eds), *Life-span developmental psychology: Personality and socialization*. Academic Press, New York.

Kohlberg, L. (1976). Moral stages and moralization: The cognitive developmental approach. In T. Lickona (Ed.), *Moral development and behaviour: Theory, research and social issues*. Holt, Rinehart, and Winston, New York.

Kohlberg, L., and Kramer, R. (1969). Continuities and discontinuities in childhood and adult moral development. *Human Development*, **12**, 93–120.

Kohlberg, L., Scharf, P., and Hickey, J. (1973). The justice structure of the prison: A theory and an intervention. *The Prison Journal*, **51**, 3–14.

Kuhn, D., Langer, J., Kohlberg, L., and Haan, N. (1977). The development of formal operations in logical and moral development. *Genetic Psychology Monographs*, **95**, 97–188.

Levine, R. A., and Campbell, D. T. (1972). *Ethnocentrism: Theories of conflict, ethnic attitudes, and group behaviour*, Wiley, New York.

Meehan, K. A., Woll, S. B., and Abbott, R. D. (1979). The role of dissimulation and social desirability in the measurement of moral reasoning. *Journal of Research and Personality*, **13**, 25–38.

Moir, D. J. (1974). Egocentrism and the emergence of conventional morality in pre-adolescent girls. *Child Development*, **45**, 299–304.

Moscovici, S. (1972). Society and theory in social psychology. In J. Israel and H. Tajfel (Eds), *The context of social psychology: A critical assessment*. Academic Press, London.

Moscovici, S. (1976). *Social influence and social change*, Academic Press, London.

Piaget, J. (1932). *The moral judgment of the child*, Routledge and Kegan Paul, London.

Piaget, J. (1951). *The psychology of intelligence*, Routledge and Kegan Paul, London.

Rest, J. (1973). Patterns of preference and comprehension in moral judgment. *Journal of Personality*, **41**, 86–109.

Rest, J. (1975a). Longitudinal study of the Defining Issues Test of moral judgment: A strategy for analysing developmental change. *Developmental Psychology*, **11**, 738–748.

Rest, J. (1975b). Recent research on an objective test of moral judgment: How the important issues of a moral dilemma are defined. In D. J. De Palma and J. M. Foley (Eds), *Moral development: Current theory and research*, Erlbaum, Hillsdale, N. J.

Rest, J. (1976). New approaches in the assessment of moral judgment. In T. Lickona (Ed.), *Moral development and behaviour: Theory, research and social issues*, Holt, Rinehart, and Winston, New York.

Rothman, S., and Lichter, S. R. (1978). The case of the student left. *Social Research*, **45**, 535–609.

Russell, B. (1946). *History of Western philosophy*, Allen and Unwin, London.

Selman, R. L. (1971). The relation of role taking to the development of moral judgment in children. *Child Development*, **42**, 79–91.

Simon, H. A. (1957). *Administrative behaviour*, Free Press, New York.

Simpson, E. L. (1974). Moral development research: A case of scientific cultural bias. *Human Development*, **17**, 81–106.

Slater, P. (1971). *The pursuit of loneliness*, Penguin, Harmondsworth.

Sullivan, E. V. (1977). A study of Kohlberg's structural theory of moral development: A critique of liberal social science ideology. *Human Development*, **20**, 352–376.

Sullivan, E. V., and Quarter, J. (1972). Psychological correlates of certain postconventional moral types: A perspective on hybrid types. *Journal of Personality*, **40**, 149–161.

Tomkins, S. S. (1965). Affect and the psychology of knowledge. In S. S. Tomkins and C. E. Izard (Eds), *Affect, cognition and personality*, Springer, New York.

Tomlinson-Keasey, C., and Keasey, C. B. (1974). The mediating role of cognitive development in moral judgment. *Child Development*, **45**, 291–298.

Turner, T. (1973). Piaget's structuralism. *American Anthropologist*, **75**, 351–373.

Weisbroth, S. (1970). Moral judgment, sex, and parental identification in adults. *Developmental Psychology*, **2**, 369–402.

White, C. B. (1975). Moral development in Bahamian school children: A cross-cultural examination of Kohlberg's stages of moral reasoning. *Developmental Psychology*, **11**, 535–536.

Yussen, S. R. (1976). Moral reasoning from the perspective of others. *Child Development*, **47**, 551–555.

Morality in the Making
Edited by H. Weinreich-Haste and D. Locke
© 1983, John Wiley & Sons, Ltd.

CHAPTER 4

Structure, Content, and the Direction of Development in Kohlberg's Theory

DAVID and STEPHANIE THORNTON

Introduction and Overview

The purpose of this chapter is to present a reformulation of the cognitive-developmental theory of moral judgment originated by Kohlberg (1958, 1969, 1976). Kohlberg's theory can be conceptualized as consisting of three central hypotheses:

A that the way in which people make moral judgments undergoes a succession of qualitative changes as they get older: the pattern of changes conforming to a stage-developmental model,
B that these developmental trends in moral judgment result primarily from developmental increases in the ability to understand high-stage moral ideas,
C that people tend to adopt high-stage moral ideas, once they understand them, because they are more moral: that is, high-stage moral ideas are adopted because they correspond better to formal criteria for distinguishing moral statements of the sort proposed by Hare.

The first part of this chapter examines the empirical basis for hypotheses A and B. We argue that existing evidence broadly supports Kohlberg's claims. Hypothesis C is then discussed. We argue that this is unsatisfactory because it

(i) depends on a mistaken equation of the structure/content distinction with a logical-form/content distinction,
(ii) in doing so makes it difficult to give a coherent account of people's concern with moral issues, and because
(iii) in any case it is difficult to elaborate the notion of progressive approximation to the pure logical-form of a moral statement in a way which actually explains people's tendency to adopt high-stage moral ideas once they are understood.

In the second part of the chapter we then offer an alternative to Kohlberg's hypothesis C. We propose that the special character of moral prescriptions derives from their involving an appeal to a concern with furthering those practices believed to best serve the collective interest. We endeavour to show that this hypothesis enables one to explain people's tendency to adopt high-stage moral ideas once they are understood, whilst avoiding equating 'structure' to 'logical form', and makes people's concern with moral issues intelligible.

Kohlberg's Three Hypotheses

Developmental Stages

One of Kohlberg's central hypotheses is that moral reasoning changes systematically with age in a way which fits with a stage-developmental model. He argues that development involves a series of qualitative changes in the type of consideration to which one appeals in making moral judgments. Most of Kohlberg's empirical work has focused on elaborating and refining a typology (outlined in Chapter 1) which captures these developmental changes. This developmental typology has been at least partly successful, in that there is unambiguous evidence for a developmental progression through the pre-conventional and conventional stages (Kuhn, 1976; Turiel, Edwards, and Kohlberg, 1978; White, Bushnell, and Regnemer, 1978). But the claims for post-conventional development are much more contentious (see Emler, Chapter 3). There have as yet been no published longitudinal studies of the post-conventional stages using the current (post 1972) version of Kohlberg's moral judgment interview. The only data bearing on the question of the developmental progression through the higher stages is that provided by Rest's Defining Issues test—the DIT (Rest *et al.*, 1974). Developmental trends for Stages 4, 5, and 6 on the DIT are summarized in Table 1 (the data here are taken from Rest, 1975). Table 1(a) refers to a 2 year longitudinal follow-up of junior high school students. It shows all three of these higher stages increasing over time. Table 1(b) refers to a similar longitudinal study of senior high school students. Here, Stage 4 declined over time, whereas Stages 5 and 6 increased. Taken together, these results suggest that moral reasoning typical of Stage 4 at first increases in adolescence, but then

Table 1   Longitudinal change in Adoption of Stage 4, 5, and 6 arguments in High School students

	(a) Junior High School	(b) Senior High School
Stage 4	+2.8	−2.0
Stage 5	+1.9	+7.1
Stage 6	+0.5	+0.2

Note: '+' indicates greater importance attached to arguments of this stage at 2 year follow up than at pretest. '−' indicates the reverse. Importance scores are Rest's raw weighted ranks score: see Rest (1975) for details.

decreases, to be replaced by principled moral reasoning (i.e. Stages 5 and 6). However, the data do not suggest that Stage 5 is replaced by Stage 6.

Somewhat similar results have been obtained in cross sectional studies with the DIT. Table 2 summarizes the results for junior high school students, senior high school students, and undergraduate and postgraduate university students. Again, the data suggest that Stage 4 was indeed succeeded by Stages 5 and 6.

Table 2   Cross-sectional analysis of percentages of subjects at each of Stages 4, 5, and 6

	Junior High students	Senior High students	College students	Graduate students
Stage 4	20.0	15.0	7.5	2.5
Stage 5	5.0	5.0	35.0	30.0
Stage 6	0.0	7.5	17.5	22.5

Note: Subjects were counted as being at a stage if the degree of importance they attached to arguments of that stage was exceptionally high (see Rest, 1976, for details of stage classification method). As in Table 1, the A and B forms of Stage 5 (which are distinguished by Rest) have been collapsed: subjects are here classified as being Stage 5 if Rest classified them as being at either the A or B form of Stage 5.

If one is prepared to give it a mathematical interpretation, the idea that moral reasoning fits a stage-developmental model can also be tested in other ways. Davison, Robbins, and Swanson (1978) have argued that the stage-developmental hypothesis implies that moral judgments should fit a unidimensional metric unfolding model. This model involves the assumptions that:

(a) both individual people, and particular moral arguments, can be located on a single continuum,

(b) the importance a given person attaches to a particular type of moral argument is an inverse function of the square of the distance on the continuum between that person and that argument.

There are statistical procedures for evaluating the fit of this model to a given set of variables. Davison *et al.* applied these to data from the DIT. Their results showed that the model fits these data well. This indicates that the different types of moral arguments involved in the DIT can be regarded as falling along a single continuum. Since the mathematical model fits the data, it can be used to estimate the relative positions of the different types of moral argument on the continuum. Table 3 gives the coefficients estimated by Davison *et al.*, using a sample of over a thousand cases. (As in all these tables, we have averaged the results for the A and B forms of Stage 5.) These data too support the idea of a developmental progression through Stages 3 and 4 to the principled stages of reasoning. However, as before, the data provide no support for the idea that Stage 6 is more advanced than Stage 5.

In summary, then, Kohlberg's claims concerning a developmental sequence in moral reasoning have been fairly successful. The hypothesized developmental sequence is well supported by data, at least as far as Stage 5. Only the claim that Stage 6 replaces Stage 5 is really contentious.

Table 3 Coefficients indicating position on the continuum

Stage 2	Stage 3	Stage 4	Stage 5	Stage 6
−0.33	−0.26	−0.02	+0.35	+0.31

Note: Data are from Davison and Robbins (1978) group 2. The sample size was 1080. The coefficient given for Stage 5 is the average of those reported by Davison and Robbins for the two substages of Stage 5.

Understanding Moral Ideas

Kohlberg's second central hypothesis is that individuals who reject (or fail to adopt) the moral arguments characteristic of the higher stages do so because they do not understand these high stage moral ideas. (In this context, the word 'understand' is used in a purely cognitive sense: that is, it is used in the sense in which one can understand a point of view whilst vehemently disagreeing with it.)

This hypothesis has two empirical implications: it implies that high stage moral ideas should be more difficult to understand than low stage moral ideas; in fact, it implies that the arguments characteristic of the stages should form a Guttman scale in terms of how easily they can be understood. Secondly, it implies that there will be a substantial correlation between an individual's score on a measure of the ability to understand high stage moral ideas and the extent to which she adopts them.

Rest (1976) describes several measures which may be used to test these hypotheses. The two most frequently used involve either asking people to paraphrase moral arguments, or asking them to select the best of several alternative paraphrases of a given moral argument. Using the first of these measures, Rest (1973) reported that the stages do indeed form a Guttman scale; if one understands the moral ideas of a given stage, one will also understand the moral ides of all the lower stages. In addition, Rest (1976) reported a correlation of 0.6 between the moral arguments an individual understood, and the arguments she produced in the Kohlberg moral judgment interview. Similarly, studies using Rest's DIT and the second type of comprehension measure have found correlations averaging in the 0.6s between moral judgment development and comprehension of high stage ideas (Rest, 1976; Davison and Robbins, 1978). Interestingly, these correlations remained in excess of 0.5 even when social class, age, and verbal intelligence were taken into account.

The claim that the stage of moral reasoning an individual characteristically adopts is correlated with the highest stage whose arguments she understands perhaps needs special discussion vis à vis the higher stages in the light of the analysis of this point in Emler's chapter.

Emler challenges the idea that understanding principled (Stages 5 and 6) arguments leads to their being adopted. He suggests that people who use Stage 4 moral arguments are as able to understand the arguments characteristic of the principled stages as are individuals who themselves use principled moral reasoning. And he summarizes Rest (1973)'s data in a way which appears to support this claim. In fact however Emler's way of presenting Rest's data is misleading. In Rest's data there appears to be a slight lag between the comprehension and adoption of a given level of arguments. It is as if once somebody becomes able to understand a higher stage they gradually shift to using it. Thus the highest stage comprehended predicts the highest stage of substantial use (where substantial is operationally defined as at least 20% of responses being at that stage) rather than to the most used stage. In examining Emler's suggestion it is necessary then to distinguish those individuals who are beginning to shift towards principled reasoning from Stage 4 (i.e. those whose most used stage is 4 but whose highest stage of substantial use is principled) from those who use Stage 4 and do not use principled reasoning. Sixteen of Rest's subjects used Stage 4 but did not use principled reasoning. Only one of these was scored as understanding principled moral arguments. 12 of them were scored as understanding Stage 4 (but not principled) arguments, and 3 actually failed on the Stage 4 comprehension items. This last group presumably reflected the presence of measurement error. Of the 15 subjects who were scored as comprehending principled moral arguments, 12 had a principled stage as the highest stage of substantial use. Thus, to sum up, if people show evidence of understanding principled moral arguments then they are very likely (80%) to show evidence of beginning to use principled moral reasoning. And if people use Stage 4 and do not use principled moral reasoning then they are very unlikely to understand principled moral ideas (only about 6% showing evidence of understanding). Thus the relationship between comprehending and adopting principled moral ideas in Rest (1973)'s data is closer than Emler suggests.

This redescription of Rest's data does not wholly undercut Emler's claim that understanding and adoption of the higher stages are not correlated, since Emler has also provided independent evidence on this point. He has reported that right wing students tend to attach more importance to Stage 4 moral arguments, and less importance to principled arguments, than is the case for left wing students. However, when these right wing students were asked to complete the DIT as a left winger would, they were able to produce scores similar to those produced by actual left wingers. Emler argues that this implies that the right wingers understood principled arguments, even though they used Stage 4 reasoning themselves. He argues that this implies that the use of Stage 4 as opposed to principled moral arguments is a matter of attitude, rather than a consequence of a failure to understand principled ideas. But these data are open to another interpretation. The fact that right wingers can 'fake good' as left wingers on the DIT does not necessarily indicate that they understand the arguments endorsed by left wingers. All that we can be sure of is that right wingers can systematically discriminate arguments which will appeal to left wingers. The cues they use in making this discrimination may be peripheral to the form of the argument per se. For example, right wingers may think of left wingers as given to fancy sounding, but rather vague, justifications of anti-authority views.

A right wing individual who did not understand principled thought, but who, in role playing a left winger, selected items which seemed to be fancy sounding, rather vague, considerations questioning the existing social order might well check a large proportion of principled moral arguments on the DIT. This account would undercut Emler's claim that his data challenge the notion of a correlation between understanding and adopting the highest stages.

Thus the data are commensurate with the view that the stage of moral reasoning an individual uses is correlated with the highest stage whose argument she understands, at least up to Stage 5. However, this correlation is not perfect. The correlations reported by Rest (1976) of around 0.6 do not allow one to simply equate an individual's understanding of high stage moral ideas with her adoption of those ideas. In addition, Rest (1973)'s data suggest that there is a lag between when individuals first comprehend principled moral thought, and when they actually adopt it as their predominant mode of thinking.

This discrepancy between the highest stage whose arguments an individual understands and the stage she adopts must, however, be put in perspective. The correlations in the 0.6s reported by Rest (1976) and Davison and Robbins (1978) are more substantial than they appear. The reliability (internal consistency) of the DIT principled morality score is only 0.77 (Davison and Robbins, 1978), and the reliability of the comprehension test (which has only 14 items) is 0.56 (Rest *et al.*, 1974). The maximum population correlation between measures of these reliabilities is only 0.66. Thus replicable sample correlations in the 0.6s between understanding, and adopting, principled moral arguments, indicate an underlying relationship between the two variables which is very nearly perfect. Further, the lag in Rest's study between comprehension and use occurred not just for the higher stage moral arguments, but also for the lower stage arguments. The size of this lag was generally small, amounting to about half a stage. Given that moral thought develops fairly rapidly in adolescence (e.g. Rest *et al.*, 1978), which was the age range studied by Rest (1973), such a small discrepancy between comprehension and use could only be maintained if there was a strong tendency to adopt the moral arguments of a higher stage shortly after comprehending them.

Nevertheless, the existence of any lag between comprehending a moral argument and adopting it implies that adopting the arguments of a higher stage involves something more than merely understanding them. Rest (1976) has argued that the lag between comprehending high stage arguments, and using them in a moral judgment interview, reflects the greater difficulties associated with producing an argument (where the subject must identify the relevant issues, imagine the consequences of the various courses of action, and integrate them into a coherent justification) as opposed to recognizing and interpreting an argument that is presented by the experimenter (where much of this work has already been done for the subject). In support of this contention, Rest (1976) refers to his 1973 finding that subjects tend to prefer (when presented with different stage arguments and asked to choose between them) arguments from stages higher than that which they spontaneously use in the moral judgment interview.

Why High Stage Ideas are Preferred

The evidence reviewed in the preceding section suggests that there is a strong tendency to prefer higher stage moral ideas to lower stage moral ideas, once both are understood. Kohlberg (1971) has attempted to explain why this should be so. He argues that the progression through the stages of moral reasoning reflects a progressive differentiation between moral and non-moral considerations. Initially children confuse moral considerations with other sorts of consideration. As their cognitive structures develop they become better able to distinguish between the moral and the non-moral. Naturally, in trying to make moral judgments, individuals will try to invoke only moral considerations. Hence they will progressively adopt higher stage arguments, rejecting the lower stage ideas as they come to recognize the way in which these ideas confuse moral and non-moral considerations. Ultimately the end point of this developmental sequence is reached at Stage 6, when only purely moral considerations are invoked in making moral judgments.

This explanation has a certain plausibility. It is easy to construe the stages in Kohlberg's typology in terms of what they confuse with the moral. For example Stage 3 can be seen as confusing interpersonal harmony with 'the moral'; Stage 4 can be seen as confusing the maintenance of social order with 'the moral'; and so on. However, this hypothesis requires a clear specification of 'the moral' if it is to be coherent. Kohlberg takes the line that moral propositions can be distinguished from non-moral propositions in terms of their logical form. A variety of criteria of this type for identifying 'the moral' has been proposed by philosophers. Kohlberg has adopted some of the views proposed by Hare (1952, 1963): he emphasizes that to be moral, a proposition must be universalizable and prescriptive. Kohlberg's claim then is that the stages of moral reasoning represent a progressive evolution towards fulfilling these criteria.

There are several difficulties with this position. First, it equates the structure/content distinction to a logical-form/content distinction. Kohlberg's use of the terms 'structure' and 'content' is not entirely consistent, but in most places 'structure' appears to refer to the general system which underlies a person's moral judgments and which undergoes developmental change. Aspects of moral reasoning which either lack this general quality or which do not change developmentally are referred to as 'content'. Now if the differences between stages which determines their developmental ordering is the degree to which they conform to a particular logical form, then we should expect the structures which underlie the stages to be defined as distinctive types of logical form. At least in Kohlberg's recent writings, though, this is not so. 'Structure' is identified with what Kohlberg (1976) refers to as the 'socio-moral perspective' of a stage. And this would seem to have more to do with the model of social relationships implicitly assumed in making moral judgments, than it does with the logical form of these judgments.

Of course, it could be that moral judgments made within different frameworks for understanding social relationships necessarily involve different logical forms, so this first objection is not by itself fatal to Kohlberg's hypothesis. However, this brings us to the second objection. It is not at all clear that the different stages, as defined by Kohlberg, are in fact progressive approximations to universalizability. If this were so then Stage 6 should include all those prescriptive principles which fully meet the logical criterion of universalizability. But this is not the case: Kohlberg (1976) regards the notion of 'equal respect for the dignity of all persons' as a central and defining notion for Stage 6. However, principles like 'all men of superhuman will deserve to be unconditionally obeyed', an idea which would be anathema to Kohlberg's Stage 6, or 'behave so as to minimize the chances of being punished' which Kohlberg would probably regard as preconventional, are equally universalizable (see Locke, 1979).

Finally, identifying moral prescriptions with universalizable prescriptions makes it difficult to give a coherent account of moral motivation. Morality is not a neutral topic. People appear to be both highly motivated to persuade others to conform to their moral prescriptions and concerned that their own behaviour appears morally justifiable. It is difficult to see why this should be so if moral judgments are merely universalizable prescriptions. A huge number of prescriptions can be universalized. But it is hard to imagine that everyone, or, in the case of some prescriptions ('always scratch your left ear before sneezing'; 'every seventh seagull must be shot'; 'curtsey 20 times to every aunt'), anyone would be the least concerned to see that they were implemented merely because they are universalizable. The fact that one can formulate a prescription in universalizable terms does not in and of itself give one a reason for being interested in whether people carry it out.

An Alternative Explanation of Kohlberg's Developmental Stages

The Problem

So far our discussion has suggested three conclusions:

(i) that the way in which people make moral judgments undergoes a series of qualitative changes as they get older: the pattern corresponding reasonably well to the stage-developmental model proposed by Kohlberg with the exception of the distinction between Stages 5 and 6 for which there is no evidence,

(ii) that these developmental trends in moral judgment result primarily from developmental increases in the ability to understand higher stage moral ideas,

(iii) that Kohlberg's explanation of the tendency to prefer higher stage moral ideas, once they are understood, is unsatisfactory.

The problem to which the second part of this chapter is addressed is that of constructing a more satisfactory explanation for people's tendency to prefer higher stage ideas. To be satisfactory we believe that any proposed explanation of this tendency should also

(a) define structure as socio-moral perspective in a manner compatible with Kohlberg's recent writings (Kohlberg, 1976). Without this feature contact would be lost with the existing body of cognitive-developmental theory,

(b) account for the type of moral judgment characteristically generated by a particular perspective. Without this one loses contact with the actual phenomena (moral judgments) that we wish to understand,

(c) do this in a way which makes intelligible people's concern about moral issues.

The Collective Interest Hypothesis

Whereas Hare (1952) has suggested that moral prescriptions can be distinguished by their logical form, other philosophers (e.g. Warnock, 1971) have suggested that what is peculiar to moral prescriptions is their function. Following on this line our own proposal is that moral prescriptions can be understood as prescriptions stemming from a concern to further those practices which one believes will best serve the collective interest. In passing it should be noted that we are not suggesting that people are necessarily conscious of doing this when making moral judgments anymore than one is conscious of using rules of grammar when speaking. However, people do consciously distinguish orientating one's actions in terms of one's conception of collective interests from acting selfishly.

The collective interest hypothesis meets one of our criteria for a satisfactory explanation: collective interests are by definition things in which we all have an interest. Thus the collective interest hypothesis makes intelligible people's concern over moral issues. The hypothesis does not imply that a person's share in the collective interest will necessarily be more important to her than her private interests. And it is of course common sense that from time to time our concern with moral issues is overwhelmed by some other concern. The collective interest hypothesis also makes it possible to define structure in a way which is broadly compatible with Kohlberg's concept of a socio-moral perspective.

We suggest that the structures underlying Kohlberg's stages be seen as conceptual frameworks for identifying people's collective interests. The plausibility of this suggestion can best be shown by analysing each of Kohlberg's stages in this way. In doing this we shall attempt to meet the other criteria suggested for a satisfactory explanation. That is, we attempt to account for the type of moral judgments characteristically generated by each framework, and also to show why higher stage frameworks are adopted in preference to lower stage frameworks once cognitive development has made this possible.

The hypothesis that moral thought is characterized by a concern with furthering collective interests suggests that cognitive development should impact on moral reasoning in two ways.

First, a certain amount of cognitive development is necessary, to enable the individual to abstract the idea of collective interests from her conception of the particular interests of particular individuals. Initially, other people's interests impinge on the child's awareness purely through the sanctions imposed upon her. Thus, for her, they are simply constraints upon her behaviour imposed by powerful others. The question of collective interests simply does not arise (this is Kohlberg's Stage 1). The first step towards distinguishing people's personal interests from collective interests is taken when the child notes that different people have different interests in social arrangements. This enables her to distinguish occasions on which she and another individual have a common interest, from occasions when only one individual's interests are satisfied by a particular course of action. At this point, though, occasions involving common interests are distinctive for the child primarily because her own interests are more easily fulfilled within them. Thus evaluation in terms of private interests is still not really distinguished from evaluation in terms of collective interests (this is Kohlberg's Stage 2). Abstracting the idea of collective interests from the conception of the particular interests of individuals occurs at what Kohlberg calls Stage 3. This step depends on an advance in social perspective-taking ability (Selman, 1976), which enables the individual to view a transaction between two people from a third, uninvolved, perspective. This uninvolved perspective allows an impartial grasp on the collective interests of the participants in the transaction (in contrast to the partisan evaluation of collective interests characteristic of Stage 2). To say that the individual at Stage 3 has the idea of an impartial assessment of collective interests does not, of course, necessarily mean that she is objectively correct in her identification of such interests, or that she is in fact impartial, even when she is trying to be so.

Secondly, cognitive development should impinge on moral reasoning by allowing the individual to identify a wider spectrum of collective interests. We hypothesize that, from Stage 3 onwards, each of Kohlberg's stages results from the attempt to *impartially* identify collective interests, given a particular (stage specific) framework for identifying collective interests. High stage ideas are preferred to low stage ideas (once they are understood) because high stage ideas are based on a more comprehensive identification of types of collective interests. Once an additional type of collective interest has been identified, it would seem (to the individual making the judgment) purely arbitrary to ignore it. We show how Kohlberg's Stages 3, 4, and 5 can be understood in this way.

At Stage 3, the individual is aware of the possibility of collective interests arising within mutual interpersonal relations. She is not aware of the possibility of collective interests arising at the level of a social system. This is the general specification, or structure, of Stage 3 moral reasoning. The use of such a perspective is likely to lead the individual to believe that people have a collective interest in such practices as: reciprocating affection; maintaining interpersonal trust; considering the feelings of others; and so on. This follows from the general belief that it is unpleasant to be involved in interpersonal relations in which our affections are unreciprocated, our trust is betrayed, or our feelings disregarded. These more specific operationalizations of the general stage structure are necessary for actual moral reasoning to occur. However, people using the same structure (i.e. referring to the same considerations) may disagree about the precise collective interests which may exist. Thus, although the structure in use influences the actual conclusions of moral thought, it does not determine these conclusions absolutely.

At Stage 4, mutual dyadic relationships are understood in the context of an integrated social system; and this, more comprehensive, framework is used for identifying collective interests. Thus, in addition to collective interests arising at the level of interpersonal relationships, Stage 4 sees the possibility of there being collective interests in how people's roles are integrated into an overall social system. This is the general specification, or 'structure', of Stage 4. Such a perspective will lead to an emphasis on a fair, consistent, impartial, and benevolent social system: people at Stage 4 will tend to judge that we have a collective interest in living in a social system which is predictable, and which does not treat us unfairly, disregarding our interests in favour of those of others, and so on. This is not to say that, at Stage 4, social systems considerations are inevitably given precedence over interpersonal considerations. Rather, the difference between Stage 3 and Stage 4 moral reasoning is that, when social system and interpersonal considerations clash, individuals at Stage 4 are aware of this clash as a problem to be resolved. For individuals at Stage 3, in contrast, the issue simply does not arise.

At Stage 4 the prevailing social order is taken very much for granted. Many aspects of it are treated as necessary when they are, in fact, merely contingent. At the post-conventional level, any given social order is seen as merely one among possible forms of social coordination. The initial effect of trying to use such a framework to identify collective interests may be a form of disorientation. The type of collective interest previously identified, particularly those at the social system level, will appear to be relative to a particular social system. Since this system is seen as but one among many possible alternatives, a focus on any particular set of collective interests associated with it may seem arbitrary. This corresponds to the position, transitional between Stages 4 and 5, which Kohlberg labelled Stage 4½. This disorientation ends, however, as the individual begins to be able to identify collective interests which are general across social orders. This is the form of moral reasoning which Kohlberg calls Stage 5.

We have not yet attempted to extend our analysis to cover Kohlberg's Stage 6. Partly this is because we do not feel that the existing evidence justifies the claim that the different forms of principled reasoning are developmentally ordered in the way Kohlberg proposes. There is also a more profound reason. We suspect that it is difficult to distinguish the general structure of a stage from the idiosyncracies of one's own moral thought unless one is oneself at least one stage ahead of the stage under analysis. This makes it particularly difficult to analyse the different forms of principled reasoning and perhaps explains why only Kohlberg, receding towards the nirvana of his hypothetical Stage 7, can seem to get a handle on Stage 6.

References

Davison, M. L., and Robbins, S. (1978). The reliability and validity of objective indices of moral development. *Applied Psychological Measurement*, 2, 389–401.

Davison, M. L., Robbins, S., and Swanson, D. (1978). Stage structure in objective moral judgements. *Developmental Psychology*, 14, 137–146.

Hare, R. M. (1952). *The language of morals*, Clarendon Press, Oxford.

Hare, R. M. (1963). Descriptivism. *Proceedings of the British Academy*.

Kohlberg, L. (1958). The development of modes of moral thinking and choice in the years 10 to 16. Unpublished doctoral dissertation, University of Chicago.

Kohlberg, L. (1969). Stage and sequence: the cognitive developmental approach to socialisation. In D. A. Goslin (Ed.), *Handbook of socialisation theory and research*, Rand McNally, Chicago.

Kohlberg, L. (1971). From is to ought: how to commit the naturalistic fallacy and get away with it in the study of moral development. In T. Mischel (Ed.), *Cognitive development and epistemology*, Academic Press, New York.

Kohlberg, L. (1976). Moral stages and moralisation: the cognitive developmental approach. In T. Lickona (Ed.), *Moral development and behaviour: theory, research and social issues*, Holt, Rinehart, and Winston, New York.

Kuhn, D. (1976). Short term longitudinal evidence for the sequentiality of Kohlberg's early stages of moral judgement. *Developmental Psychology*, 12, 162–166.

Locke, D. (1979). The illusion of stage six. *Journal of Moral Education*, 9, 103–109.

Rest, J. (1973). Patterns of preference and comprehension in moral judgment. *Journal of personality*, 41, 86–109.

Rest, J. (1975). Longitudinal study of the defining issues test. *Developmental Psychology*, 11, 738–748.

Rest, J. (1976). New approaches in the assessment of moral judgement. In T. Lickona (Ed.), *Moral development and behaviour: theory, research and social issues*, Holt, Rinehart, and Winston, New York.

Rest, J., Cooper, D., Coder, R., Masanz, J., and Anderson, D. (1974). Judging the important issues in moral dilemmas—an objective test of development. *Developmental Psychology*, 10, 491–501.

Rest, J., Davison, J., and Robbins, M. L. (1978). Age trends in judging moral issues: a review of cross-sectional, longitudinal, and sequential studies of the defining issues test. *Child Development*, 49, 263–279.

Selman, R. L. (1976). Social-cognitive understanding: a guide to educational and clinical practice. In T. Lickona (Ed.), *Moral development and behaviour: theory, research, and social issues*, Holt, Rinehart, and Winston, New York.

Turiel, E., Edwards, C. P., and Kohlberg, L. (1978). Moral development in Turkish children, adolescents, and young adults. *Journal of cross-cultural psychology*, **9**, 75–86.

Warnock, G. J. (1971). *The object of morality*, Methuen, London.

White, C. B., Bushnell, N., and Regnemer, J. L. (1978). Moral development in Bahamian school children: a three year examination of Kohlberg's stages of moral development. *Developmental Psychology*, **14**, 58–65.

Morality in the Making
Edited by H. Weinreich-Haste and D. Locke
© 1983, John Wiley & Sons, Ltd.

CHAPTER 5

Social and Moral Cognition

HELEN WEINREICH-HASTE

Morality has always been a popular issue. Until relatively recently, however, the dominant ethos of psychological science limited the discussion of morality to motivation and learning associated with the control of anti-social behaviour. With the general resurgence of interest in reasoning and cognition, judgment processes and moral reasoning have become a legitimate area of investigation. There is now an extensive body of evidence on the development and correlates of moral reasoning. A major effect of this activity has been to reintroduce into psychology most of the debates which have preoccupied moral philosophers for a couple of millenia; it is clear that psychologists and philosophers can no longer afford to ignore each other in this area. Many of the products of this cross-fertilization will undoubtedly enrich psychological explanation; as other chapters in this book illustrate, psychologists are being forced to consider the implications of such issues as thought vs. action, the relationship between ideology and theory, and the fact that 'morality' is not a unitary concept.

In this chapter, however, I want to argue that a too easy acceptance of what are perceived to be philosophical criteria of 'moral' reasoning has obscured some of the important conclusions for both social and developmental psychology which can be drawn from the evidence. I shall argue, firstly, that the evidence indicates considerable overlap between 'moral' and other forms of 'social' reasoning—by which I mean reasoning about the relationship between individuals and between the individual and society. This overlap has considerable implications for the psychological use of the category, 'moral', and for the development of 'social' cognition generally. Secondly, I shall argue that the emphasis on a theory of *morality* has led to a lot of attention being paid, especially by critics, to the *content* of stages of moral development, and less to the processes by which development between the stages occurs. My general thesis is that we should look more closely at what is actually going on in 'moral' reasoning studies, and consider the implications of this for an understanding of developmental processes.

The primary source of material which I shall use in pursuing these arguments is the theoretical and empirical work of Kohlberg and his followers. Kohlberg's is not the only rationalist model of moral development, nor are the general problems which I shall consider only to be found in cognitive-developmental theory. But in cognitive-developmental theory on the whole the concepts are well-articulated, the research is extensive and follows a consistent pattern, and the limitations of the perspective are therefore apparent. Kohlberg (1969, 1971) has made explicit his assumptions about the nature and development of morality, and about the kinds of questions that psychologists should be asking about development.

In Chapter 2, Vine defined Piaget as a 'moderate constructivist'. Although he argued that Kohlberg departed from this approach in the way he deals with *ethics*, I will work with the premise that Kohlberg's developmental theory does conform to the 'moderate constructivist' position. It also applies to a wide range of current perspectives in social and developmental psychology, especially approaches to various aspects of social reasoning. The general principle is that the individual *constructs* her social and conceptual world. Individual construal is the outcome of interaction between the individual's own implicit theory about the situation, collective representations shared by others, and group dynamics which affect what emphasis or elements of those representations will be deemed relevant at any one point in time (Weinreich-Haste, 1981). This approach focuses on *processes* of the formation, development, and change in constructions and representations.

Social and developmental psychologists have somewhat different orientations within this general framework. The social psychologist seeks structural explanations in the interaction between individual and social, preferring to analyse the group and situational context rather than individual variables. Developmental psychologists focus on individual cognitive structure, how this limits the construal processes, and how the structure changes through growth. Social psychologists tend to criticize the orthodox cognitive-developmental model as too rigidly structuralist, and too tied up with individual processes at the expense of the social, cultural, and situational factors which may affect the child's construal.

According to the constructivist position, development is not a matter of the acquisition of more knowledge, but of increasing differentiation and integration in the construal process. Development means increasing ability to comprehend what is relevant, what should be taken into consideration, and increasing capacity to organize and reorganize conceptualization and construal to take account of this comprehension. Changes in the course of development are qualitative. The argument for 'stages' is that the organization of construal forms a 'structured whole'. The underlying structure of thinking within a 'stage' is the *common principle* of construal, the common set of criteria for organization and interpretation. Developmental change from stage to stage involves the breakdown of this structure and the development of a new, more complex and more differentiated structure.

Each stage is characterized by *limitations* of thinking which prevent the individual from (a) perceiving all the possible parameters and variables which may be relevant to the situation, (b) perceiving contradictions inherent in her existing mode of reasoning, and (c) dealing with such contradictions or alternatives if they are pointed out to her. The evidence in all areas of reasoning indicates that these limitations are overcome only when the dominant mode of reasoning, the dominant organization of criteria for judgment, is broken down and replaced by more complex structures. In the interim, novel or more complex material is interpreted in terms of the existing categories and criteria.

The Nature of 'Morality'

My first argument is that the research area current labelled 'moral' judgment is a misleading categorization. The 'moral' category reflects the place which the study of moral development has had in psychology, and the way in which psychologists' implicit theories of morality have remained largely unquestioned, their philosophical roots unexamined. From being an unacceptable topic in the heyday of behaviourism, the study of moral development gradually crept back into the literature of social-learning theory, via the socialization of values and social constraints. In psychoanalytic theory the concept of morality has always had a central, if sometimes implicit, position (Freud, 1930; Rieff, 1960).

Hogan *et al.* (1978) argue that the social-learning perspective represents a form of extreme moral relativism, because 'moral' values and constraints are defined by arbitrary cultural or subcultural contingencies. Eysenck and Skinner, for example, in different ways express extreme forms of the conditioning model. Both define 'moral' explicitly in terms of conformity to or deviation from the current social code; both consider this to be the only way in which a 'scientific' psychologist can use the term (Eysenck, 1976; Skinner, 1971). In this relativistic perspective, there is no *a priori* differentiation between moral, social, and conventional values; any differentiation arises only insofar as the labels have some meaning within the culture. The model is explicitly normative, the goal of socialization must be conformity to the currently accepted social values and behaviours.

Cognitive-developmental models of moral development, in contrast, have adopted a more objective moral perspective, which several critics have argued leads to a form of moral absolutism (see Vine, Chapter 2). The assumption held by Kohlberg, and also by Piaget, is that there are universal moral principles, held by any *rational* person, which pertain across time and culture. Moral development is the increasing comprehension of these principles, and increasing capacity to organize moral cognitions in accordance with them. In this perspective a strong distinction is made between 'moral' and other kinds of reasoning. This in part arises from their acceptance of formalist criteria of morality, in particular the criteria of prescriptiveness and universalizability. In the cognitive-developmental model these general criteria are translated into specific principles of justice and equity; these are the core concepts of morality from which, it is argued, all else is derived (Kohlberg, 1971). This is explicit in Kohlberg's theory, but only implicit in Piaget's. Piaget was much more preoccupied with the mechanism by which the child generates a rational, autonomous understanding of the rule, and mutual respect; conceptions of justice and equity may be constitutive of autonomous morality, but this was largely incidental to Piaget's main concerns (Piaget, 1932; Weinreich-Haste, 1982; see Wright, Chapter 8).

One of the major objections levelled at the cognitive-developmental model is that it focuses on rational processes and ignores both motive and action. The basic position of both rationalist psychologists (e.g. Kohlberg, 1971) and philosophers (e.g. Rawls, 1971) is that actions, however commendable in their consequences or their motives of sympathy, are morally meaningless unless springing from moral reasoning.

It happens that the traditional distinctions between a Kantian, reason-based definition of reality and a Humean, virtue-based definition of morality have become aligned with two contrasting psychological theories of moral development, which also, for historical reasons, happen to coincide with the relativist vs. absolutist distinction. The accident of this dual dichotomy leads to some confusions and a complex range of criticisms. Kohlberg's theory, for example, has been subject to criticism for both its rationalist *and* its absolutist orientations, and the two criticisms are frequently confused. Interestingly, relatively little attention has been paid to the relativist *or* motivational assumptions of the social-learning perspective, except by cognitive-developmental psychologists. An enduring exception is Peters, who has consistently criticized both schools of thought (Peters, 1963, 1971, 1974, 1978). Kohlberg's narrowly rational conception of morality has been criticized by psychologists and philosophers (e.g. Hogan, 1970, 1973; Alston, 1971). His absolutism has been attacked on both theoretical and empirical grounds. While the evidence for the earlier stages of moral reasoning is good, that supporting the post-conventional Stages 5 and 6 is sketchy. Several writers have argued that there are possibly several 'final' forms of moral thinking (Gibbs, 1977; Locke, 1980). If this is the case, then the moral absolutism supposedly inherent in the present conceptualization of Stage 6 thought need not necessarily be the *logical* corolloary of the cognitive-developmental position.

There are, therefore, several possible objections to the theories of morality implicit in psychological models. My position is that much of the problem derives from a false premise, the premise that there is a real difference between the processes of reasoning applied to 'moral' questions and those applied to other social issues. It is undoubtedly the case that the philosopher is trained to make a valid distinction between moral and other categories, which she is capable of applying to her own actions; it is evident also that post-conventional reasoners are at least *aware* of the distinction. It is however a dangerous assumption in my view that there is, *for most people most of the time*, anything special or separate about the kinds of reasoning employed in discussing moral issues. There are three premises on which I shall base my defence of this position. Firstly, the methods employed by researchers to tap moral judgment are in fact accessing a wide range of social reasoning. Secondly, the stages of moral reasoning are manifestations of development over a broad range of social cognition. Thirdly, the current view, which separates reasoning development into a sequence which starts from intellectual-logical areas and progresses to social, moral, and then political domains, is a distorted perception and an artefactual consequence of methodology.

The Evidence

The data on moral reasoning development and its correlates is now substantial (see Chapter 1). It can be divided broadly into (1) material which bears directly on developmental processes, and (2) material on the correlates of level of moral reasoning:

1(a) The ways in which the moral dilemmas are resolved change significantly with age. There are substantial shifts in the basis of reasoning utilized. These changes include the kind and range of factors which are considered to be relevant to the issue.

 (b) Development is manifested by increased complexity of thinking on both social and moral issues, and increase in the number and subtlety of the variables taken into account and integrated into the reasoning process.

 (c) The changes are qualitative, and at any point in time the individual demonstrates a consistency in the kind of reasoning utilized across several issues or problems; the same criteria for judgment are invoked, and the same dominant themes occur. The concept of 'stage' reflects this consistency. Additionally, the invariant sequence of stages meets the criterion of hierarchization proposed by Pinard and Laurendeau (1969). (Kohlberg, 1969; Kohlberg and Kramer, 1969; Holstein, 1976; Davison *et al.*, 1978.)

 (d) The hierarchical nature of the stages, and the increasing complexity, differentiation, and organization of later forms of thinking are demonstrated by the fact that individuals reject the arguments of a lower stage of thinking, when they are presented, and reinterpret arguments presented in the concepts of stages higher than their own, in terms of the reasoning of their own stage (Rest, 1973, 1979; Rest *et al.*, 1969; Turiel, 1966, 1972.)

2(a) The development of logical-cognitive operations, as represented by Piaget's stages, is a prerequisite for the development of moral stages. It is, however, not a sufficient condition.

 (b) Moral judgment stages appear to depend on the stages of 'social perspective-taking' which itself follows upon the development of the parallel logical stages. Social perspective-taking, therefore, would seem to be the intervening variable between logical and moral operations. (Selman, 1980; Walker, 1980.)

(c) There is a relationship between moral reasoning, political reasoning, and political action. Moral reasoning level is predictive of direct political action, and there is also evidence of considerable overlap between the dominant themes expressed in the two areas (Haan *et al.*, 1968; Fishkin *et al.*, 1973; Haan, 1975). Studies of the development of political understanding and reasoning show similar kinds of changes in criteria, factors considered significant, and dominant themes, to those found in moral judgment development (Adelson and O'Neil, 1966, 1969; Adelson, 1971).

(d) Evidence from a number of studies using 'self' and 'ego' measures of various kinds indicate a relationship between moral reasoning and ego functions. Some of these studies concern the integrative processes of the ego (e.g. Podd, 1972); others concern the parallels between organizing functions of the ego (cognitions about the self and others in the social world) and moral reasoning (Loevinger, 1976; Lambert, 1971; Haan *et al.*, 1968; Candee, 1974; Haan, 1978; Erickson, 1980).

Three issues are raised by this evidence. Firstly, it is obvious that moral judgment does not exist in isolation; it is closely related to several other aspects of development. The current interpretation of the data is that these relationships are causal. Secondly, given that movement through the stage is *qualitative* change, what is the *meaning* of the consistency found at each stage? By what *processes* does the individual progress to greater integration and differentiation; by what processes does reorganization and restructuring take place? Thirdly, what is actually the nature of the decision-making process? In order to understand what is going on when *this* person at *this* stage of moral reasoning tackles a moral dilemma, we must understand, (a) what are the limits of her conceptual capacities; (b) what factors does she consider relevant to the situation a she perceives it, and (c) how has she *categorized* and *organized* the elements of the situation. We need to know the elements involved in the decision-making process in order to comprehend how they are changed by reorganization.

These questions relate to two distinct problem areas. Firstly, they each apply to the issue of *construal*, and cognitive organization. Secondly, they each have implications for the theory of how construal and organization develops and changes.

'Moral' and 'Social' Reasoning

The usual interpretation of the relationship between reasoning on moral dilemmas and other areas of reasoning is that there is a *series*; the individual's reasoning about physical and logical phenomena matures first. Through the application of role-taking skills to social interaction and taking the perspective of others, the individual develops comprehension of the social situation and its implications, which enables her to generate prescriptive judgments about the moral and social order (see Thornton and Thornton, Chapter 4).

However, role-taking, as Vine has argued in Chapter 2, is a very confused concept. It is used in the literature to mean both the affective process of sympathy and the cognitive process of empathy. In his early writings Kohlberg, in common with other writers, confused the two kinds of role-taking, and, in effect, argued that moral reasoning sprang from sympathy. He attempted to test this by correlating moral judgment level and degree of peer-group involvement, which he used as an indirect measure of role-taking skills (Kohlberg, 1958). Latterly, through Selman's work, role-taking has been defined more precisely as 'social perspective-taking' (Selman, 1980). In the early stages social perspective-taking is very limited and egoistic. Smith's evidence that stage 1 moral thought is in many ways an expression of pre-operational thinking is consistent with this; Stage 1 thinkers characteristically focus on only one aspect of the situation—usually Heinz's rule-breaking—demonstrating limited capacity for decentration and no capacity for social reciprocity (Smith, 1978). Stage 2 thinking represents a simple dyadic reciprocity; 'if I were her' means just that, with no account taken of 'her' different experience and situation. A more reflexive perspective-taking is found in Stage 3 thought, where the individual can perceive the situation as the other would. With the acquisition of formal operational thought the individual is able to take a perspective which begins to include 'society' as well as the individual, and to see the symbolic effect of actions upon the social system as well as on the person. This perspective also permits the observer to include the role of the impartial judge. In Stage 5 the capacity extends further, to include not only all points of view *within* the situation, but all possible points of view on the issue. Selman and Kohlberg refer to this as the 'prior to society' perspective; in logical terms it is the capacity to see the actual as a subcategory of the possible, a capacity which marks formal operational thinking in contrast to the concrete operational tendency to see the possible as a subcategory of the actual (Kohlberg, 1976; Selman, 1980).

The argument is that social perspective delineates the individual's understanding of the social order, and this provides the reference points for judging what is 'fair' and 'right'. The principle of justice is central to Kohlberg's theory of morality, consequently, the capacity to judge 'fair' is sufficient to define 'right', and therefore to define 'moral' reasoning. Kohlberg identifies as 'sociomoral' perspectives the perception of social *facts* and the *prescription* of right and good. In Kohlberg's theory of morality there are four components: normative order, utility, ideal self, and justice—but justice is the core component. Social perspective-taking is a necessary but not sufficient condition for moral thinking, because of itself it does not include justice, though justice will follow from social perspective-taking.

I want to propose an alternative interpretation of the evidence, which argues against a sequential model of the different kinds of reasoning. The distinction between 'moral' and other kinds of reasoning about interpersonal and social issues has its origin in certain philosophical positions which have been accepted uncritically by psychologists. This acceptance creates a number of problems. Philosophers argue on the assumption that the agent or judge is an adult, usually a rational adult with a capacity for reflective consciousness. Although this necessarily implies some preceding period of development, it has been left to psychologists to establish how the individual arrives at the adult moral position postulated. The developmental psychologist is not dealing with a rational, self-conscious adult, yet it is remarkable that there has been little recognition of the implications of this. The main implication is that the psychologist ultimately has to account for the 'specialness' of moral function in the child or adolescent by appeal to psychological, rather than philosophical, criteria.

There is some evidence which supports a psychological distinction between moral and other forms of reasoning. It comes from studies which compare children's reasoning on social conventions and their reasoning on rules of right and wrong (Turiel, 1974, 1979; Much and Schweder, 1978; Damon, 1977). Rules which concern issues which an adult would deem 'moral' are seen by the child as having an *intrinsic* quality, and are less likely than conventions to be subject to negotiation or exception. This indicates that, at the very least, the child has picked up the *notion* that moral rules are 'special', that their observance is mandatory in the way that other rules are not. But the same studies show that the processes of reasoning about all rules, whether moral or conventional or instructional, are the same; the same *kinds* of justifications, and the same underlying conceptions of social order, are invoked for all kinds of rules in the 'social' domain. Damon found that friendship and justice are confused, as criteria for judgment, up to the equivalent of Kohlberg's Stage 4 moral reasoning. Turiel found that in the *early* stages of reasoning, the child does distinguish between 'moral' and 'conventional' rules, but in Stages 3 and 4 she gives the same kinds of justifications for both—namely that they serve social cohesiveness. The common feature of reasoning in all areas concerned with social and interpersonal rules is the interrelationship of fact and value, the failure to distinguish between what *is* and *should be*, and the lack of distinction between what is right and what is desirable. This confusion of fact and value is a *psychological* reality, despite the categorization which philosophers might wish to apply.

My argument is that the moral dilemma is much more usefully conceived as a very effective technique for eliciting the much broader processes of social cognition and social reasoning. In resolving the dilemma the individual is made to consider evaluative and prescriptive criteria to justify her decision about what is the 'right' action, and these arguments and reasons reveal the processes by which social reasoning in general is organized. It is by no means the only technique for eliciting such reasoning; in many ways it is a very restricted tool, but my argument is that because researchers have focused on 'morality', as defined by criteria extrinsic to psychology, the depth and range of the data already collected have not been fully appreciated. One reason why the technique is effective, is common to all hypothetical or projective methods. However remote from one's own experience the situation presented may be the only reasoning available to the individual is that which does derive from her own experience. Her construals and representations of the world have developed out of the organization of that experience: in resolving the hypothetical moral dilemma, she must invoke a *real* world view of proper and necessary rules and roles, and of interrelationships between the individual and society. The overt conflict in the Heinz dilemma (Figure 1, Chapter 1) is between life and law, but to resolve the dilemma the individual will take into account the conflicts between personal and social demands portrayed in the situation, and the ideal versus the immediate instrumental consequence—all of this construed in terms of her ordinary social cognitions, and limited by them. Thus the resolution and its arguments exposes the *ordinary* reasoning of the individual.

My major contention is that in deciding whether Heinz should steal the medicine the individual is utilizing a much wider conception of 'the good' than that encompassed by a narrowly formalistic definition of 'the moral'. It is undoubtedly the case that individuals of all ages engage in moral rhetoric and moral indignation, and make distinctive certain rules which they subjectively sense as mandatory (see Breakwell, Chapter 13). In response to a moral dilemma, the individual will frequently make quite simple moral-rhetorical statements, which are heavily prescriptive, but the processes of reasoning behind that rhetoric are extensive and complex. The wider 'good' includes outcomes which are desirable because of their consequences for interpersonal relations and the social world in general. Role performance, for example, may be good *in itself*, either because it is seen to be *of itself* a virtue, or because it is seen as functional to the maintenance of social order. A justification such as that is made in terms of beliefs about the consequences of events and these are seen by the individual to be *factual* beliefs, even though to the sophisticated observer they are indistinguishable from values. The interesting questions about the judgmental process therefore concern the conception of the wider 'good', how it is justified and what factors contribute to that justification.

Let us consider the changes which take place in the conception of 'the good' at different stages of reasoning, and see in what way they represent an implicit theory, not of morality, but of society, which has wider implications. We shall see that the implicit 'good' of each stage of thought effectively delineates the dominant criteria of judgment in the stage. The theory of society reflected in the conceptualization of the good reveals the limitations of the world-view at that particular stage, but more important, it reflects the way in which the individual has organized her construal within those limitations.

In Stage 1 thought, the implicit good elicited in response to the Heinz dilemma is unequivocal; it is defined by the rule in most cases, though some individuals focus on the material good, and speculate on whether Heinz's wife should be saved if she is an especially important or rich person. In this case, the rule is a *self-evident* good, and obedience follows from this. The simplicity of the 'good' at this stage—combined with the tendency to focus on only one aspect of the situation—means that for the Stage 1 thinker there is no conflict, no dilemma.

In Stage 2 thinking, the wider 'good' is easily hidden in the general moral rhetoric which attaches to the broadly instrumental perspective; 'fairness' is the rallying cry—but this is not a sophisticated plea for justice. The Stage 2 thinker construes the world in terms of conflict—between persons and between groups. At the purely instrumental level, the good is defined in personal terms, the survival of one's own rights and goals. In the context of the wider community this is a perception of the legitimacy of everyone's right to a 'fair' distribution of rewards and assets. Individuals have the right to attempt to gain these, within certain limits which are defined by the concept of 'fairness'. This conceptualization gives Heinz the right to steal, but it also gives the chemist the right to charge what he wants. In one study of an adult population, the real-life situation of the Berkeley Free Speech Movement sit-in in 1964 was construed by Stage 2 thinkers as a power struggle between 'we' the students and 'they' the unfair establishment (Haan, 1975).

For the Stage 3 thinker, the good is social and interpersonal harmony. It is implicitly understood that roles and rules evolved through law and custom as a means of maintaining this harmony, therefore the maintenance of both is regarded as desirable, and is a criterion for judgment. The primary categorization is in terms of the 'good person'—the person who fulfils role and rule expectations. The codification of the good person is in terms of traits and virtues; if everyone was nice, kind, honest, etc., social harmony would be automatic. The Heinz story is a particular problem for Stage 3 thinkers, because of the conflict of rule and role. The conflict between Heinz and the chemist is between the *good* husband and the *greedy* chemist; if Heinz is unable to persuade the chemist to become *generous*, he will be forced to act as a *bad* citizen, and steal the medicine. The conceptions of 'good' applied here to people have only indirectly 'moral' connotations; they apply to *effective role performance*, and reflect an essentially *gemeinschaft* conception of social order as the interrelationship of roles and functional reciprocity.

The 'good' for Stage 4 is *order*, rather than harmony. The shift from concrete to formal operations facilitates a much more complex, holistic conception of the social system than the Stage 3 communalistic extrapolations from the face-to-face group. The capacity to conceive of society as a whole enables the individual to be aware of the wider effects of individual action, and also of the limited efficacy of mere norms as constraints. Rules and a system of sanctions are necessary not simply to sustain norms—and keep order—but also to establish some impartial basis for the distribution of goods and rights, and to provide means to redress inequalities. An impartial justice system is necessary to control offenders, but also to prevent the escalation of interpersonal strife or conflict of interest. Justice must be *seen* to be done, because of its deterrent and exemplary function; it is not a moral ideal, but an efficient means of maintaining social order. The conflict between Heinz and the chemist reflects these processes. Both have rights and obligations within the law, but their conflict of interests has led to a possibility that social order may be disturbed.

The conception of the good is also reflected in the personality traits considered desirable by Stage 4 thinkers. These are apparent from analysis of responses to moral dilemmas, but they also emerged in an independent study of self and ideal-self by Haan *et al.* (1968). For the Stage 3 thinker, qualities associated with virtue and interpersonal skills—such as niceness—are valid. The Stage 4 thinker rates highly those characteristics likely to ensure effective performance of *institutional* roles, and the maintenance of social order, such as reliability and trustworthiness. A view of virtue which is societal, rather than a dyadic, values symbolic and publicly identifiable characteristics which predict the continued performance of obligations, even in private.

For the Stage 5 thinker there are four kinds of 'good' to be balanced; the personal, the societal, the legal, and the moral. The overriding good is the protection of the rights and goals of the individual while at the same time maintaining the institutions of society for the benefit of the majority. An act has immediate personal implications and consequences, and symbolic effects upon the wider social system. If Heinz steals (the personal-moral choice), what effect will this have in terms of setting precedents? If the respondent decides he should not steal (the legal good) is this denying the purpose of the law, namely to provide impartial support for the rights of all and to codify moral principles? The chemist is not legally wrong, but he may be seen as morally wrong. This has implications for the legal system; should it be able to control his actions? Furthermore, Heinz's moral rightness in stealing has as much implication for wider society as his legal wrongness. The Stage 5 thinker juggles with all these factors in her construal of the situation; the overriding good does not in fact offer easy criteria for prioritization of the variables. The solution tends to be pragmatic in this case; the single event of Heinz's theft is hardly likely to bring the social system tumbling down, and Heinz's problem is a very immediate one, with moral if not legal right on his side.

The foregoing has outlined the changes in the conception of 'the good', and the way in which it is utilized in reasoning on moral dilemmas. The moral dilemma, although itself narrow and specific, brings out the way in which the respondent sees 'the good', and how several 'goods' may be seen to be in conflict or in interrelationship. The process of construal of 'the good' is part of the organization of perceptions of the social world, and of existing values and beliefs. At each stage of thinking, there are *pre-eminent* categories and criteria for construing the situation. These criteria and categories reflect implicit 'theories' which the individual has about the desirable basis for human interaction, the resolution of conflict, and the attainment of various forms of the 'good'. The conception of 'the good' itself is both a factor in the organization, and a reflection of the organization, of the individual's conceptual world.

The Implications of Political Reasoning Correlates

The relationship between moral and political reasoning which has been empirically demonstrated by a number of studies provides a case-history of the problems arising from undue focus on the narrow definition of 'moral' reasoning. The question raised by these studies is how far is 'political' thinking *confused* with 'moral' thinking, and how far is 'moral' thinking *applied* to 'political' issues?

There is good documentation of a relationship between the development of moral thought, and action and reasoning in the broadly defined 'political' domain. Extensive research in the restive campuses of the last two decades has demonstrated a powerful and complex relationship between political beliefs, practical action, and moral reasoning (Haan *et al.*, 1968; Fishkin *et al.*, 1973, *inter alia*). Secondly, Adelson and his associates have studied the interesting parallels with the development of social and moral reasoning (Adelson and O'Neil, 1966; Adelson *et al.*, 1969; Adelson, 1971). There is an important sampling difference between the studies of student activists and the Adelson studies. In the former, the correlations between reasoning and action were found in a population of heterogeneous *stage* but homogeneous age; Adelson's subjects were adolescents of different ages.

Haan *et al.* (1968), and others, have produced evidence suggestive of the effect of different family environments (which may be causal), and of differences in ego-ideal and in political thought (whose causal direction is not clear) (Candee, 1974; Haan, 1978). Other research suggests that the organization of social and moral reasoning becomes 'set' in a particular stage, around the age at which formal education finishes, and is only shaken into disequilibrium by a major life experience (Turiel, 1974; Podd, 1972: Kohlberg, 1976; Gilligan, 1977, 1982). Because of these theoretical problems, there are some difficulties in taking the correlates of moral reasoning in an age-homogeneous sample as being indicative of *developmental* relationships. However, despite these caveats, it is clear that the kind of moral reasoning used by the students was associated with a whole range of attitudinal and behavioural variables. Firstly, individuals using post-conventional reasoning were more likely to support action and ideologies associated with reform or even revolution than were conventional (Stage 3 and 4) reasoners. Individuals using Stage 2 reasoning were instrumental and quixotic; they supported whichever mode of action was perceived to serve their immediate interests. Secondly, these relationships predicted both direct political action and wider community action (e.g. Peace Corps activity).

Some commentators have argued that these results are evidence of an inherent political conservatism in conventional-level thinking, and of radicalism in post-conventional thinking (Hampden-Turner and Whitten, 1971). It may be, however, that this is a *zeitgeist* effect; the sophisticated moral rhetoric of the period favoured the Left rather than the Right. At any point in time, the capacity to see beyond the current dominant social and political paradigm requires a capacity for complex sociopolitical reasoning. It would follow from my position that more complex *social* reasoning is an integral aspect of the higher stages of *moral* thinking, that post-conventional moral reasoners by definition comprehend the wider social and political implications of what is going on in the situation, and then also bring more complex and sophisticated theoretical viewpoint to the issues. It is not necessarily the case that the theories of the Left are more complex in their analysis of the social order than those of the Right (though some would certainly argue this), but for historical and sociological reasons these were the arguments advanced most vociferously at the time, and attracted the most attention amongst those capable of post-conventional sociomoral reasoning.

It is also arguable that the conventional terms 'political' and 'moral' are only loosely applicable to the situation on the campuses. In later writings Haan talked not about *political* thinking, but about actual vs. hypothetical *moral* thinking; the moral dilemma is an example of hypothetical moral reasoning, the campus situation an actual case of moral reasoning (and action). According to her evidence and analysis, the lack of involvement of the students whose thinking was Stage 3 or 4 can partly be accounted for by their failure to see the issues as being *moral* issues—rather than that their general ideology was opposed to direct action, which would be the Hampden-Turner interpretation. This interpretation places much more emphasis on structural factors—the overall construal of the situation and the limitations of what is perceived to be relevant—than on content factors of ideology and attitude. Commensurate with this is the evidence that Stage 2 thinkers construed the situation in considerably more simplistic terms than did post-conventional thinkers, although their *actions*, and to some extent their superficial expression of opinion, were similar.

A study by Candee further illuminates the relationship between 'political' thinking and construal of the social world (Candee, 1974). He investigated the relationship between ego stages (according to Loevinger's model) and ideology (Loevinger, 1976). He found that at different ego stages the students viewed their left-wing activities in very different ways. At the lower ego stages, students construed the situation and the issues in terms of self-other relations; increasingly, through the stages, they demonstrated wider social and societal perspectives.

In a study of women contemplating abortion, Gilligan identified a number of levels of reasoning which overlap with Kohlberg's moral stages, but differ from them in important details (Gilligan, 1977, 1980, 1982). Gilligan argues, as others have (e.g. Holstein, 1976), that the moral stages which Kohlberg originally identified in adolescent boys do not take into account the much greater part which interpersonal caring and responsibility play in women's moral reasoning. The real-life issue of abortion provided a focus for drawing out a wide range of reasoning on interpersonal and role obligations. The main departures from Kohlberg's scheme are in the differential emphases placed on justice and caring. According to Kohlberg's data—and in line with his moral theory—justice does have an imperative quality for males. For females, however, the moral imperative takes the form of injunction to care, to alleviate suffering, and to prevent violence.

Gilligan's levels reflect, like the other studies, changes in integration, organization, and construal of the social world. Her findings on changes in the concept of 'the good' are particularly interesting; for women, the 'good' is defined in terms of various kinds of self-sacrifice, even of self-abnegation, which are perceived as necessary for fulfilling the moral imperative of responsibility for others. The significant developmental change which Gilligan identifies is the realization that 'responsibility' also included responsibility for the self and for the autonomy of one's own actions.

In Adelson's developmental studies the term 'political' has a somewhat different meaning. Adelson and his co-workers asked children to devise and justify an ideal political system for a hypothetical population of a thousand people on an isolated island. Development was manifested by increasing awareness of historical perspective, of possible alternatives, of social variables to be considered, and, ultimately, in the use of general principles for evaluating rules and institutions. The kind of changes in reasoning which Adelson found are very similar to the change found in other areas of social reasoning, the same increasing awareness of the wider implications of individual and social events and their consequences, and of the function of rules and roles (Adelson and O'Neil, 1966; Adelson et al., 1969; Adelson, 1971).

Tomlinson (1975) has argued that 'the political constitutes a specification and extension of the moral'—in other words, political thinking develops later than, and is consequent upon, moral reasoning. He also argued that the values under consideration in studies of political reasoning are 'procedural', in contrast with moral values, which are 'terminal'. As a consequence, he argued, the processes in political reasoning are more *apparent* than those involved in moral reasoning. This, in my view, is an imposed criterion; the foregoing analysis has on the whole indicated that most of the values involved in the social and moral construal processes are in fact procedural. The explicit organization of terminal values only really occurs in post-conventional reasoning, and, as we have seen, this organization occurs as much in the sphere deemed 'political' by researchers as it does in the sphere deemed 'moral'.

The overlap between the different areas of reasoning becomes even more obvious when we take into account the constraints imposed by methodology. In a 'real-life' situation, where the individual's own actions and appraisals are currently and practically involved in the event, the experimenter does not impose the criteria by which the event shall be judged; she interprets the categories used by the respondents. Although this is what in fact should be happening in any open-ended technique, it is my contention that the categories of 'moral' and 'political' imposed on the data by the experimenters have distorted and limited the interpretation of the material. From Haan's later analysis of the Berkeley Free Speech Movement data, it is clear that the distinction between 'moral' and 'political' was not made in the minds of the majority of students. Social, personal, moral, and political arguments were all invoked in their construal of the situation. Haan, in fact, found that nearly half of the sample reasoned about the 'real' (i.e. 'political') situation at a *higher* stage than they did about the hypothetical (i.e. 'moral') situation of the dilemma. This of itself is counter-evidence for the argument that political development is consequent upon moral development, but more important for the present discussion, it is evidence of considerable overlap in reasoning. The conclusion which Haan draws is that, for these students at least, the actuality of the event created a general state of disequilibrium which focused their thinking and effected a greater organization and integration of *all* the construals in the situation (Haan, 1975).

The same overlap and interaction between various kinds of reasoning, and lack of subjective distinction between them, is found in all the studies which looked at 'real-life' situations (e.g. Candee, 1974; Gilligan, 1977, 1980). From these studies it is clear that some arguments do have an imperative quality, but this quality cannot be satisfactorily labelled as 'moral' or 'political'—for Gilligan's subjects it was role obligations, attached to a particular ideal image of 'womanhood'. As we have seen, in hypothetical situations, the experimenter may impose parameters which delineate the situation, but irrespective of the label that is hung on the task, the technique effectively picks up a very wide range of 'social' reasoning. On the basis of all the foregoing, it would seem that there is now a need for research which examines the interrelationship *within* the broad area of social cognition, as opposed to research which looks at the correlations *between* areas of social cognition.

The Developmental Process

In the foregoing, I have spelt out what I see to be the limitations of applying a *moral* theory to what is in fact the development of social reasoning. I now shall look at the effect of the emphasis on the *moral* aspect of the theory, on analysis of developmental processes. Firstly, it has enforced a teleological perspective on supporters and critics of Kohlberg alike; the role of Stage 6 in the *moral* theory has been exaggerated out of all proportion to its distribution in the population. Secondly, it has focused attention on the specific contingencies of development relating to those areas which fit the definition of 'moral'—including moral action—at the cost of attention to the general processes of reasoning and changes in reasoning. Thirdly, the preoccupation with the ideological consistency of the *moral* stages has led to a somewhat static picture, which tends to focus on content rather than structure, and consequently underplays the essentially dynamic model of development which is inherent in cognitive-developmental theory. Fourthly, emphasis on the narrow ideology of morality has limited the attention paid to interaction between the individual and society, in particular, the individual in her own social world. This interaction is important in the developmental process partly because of its role in *what* the individual learns about construal—in other words, what categories are offered to her by her immediate environment. However, it is also important because interpersonal discussion, conflict, and dissonance affects the restructuring process.

The kinds of change which occur developmentally have been discussed in detail in the first part of this chapter. Let us for example consider what happens to decision-making about a *rule*: (a) it is comprehended with increasing complexity; (b) it is perceived as being applicable to different people and different individuals; (c) it is seen as serving the interests of different groups of people; (d) different immediate and long-term effects are seen to accrue from obeying (or failing to obey) the rule. A developmental explanation requires explication of the mechanisms involved in these changes. Required for this is analysis of the transition processes, and the dynamic interactions between the individual's existing construals, and between the individual and the construals of other individuals. The extent to which this explication would be better served by a model of social reasoning rather than moral reasoning can best be examined by seeing in detail how the 'moral theory' approach impedes analysis.

A substantial part of the debate on moral development has been caught in the trap which arises from the teleological model. This takes the form of discussion about the *moral* validity of the ideologies manifested at various stages, or else about the explicit *telos* of the developmental sequence—the content of Stage 6 thought. Supporters of the Kohlberg model argue that the later stages are more 'moral' because they approximate more closely to the thinking of certain moral philosophers, and in particular because the sequence indicates progress towards a justice-based liberal ethic (Kohlberg, 1971, 1973). Critics of the model have also shown the same preoccupation with the definition of morality; they argue that Kohlberg's stages are culturally or politically biased because Stage 6 reflects the dominant ideological perspective of a liberal Western culture (Simpson, 1974; Sullivan, 1977; Trainer, 1977; see Emler, Chapter 3). *Both* sides in this debate are preoccupied with the same issue, namely moral 'maturity'.

By any criterion, the later stages of reasoning are more complex, more subtle, and invoke more factors for consideration, but these characteristics refer to the *reasoning processes*. They are not an evaluation of the moral content. In other words, the criticisms are valid as objections to the implicit theory of *morality*, but they are not valid as objections to the implicit theory of *development*. Hierarchical stage models are particularly vulnerable to teleological, evaluative, fallacies; Piaget has been criticized for using an implicit *telos* which reflects only one, ahistorical view of science. His natural science paradigm of formal operational thinking carries the implication that knowledge *equals* science, rather than that science equals one *form* of knowledge (Riegel, 1972; Wilden, 1975; Wozniak, 1975). However, the developmental theory of both Piaget and

Kohlberg is about the explanation of *progression* and *transformation*. These processes are of psychological significance irrespective of whether or not the individual completes the sequence of development—in the case of moral reasoning, of course, the vast majority of people do not.

These problems reflect the recurrent issue of 'structure vs. content'. The structure of thinking is the underlying organization of beliefs, which is only partly manifested in the content, i.e. the expressed opinion. There are two approaches to structure, and it is these two approaches which reflect the kinds of confusions above. One approach is to look at the *moral* structure, that is those consistent *moral* principles and themes which underlie the attitudes expressed, and represent the moral origin of the reasoning. It this type of structure which has predominated in many discussions of the moral theory. A second approach to structure, which is consistent with my argument in this chapter, is to see the structure of reasoning as the organization of cognitions about the social world, *some* of which may be expressed in moral opinions. A structural view based on social cognition includes a wide understanding of society, and social relations, norms, conventions, and obligations, which is only partly relevant to any specific 'moral' issue. This structure also includes the ways in which the individual construes causal relations between social events and individual attributes.

The focus of a developmental theory should be upon the growth process; in the case of stage theory, in particular on the transition process from stage to stage. Undue focus on the *telos* distracts from this analysis, especially if that focus is on description. The growth or transition process, according to the tenets of cognitive-developmental theory, is a process of increased disequilibrium which creates reconstruction and restructuring (Langer, 1969). Disequilibrium arises from a disjunction between assimilative and accommodative processes. The origins of disequilibrium must be sought, therefore, not only in the relationships within the existing construal system, but also in the relationship between the individual and other individuals, and the relationship between the individual and the values and construal processes of the wider society. The constant interaction between the self and the environment, and the process of conscious realization of action in thought, is explicit in Piaget's cognitive theory (see Wright, Chapter 8). It is barely touched upon in moral development theory.

Research on development has focused largely on the independent variables associated with developmental change. Some evidence of the effects of group dynamics and social interaction has been collected, but this has been primarily designed to test the hierarchical criterion of the moral stages—to demonstrate that the reasoning of stages higher than the individual's own are seen as more effective and attractive arguments. The relationship between the individual and the wider values, rhetoric, and construals of society is virtually unresearched. Two pieces of research, however, are illuminating on the transition processes. Both pieces of research concentrate on the development of moral thought, but in fact demonstrate a complex interaction between construals of the social situation, and the organization of beliefs about social relations.

The first, by Turiel, studied the transition between Stages 4 and 5. This particular transition originally aroused interest because in the longitudinal study, Kohlberg and Kramer found that students who came to university with well-established Stage 4 thought appeared to regress to a form of Stage 2 thinking, especially if they became exposed to 'radical' ideologies (Kohlberg and Kramer, 1969). Subsequently they moved on to Stage 5. Turiel identified this 'regression' as a transitional 'Stage 4½'. The décalage process involved in moving out of Stage 4 thought is manifested by increased awareness of relativistic possibilities, and in particular by the realization of the possibility of more than one viable form of social system. The transition phase is marked by the rejection of the well-ordered system of rules which has characterized Stage 4 thinking, and a temporary period of anarchic relativism. Eventually this becomes organized into the characteristically non-rigid, dynamically structured, conception of individual-societal interdependence of Stage 5. The anarchy found in Stage 4½ has interesting parallels with the 'epistemological loneliness' which Chandler found in intellectual development, following the initial shock of realizing a relativistic perspective at the beginning of formal operations (Chandler, 1975).

The second area of research is the various practical applications of the concept of the 'just community' in prison and school settings. By restructuring the social system in the prison or school to establish a 'just community' based on cooperation and egalitarian roles, the researchers and teachers created a setting in which the implicit moral atmosphere is that of Stage 3, rather than Stage 1 or 2—the normal implicit moral ideology of many institutions (Scharf and Hickey, 1976; Mosher, 1980). In these just communities, there is continual reflection upon the community needs, and on the decision-making processes involved in moral and group norm issues. This is demonstrably effective in stimulating moral development. In the work on just communities there are a number of interesting factors. Real-life construals are the basis of discussion, and real-life crises of organization, in developing norms and in deciding how to deal with deviance. The data also illustrate richly the interpersonal dynamics involved. Finally it is very apparent that reconstrual and developmental change involve changes in conceptions of roles and of interpersonal interaction. It is these conceptions which are the origin of any sense of rule *or* role obligation.

If we wish to progress in our understanding of the processes of development of moral, social, and political reasoning then perhaps we should be addressing two issues in detail: the social psychological processes which contribute to disequilibrium in the individual's present structure, and the consequences of this, in other words the processes by which the disequilibrium is resolved. The now extensive material on the school 'just communities' is adequate to document the way in which *negotiated social meaning* is generated by the discussion of moral issues and the democracy-building events which are part of the ongoing life of the just community (Mosher, 1980). There is also a considerable amount of material in Gilligan's and Erickson's work, and in Kohlberg's own longitudinal data, on the ways in which life crises act as a catalyst for disequilibrium, and for restructuring of the individual's understanding and organization of roles, relationships, and rules (Gilligan, 1977, 1982; Erickson, 1980).

In this chapter I have been exploring two related issues. The first is that Kohlberg's theory of moral development is not one, but two theories, a theory of development and a theory of morality. The former is an orthodox extension of cognitive-developmental theory, and is substantively supported by the empirical data on stages of reasoning. The latter is a definition of morality derived from a particular philosophical position, which places great emphasis upon rationality and upon justice as the core and essence of 'morality'. Kohlberg's argument that the evidence of the one supports the other has led, in my view, to a number of important and in some ways misleading conclusions. It has led critics of the theory to confuse the two, to criticize the theory of morality (particularly the hypothetical *telos* of Stage 6) and in doing so to also reject the more solidly founded and practically-relevant material on the first four stages of reasoning. Supporters of the theory have made the same mistake, filtering their perceptions of the earlier stages through a view that they are less adequate insofar as they do not approximate to the Stage 6 form.

The emphasis on the theory of morality has also, I have argued, led to greater attention to the question of how people become more 'moral', rather than upon what is actually going on when they *develop*—i.e. change and transform their reasoning. But my most extensive criticism comes from the biases I see arising from the definition of the moral domain itself. A main consequence of recognizing the distinction between the theory of morality and the theory of development is that it permits modification of one without rejection of the other. Gilligan's research has had an important effect upon the theory of morality. Her findings that women focus on the interpersonal, on negotiation, and on mutual responsibility are a contradiction to Kohlberg's position that morality reflects the delineation of rights and obligations, and the understanding of justice in terms of rational 'fairness'. The stages of development which she is currently working on parallel Kohlberg's in their conceptual structure; her work in other words is firmly within the cognitive-developmental paradigm. This work is an extension of Kohlberg's, but its implications are that one may take a broader view of moral reasoning which allows for several styles of thought within a single cognitive structure.

In this chapter I have tried to go further than this, and explore the argument that the tools of moral reasoning research set their own artefactual boundaries of a 'moral domain', and that, however valid the measures are of the development of a specific sort of reasoning, the data do not support the view that there is a 'moral domain' with special characteristics. The specialness arises from the coding of only prescriptive statements. I have argued that what is being elicited from the individual is a broad understanding of social and political relationships and systems which *facilitate* the making of moral judgments in both hypothetical and real-life situations.

References

Adelson, J. (1971). The political imagination of the young adolescent. *Daedalus*, **100**, 1013–1050.
Adelson, J., and O'Neil, R. (1966). The growth of political ideas in adolescence; the sense of community. *J. Personality and Social Psychology*, **4**, 295–306.
Adelson, J., Green, B., and O'Neil, R. (1969). Growth of the idea of law in adolescence. *Developmental Psychology*, **1**, 327–332.
Alston, W. P. (1971). Comments on Kohlberg's 'From is to ought'. In T. Mischel (Ed.), *Cognitive development and epistemology*, Academic Press, London.
Candee, D. (1974). Ego developmental aspects of New Left ideology. *J. Personality and Social Psychology*, **30**, 620–630.
Chandler, M. J. (1975). Relativism and the problem of epistemological loneliness. *Human Development*, **18**, 171–180.
Damon, W. (1977). *The social world of the child*, Jossey-Bass, San Francisco.
Davison, M. L., Robbins, S., and Swanson, D. (1978). Stage structure in objective moral judgements. *Developmental Psychology*, **14**, 137–146.
Erickson, V. L. (1980). Deliberate psychological education for women. In V. L. Erickson and J. Whiteley (Eds), *Developmental counselling and teaching,* Brooks Cole, Belmont.
Eysenck, H. J. (1976). The biology of morality. In T. Lickona (Ed.), *Moral development and behaviour*, Holt, New York.
Fishkin, J., Keniston, K., and Mackinnon, C. (1973). Moral reasoning and political ideology. *J. Personality and Social Psychology*, **27**, 109–119.
Freud, S. (1930). *Civilisation and its discontents*, Hogarth Press, London.
Gibbs, J. C. (1977). Kohlberg's stages of moral judgement; a constructive critique. *Harvard Educational Review*, **47**, 43–61.
Gilligan, C. (1977). In a different voice; women's conceptions of the self and of morality. *Harvard Educational Review*, **47**, 481–517.
Gilligan, C. (1980). Do the social sciences have an adequate theory of moral development? In N. Haan, R. Bellah, P. Robinson, and E. Sullivan (Eds), *Social Sciences; moral inquiry*, University of California Press.
Gilligan, C. (1982). *In a Different Voice*, Harvard U.P., Cambridge, Mass.
Haan, N. (1975). Hypothetical and actual moral reasoning in a situation of civil disobedience. *J. Personality and Social Psychology*, **32**, 253–270.
Haan, N. (1978). Two moralities in action contexts; relationships to thought, ego regulation and development. *J. Personality and Social Psychology*, **36**, 286–305.
Haan, N., Smith, M. B., and Block, J. (1968). Moral reasoning of young adults. *J. Personality and Social Psychology*, **10**, 183–201.
Hampden-Turner, C., and Whitten, P. (1971). Morals left and right. *Psychology Today*, **4**, 39–43, 74–76.
Hogan, R. (1970). A dimension of moral judgement. *J. Consulting and Clinical Psychology*, **35**, 205–213.
Hogan, R. (1973). Moral conduct and moral character, *Psychological Bulletin*, **79**, 217–32.
Hogan, R., Johnson, J. A., and Emler, N. P. (1978). A socioanalytic theory of moral

development. In W. Damon (ed.), *New directions for child development 2; moral development*, Jossey-Bass, San Francisco.

Holstein, C. B. (1976). Irreversible, stepwise sequence in the development of moral judgement; a longitudinal study of males and females. *Child Development*, **47**, 51–61.

Kohlberg, L. (1958). The development of modes of moral thinking and choice in the years ten to sixteen. Unpublished PhD thesis, University of Chicago.

Kohlberg, L. (1969). Stage and sequence; the cognitive-developmental approach to socialisation. In D. A. Goslin (Ed.), *Handbook of socialisation theory and research*, Rand McNally, Chicago.

Kohlberg, L. (1971). From is to ought; how to commit the naturalistic fallacy and get away with it in the study of moral development. In T. Mischel (Ed.), *Cognitive development and epistemology*, Academic Press, New York.

Kohlberg, L. (1973). The claim to moral adequacy of a highest stage of moral judgment. *Journal of Philosophy*, **70**, 630–646.

Kohlberg, L. (1976). Moral stages and moralisation; the cognitive-developmental approach. In T. Lickona (Ed.), *Moral development and behaviour*, Holt, New York.

Kohlberg, L., and Kramer, R. B. (1969). Continuities and discontinuities in childhood and adult moral development. *Human Development*, **12**, 93–120.

Langer, J. (1969). *Theories of development*, Holt, New York.

Lambert, H. V. (1971). A comparison of Jane Loevinger's theory of ego development and Kohlberg's theory of moral development. Unpublished PhD thesis, University of Chicago.

Locke, D. B. (1980). The illusion of stage six. *J. Moral Education*, **9**, 103–110.

Loevinger, J. (1976). *Ego development*, Jossey-Bass, San Francisco.

Mosher, R. (1980). *Moral Education: a first generation of research*, Praeger, New York.

Much, N. C., and Schweder, R. A. (1978). Speaking of rules; the analysis of culture in breach. In W. Damon (Ed.), *New directions for child development 2; moral development*, Jossey-Bass, San Francisco.

Peters, R. S. (1963). Reason and habit; the paradox of moral education. In W. R. Niblett (Ed.), *Moral education in a changing society*, Faber and Faber, London.

Peters, R. S. (1971). Moral development; a plea for pluralism. In T. Mischel (Ed.), *Cognitive development and epistemology*, Academic Press, New York.

Peters, R. S. (1974). Moral development and moral learning. *The Monist*, 58.

Peters, R. S. (1978). The place of Kohlberg's theory in moral education. *J. Moral Education*, 7, 147–57.

Piaget, J. (1932). *The moral judgement of the child*, Routledge, London.

Pinard, A., and Laurendeau, M. (1969). 'Stage' in Piaget's congitive-developmental theory. In D. Elkind and J. H. Flavell (Eds), *Studies in cognitive development*, Oxford University Press, Oxford.

Podd, M. (1972). Ego-identity status and morality. *Developmental Psychology*, **6**, 497–507.

Rawls, J. (1971). *A theory of justice*, Oxford University Press, Oxford.

Rest, J. R. (1973). Patterns of preference and comprehension in moral judgement. *J. Personality*, **41**, 86–109.

Rest, J. R. (1979). *Development in judging moral issues*, University of Minnesota Press, Minneapolis.

Rest, J. R., Turiel, E., and Kohlberg, L. (1969). Level of moral development as a determinant of preference and comprehension of moral judgements made by others. *J. Personality*, **37**, 225–252.

Rieff, P. (1960). *Freud; the mind of a moralist*, Gollancz, London.

Riegel, K. F. (1972). Influence of economic and political ideologies on the development of developmental psychology. *Psychological Bulletin*, **78**, 129–141.

Scharf, P., and Hickey, J. (1976). The prison and the inmate's conception of legal justice. *Criminal Justice and Behaviour*, **3**, 107–122.

Selman, R. (1980). *The growth of interpersonal understanding*, Academic Press, New York.

Simpson, E. L. (1974). Moral development research; a case of scientific cultural bias. *Human Development*, 17, 81–106.

Skinner, B. F. (1971). *Beyond freedom and dignity*, Penguin Books, Harmondsworth.

Smith, M. E. (1978). Moral reasoning; its relation to logical thinking and role-taking. *J. Moral Education*, **8**, 41–50.

Sullivan, E. V. (1977). A study of Kohlberg's structural theory of moral development; a critique of liberal science ideology. *Human Development*, **20**, 352–376.

Tomlinson, P. (1975). Political education; cognitive developmental perspectives from moral education. *Oxford Review of Education*, **1**, 241–267.

Trainer, F. E. (1977). A critical analysis of Kohlberg's contributions to the study of moral thought. *J. for the Theory of Social Behaviour*, **7**, 41–63.

Turiel, E. (1966). An experimental test of the sequentiality of developmental stages in the child's moral judgements. *J. Personality and Social Psychology*, **3**, 611–618.

Turiel, E. (1972). Stage transition in moral development. In R. M. Travers (Ed.), *Second handbook of research on teaching*, Rand McNally, Chicago.

Turiel, E. (1974). Conflict and transition in adolescent moral development. *Child Development*, **45**, 14–29.

Turiel, E. (1979). Social regulations and the domains of social concepts. In W. Damon (Ed.), *Social Cognition: New Directions for Child Development*, Jossey-Bass, San Francisco.

Walker, L. J. (1980). Cognitive and perspective-taking prerequisities for moral development. *Child Development*, **51**, 131–139.

Weinreich-Haste, H. E. (1981). Developmental and social psychological aspects of moral reasoning: the adolescent as social theorist. Paper presented to the European Association for Social Psychology, University of Sussex, April 1981.

Weinreich-Haste, H. E. (1982). Piaget's moral psychology; a critical perspective. In S. Modgil and C. Modgil (Eds), *Jean Piaget; Consensus and Controversy*, Holt-Saunders, Eastbourne.

Wilden, A. (1975). Piaget and the structure as law and order. In K. F. Riegel and G. C. Rosenwald (Eds), *Structure and Transformation*, Wiley, New York.

Wozniak, R. H. (1975). Dialecticism and structuralism: The philosophical foundation of Soviet psychology and Piagetian cognitive developmental theory. In K. F. Riegel and G. C. Rosenwald (Eds), *Structure and Transformation*, Wiley, New York.

MOSAIC

SECTION II

Moral Behaviour—The Relation Between Thought and Action

The distinctive feature of cognitive-developmental moral theory, as opposed to some other more traditional psychological approaches to morality, is its emphasis on moral reasoning. It is, in fact, a theory of moral thought, not moral action, validated not by how people behave but by how they think, and in particular by what they say about morality and its problems. But this, to many, will seem an odd place to start. Even if we avoid the positivist trap of thinking that a psychological theory is acceptable only if it is based directly on observable behaviour, it may still seem that what matters most in morality is not what people say or think, but what they actually do. The gap between thought and action, the failure to live up to our moral convictions, is as familiar to psychologists as it is to philosophers. Why, then, choose mere thinking as the prime object of study?

One familiar answer is that moral behaviour cannot be identified purely behaviourally. One and the same piece of behaviour might be right on one occasion, wrong on another, and on a third morally neutral. It depends on the circumstances, and also on the individual's motivation, on what he thinks he is doing and why. Merely obeying a command—a criterion often used by psychologists as a measure of 'resistance to temptation'—is not necessarily behaving morally. It depends on what the command is, and why you obey it.

In the first chapter in this section Don Locke carries this line of thought further, asking how we are to identify moral behaviour in the first place. The risk of prejudice and bias, of the experimenter—or the society—merely taking it for granted that the behaviour it labels moral or immoral *is* moral or immoral, is obvious. If we are to have a genuinely neutral, value-free conception of moral behaviour, Locke argues, it will have to be identified by the individual's own reasons for behaving as he does. But Locke also argues against over-emphasizing this reference to reason. It does not follow that behaviour can be classified as moral only if it is the result of explicit reasoning, conscious thought.

109

Even habitual action can be moral in the sense explained, provided it too is sensitive to reasons.

But if moral thinking is the place to begin, it is clearly not the whole story. Reasoning without action will be idle and empty, and any comprehensive account of moral functioning must include moral behaviour as well as moral thought. The problem remains of the relationship, and often enough the gap, between thought and action, between people's beliefs about what they ought to do, and how they actually behave. This is the traditional philosophical problem of *akrasia*, or weakness of will, but discussed here by Roger Straughan with reference to the psychological data as well. Indeed Straughan's solution to the philosophical problem, a thesis of 'moderate internalism' which distinguishes justification from motivation, is intended also to illuminate the psychological findings, such as that 'principled' moral thinkers are more likely to act on their moral judgments than are non-principled thinkers, or the motivational differences between shame- and guilt-based ethics.

In the chapter that follows Straughan's, however, Derek Wright approaches the problems of thought and action from a radically different perspective. His prime concern is to go back beyond Kohlberg to Piaget, and to emphasize some neglected differences between the two. For Kohlberg's account of moral reasoning is derived more from Piaget's general theory of cognitive development than from his work on moral judgment specifically: the latter, Wright suggests, can usefully be seen as more social-psychological than cognitive-developmental in nature. In particular, in contrast to Kohlberg's emphasis on moral reasoning and development as arising from cognitive conflicts, Piaget's theory focuses more on a dialectical relationship between thought and action, inasmuch as judgment is, for Piaget, a reflection upon, or conscious realization of, action.

Thus where Straughan sees a stark gap between judgment and action, and is concerned to find some bridge between the two, Wright's strategy is rather to close the gap by stressing the merging of practical and theoretical morality in the process of moral development, and especially by emphasizing the role of a sense of moral obligation, which is both cognitive and motivational in nature. In the final chapter in this section Don Locke attempts to relate and compare these two approaches: the philosophical, as it were, against the psychological.

Morality in the Making
Edited by H. Weinreich-Haste and D. Locke
© 1983, John Wiley & Sons, Ltd.

CHAPTER 6

Moral Reasons and Moral Action

DON LOCKE

Once there was a subject called moral psychology, the theory of the moral sentiments and passions, but it disappeared when scientific psychology detached itself from philosophical speculation. Now it has its heir in the psychology of morals, the empirical study of moral behaviour, the attempt to explain and understand, to predict and—more usefully—promote, moral conduct. Yet the psychology of morals retains its philosophical aspects, not least the problem of identifying the domain of moral action as a subject for empirical investigation. For if moral action is to provide a topic worthy of scientific examination then it ought to constitute its own distinctive area of human activity, one of special interest and significance. Yet it seems that almost any conduct could be, or could be classified as, moral or immoral; and it seems that particular instances of moral conduct might be explained by any of the manifold factors that affect human behaviour. For both these reasons it seems unlikely, at first sight, that there will be a specific form of behaviour called 'moral action'. Instead the explanation of moral action will range as wide and as deep as the explanation of all action, which is to say as wide and as deep as psychology itself. This, then, is the question I want to consider: how, exactly, moral action is to be understood; what, if anything, distinguishes it from behaviour of other kinds; whether there is a distinctive domain of moral action, to be studied in its own right.

Towards a Definition of Moral Action

There is first the familiar difficulty that societies, and even individuals, may differ in their moral beliefs and attitudes, not only in what they regard as right or wrong, but also in what they regard as morally relevant or irrelevant to begin with. This means that what one observer or context classifies as moral action, another may classify as immoral, or as having nothing to do with morality at all. The domain of moral action will accordingly shift in an almost arbitrary manner, depending perhaps on who is being studied, perhaps on who is studying them. This is not necessarily to endorse moral relativism: the recognition that different people have differing conceptions of morality is entirely compatible with the belief that there is only one true or correct morality, whether or not we claim to know what that true morality is. But the variability of morals from person to person, and from society to society, does seem a major obstacle to the scientific investigation of moral action. For it seems that the study of moral action must presuppose some decision as to which actions actually are moral; and that, it seems, is a matter of opinion, or evaluation, which can have no place in a properly scientific study.

The most obvious way of avoiding this difficulty is to offer a purely formal definition of moral action, e.g. that moral action consists in acting in accordance with the dictates of morality, whatever those dictates might turn out to be. But, its obvious triviality side, such a definition is of no use to the empirical researcher, who wants not to define moral action but to identify it. He needs to be able to tell which actions are moral actions and which not, so that he knows which behaviour to study. A purely formal definition does not enable him to do that.

A second, more heroic, course would be to take a stand on the moral question itself, and attempt to demonstrate that a particular morality is the one true morality, by reference to which moral action can be defined and particular moral actions identified. From his criticisms of moral relativism and his claims for the universal status of Stage 6 principles this appears to be the approach favoured by Lawrence Kohlberg. Yet any such approach will be arguable in the extreme (and I have argued against Kohlberg's claims, in particular, elsewhere) and may also unduly restrict the domain of moral action. It is sometimes suggested, for example, that moral action consists in action performed for Stage 6 reasons, thus excluding actions which may seem similar on the surface, but are performed for different, lower stage, reasons. But given the paucity of Stage 6 moral thinkers, the domain of moral action will accordingly dwindle almost to vanishing point, and almost everything that researchers in the field actually study, Kohlberg himself included, would fall outside it. Even the broader definition of moral action as action which accords with Stage 6 principles, rather than action which actually results from them, might still prove too narrow, eliminating much behaviour which we would properly want to include in the field of study. It may be, for example, that Stage 6 principles establish that there is no obligation to obey a certain unjust law. Yet someone might obey that law, even though he recognizes its injustice, because he (mistakenly) believes that, on balance, he ought to. This would not be moral action on the definition suggested; nor, for that matter, need it be immoral action; yet it is surely just the sort of action which, among others, we would want to include in the domain of moral action as an area for scientific investigation.

In effect the variability of morals presents us with a choice. We can either define moral action by reference to our own beliefs and attitudes about what is right or wrong, good or bad, in which case only those actions which actually are moral—at least in our opinion—will count as moral actions; or we can define it by reference to the attitudes and beliefs of the agent, in which case actions which, at least in our opinion, are not moral—they may be immoral, they may be neutral—may nonetheless qualify as moral actions. Either course can be confusing; both oblige us to treat as moral actions, in one sense, actions which may not be moral in the other. But just as legal theorists have distinguished between 'positive morality' which is the morality that happens to be adopted in a particular community, and 'critical morality' in terms of which that positive morality may itself be morally criticized, let us distinguish between an evaluative sense or definition of moral action, one which incorporates some decision as to which actions actually are good or bad, right or wrong, and a neutral sense or definition, which does not. The two must be clearly distinguished. A failure to do so can make it seem much easier to bridge the gap between 'is' and 'ought' than it actually is.

The question, then, is whether, from the point of view of the psychology of morals, we require an evaluative or a neutral definition of moral action. The disadvantages of the former are considerable: it obliges us to make a decision on two types of definition distinct: it obliges us to identify as moral actions actions which may seem to us morally irrelevant, or even positively immoral. The disadvantages of the former are considerable: it obliges us to take decision on matters of substantive morality which seem to lie outside the proper sphere of a scientific study; and it obliges us to limit the field of that study, restricting it to those actions which are moral by our lights, and eliminating those which seem moral to the agent himself. Accordingly I propose to work towards a neutral definition, always bearing in mind that moral action in this sense will not necessarily be action that we would ourselves regard as good or bad, right or wrong.

Three Modes of Moral Action

At its broadest, moral action might be said to include any action which could be assessed in moral terms. Yet this definition is clearly too broad for our purposes. Not only is there no limit to the actions which might in theory be categorized in moral terms, no action which nobody, no matter how bizarre their moral opinions, might be prepared to describe as good, right, or obligatory; but also, and more importantly, moral action in this broad sense will include many actions which are, so to speak, moral only by accident: actions where the agent does not realize what he is doing, or does not realize that it is moral, or perhaps recognizes that it is moral but regards that fact as irrelevant, and does it for other, quite different reasons. We might be prepared to say of such 'accidentally moral actions', as I will call them, that it was a good thing they were done, or even that it was a good thing the agent did them, but I think we would balk at describing them as good actions without qualification, let alone calling the agent good for doing them. But it is not just that we are reluctant to regard such actions as genuinely or fully moral; if even accidents and mistakes are to count as moral actions, just because they happen to be right in the circumstances, it seems extremely unlikely that moral action will constitute a homogeneous area of study. Clearly some tighter definition is required, to rule out the merely accidentally moral.

This suggests that we should identify moral action not as action which can be morally evaluated, but as action which is morally motivated. But here, too, there are difficulties. We could, for example, understand morally motivated actions as actions performed because they are moral, or more neutrally because the agent believes they are moral. Thus Kant believed that moral action consists in acting for the sake of morality itself, or as he would put it, acting out of respect for the moral law. Kohlberg, too, seems inclined to restrict genuine moral action to action based explicitly on genuine moral principles, e.g. principles of justice. But this definition seems too narrow for our purposes, for only a minority of our actions are moral in this restricted sense. The Kantian moral agent is too much the Boy Scout looking for his one good deed a day; such cases are the exception not the rule. Typically we perform a moral action not because it is right, but because of those features which make it right: when I help someone in trouble I may well appreciate that I am doing the right thing, but I do it because they are in trouble, not because justice or the moral law demand it. Indeed I may do it spontaneously, without stopping to think about morality or justice at all, and still be acting morally. To restrict moral action to those actions performed for the sake of morality itself is to restrict the study of moral action to an extent which eliminates almost all of its interest and importance.

The main reason for preferring the narrow Kantian definition, I take it, is that such 'explicitly moral actions', as I will call them, seem to provide the clearest example of moral action: what could be more obviously moral than recognizing that some action is right, and doing it for precisely that reason? Perhaps this is because explicitly moral action seems more moral than other action: the man who does the right thing just because it is right seems more admirable, more worthy, than someone who does it for other reasons, no matter how good, or someone who does it out of habit or spontaneously, without even thinking whether he ought to do it. But first of all this is not as clear-cut as it might seem: there are times when an action performed directly from sympathy or benevolence will seem morally preferable to one which required a recognition that you ought to be sympathetic or benevolent; and times when an action performed spontaneously will seem preferable to one which depended on thinking whether you ought to do it. And secondly this justification of the Kantian definition requires us to interpret it in an evaluative, not a neutral, sense, as referring to actions performed because they actually *are* moral. There is no guarantee that actions performed because the agent thinks they are moral will be morally better than other actions. History is rich in examples of misplaced conscientiousness, where people have been mistaken about what they ought to do and hence mistaken in what they have done. Indeed an action performed from a misplaced sense of duty can seem worse precisely because it is done from a sense of duty, in defiance of the palpable harm and suffering that it causes.

I prefer, therefore, a wider definition of moral action, which will include more than these explicitly moral actions, while still excluding actions which are only accidentally moral. Two sorts, in particular, need to be mentioned. First of all, there are those actions where the agent does something right or good, and does it for the reasons which make it right or good, without doing it *because* they make it right or good. It is even possible to do something for reasons which make it moral, without recognizing that they do make it moral: an official who believes it his duty to adhere strictly to the rules may make an exception in a particularly unfortunate case which arouses his sympathy; it may be that the right thing in this case is to bend the rules, though the official does not realize that, nor is it why he does it; so he does it for reasons which make it right, but not because they make it right. Or more commonly, we may recognize that something is right, and do it for the reasons which make it right, yet do it for those reasons as such is not because they make it right: it may be my duty to help someone because he is my brother, but I help him because he is my brother, not because it is my duty. Action of this sort, performed for reasons which make it moral but not for the reason that it is moral, I will call 'indirectly moral action'.

Secondly, there are those actions we perform in immediate response to a situation without consciously considering the whys and wherefores, and hence without considering whether it is moral, or the factors which make it moral. Some moral actions are performed automatically, spontaneously, or out of habit, as when I apologize at once for standing on someone's toe, or call out when I see them drop something, without stopping to think whether I should or not. But although such actions are performed without thinking, there are reasons why I act as I do, factors which both explain and, hopefully, justify my action. If these reasons have nothing to do with the morality of the action, then the action will be only accidentally moral: it is only by coincidence that I happen to react in the right way. But if those reasons include the fact that the action is moral, or various factors which make it moral—if, for example, my parents inculcated that response in me precisely because they wanted me to behave in the right and proper way, and that is why I react as I do—then the action is not merely accidentally moral. I will call such actions 'unreflective moral actions'.

Nevertheless it may be objected that unreflective actions cannot properly be called moral, in either an evaluative or a neutral sense, simply because the agent may not even realize that he is acting morally. Yet we have already seen that a spontaneous action may be morally preferable to one where the agent has to think about what he is doing. Indeed if we had to consider the reasons for truth-telling every time we told the truth, if we had to rehearse the case against stealing whenever the opportunity for theft presented itself, if we had to remind ourselves of the value of benevolence before ever helping anyone, we would devote so much time to moral thought we would have none left for moral action. And it is not just that there are situations in which someone who acts spontaneously, and therefore quickly, is more likely to do good than someone who stops to think about it. It is also that someone who reacts immediately to the morally relevant features of a situation may be more admirable, and have a more developed moral consciousness, than someone who has to think about what to do, and why. Someone who has to work out his various obligations to his family, for example, and why he has them, before he acts on them, seems to have an inadequate grasp of what those obligations are, and what they involve.

Moral theorists are temperamentally inclined to overestimate the importance of moral thinking. Devoting their time and attention to the analysis of morals and moral conduct as they do, they naturally tend to think that someone who does not fully comprehend the morality of his action cannot genuinely be acting morally. Yet moral reasoning is the exception, not the rule, something we engage in only when faced with difficult problems, or in our more philosophical moments: the majority of moral behaviour is unaccompanied by any conscious moral calculation. It is important, therefore, to distinguish moral reasons from moral reasoning, and acting for reasons from acting as a result of reasoning. Pointing a gun at someone gives him a reason for doing as you say, but it is not reasoning with him; and similarly one may have a moral reason, even be aware of that reason and act on it, without engaging in moral reasoning. By reasoning here I mean a form of conscious deliberation, trying to solve some problem or arrive at some conclusion, so that moral reasoning involves such things as trying to work out which rules, standards, or values apply to some particular case, or trying to discover what those rules, standards, or values are in the first place. So not all thinking, not even conscious thinking, will be reasoning in this sense: someone who reminds himself of what he ought to do, or idly contemplates the immorality of his conduct, may be engaged in moral thinking without indulging in moral reasoning. But more importantly people can recognize moral reasons, and act on them, without needing to think, let alone reason, about the matter at all: it needs no thought to realize that I ought to pick up a child who has hurt itself, or help a blind person across a busy road; I just recognize that I should. This is not, of course, to deny that cognitive processes are involved at some level: recognizing that I should intervene is itself a cognitive operation. It is only to insist that people can and do act morally without being consciously aware of the reasons which may explain and justify their conduct: the fact that I do not think about what to do, or whether to do it, does not prevent my action from being moral.

Accordingly I will adopt a definition of moral action which includes indirectly moral actions and unreflective moral actions alongside those which are explicitly moral. Of course all these actions might be said to be morally motivated or performed 'because they are moral': in each case it is because the action has certain features which make it moral that the agent acts as he does—if it did not have those features the agent would not perform that action—even if the agent does not explicitly take into account the fact that it is moral, or even those reasons why. But this way of defining moral action can easily be confused with the narrower, stronger, sense in which explicitly moral actions are performed because they are moral. Indeed this very confusion may be responsible for making the Kantian definition more plausible than it actually is. So let us, instead, define moral action as action which is explicable, at least in part, by moral reasons.

The Role of Moral Reasons

What I mean, more precisely, is this: if any action is right or wrong, good or bad, moral or immoral in any way, there will be various factors which make it so. Just what these factors are and where they are to be found—in the nature of the act, its circumstances or its consequences, in the agent's character or in his intentions—how they might conflict or balance, what makes them morally relevant in the first place, I will not try to say. These are issues of ethical theory or substantive morality which we are trying to avoid. But whatever those factors might be, wherever and however they arise, they constitute moral reasons, meaning by that reasons why an action is moral, not—what may be very different—reasons why it is performed. Nevertheless these moral reasons will often explain why an agent acts as he does: he may do it because he recognizes that there are these moral reasons for so acting (explicitly moral action); he may do it because he recognizes that there are these reasons for so acting, but not because he recognizes that they provide moral reasons (indirectly moral action); or he may do it because these reasons apply to his action, but without his recognizing them as reasons for so acting (unreflective moral action). In each case he acts because of moral reasons; moral reasons explain his action. But with accidentally moral action this is not so: there are moral reasons for acting, but the agent does not act because of those reasons; he may be aware of them, he may even be aware that they provide moral reasons, but that is not why he acts as he does.

Now this idea that it is, so to speak, the agent's reasons which make an action moral is a familiar one, both in philosophy and psychology. As is often pointed out, an action may be good, bad, or indifferent, depending on the context: there are times when it is wrong to lie, cheat, or steal, but there are also times when it may be right. Similarly, the same action, motivated by different reasons, may be good, bad, or indifferent, even in the same context: one man may join the demonstration because he wants to protest against a great evil, another because he wants to kick a few policemen, a third because all his friends are doing it. So it seems crucial, in assessing moral action, to understand why the agent acts as he does.

However this is *not* the point I am making here. First of all, the reasons which explain the action, and so make it moral in this technical sense, may not be reasons which the agent himself takes into account because, I have suggested, he may perform a moral action without thinking about its morality at all. But secondly, and more importantly, our present question is not whether a particular action is to be judged right or wrong, good or bad, in an evaluative sense, but whether it qualifies as moral action in some neutral sense. Accordingly the reasons which make an action moral in this sense do not necessarily make it right or good in actual fact, or in our own opinion; rather they are factors which would make it right or good in the agent's opinion, factors which *he* would regard as making his action moral. So it is entirely possible for an action to count as moral in this technical sense, even though it strikes us as morally irrelevant, or as positively wicked, provided that the action is moral in the light of the agent's own beliefs. Thus to say that the agent's attitudes and opinions in part determine whether his action is moral is not to say that they make it good, bad, or indifferent: it could, in fact, be any of these, yet still be moral action in the sense defined.

This definition serves not only to define a domain of moral action broad enough to include more than the special case of explicitly moral action, and sufficiently narrow to exclude action which is only accidentally moral. It also serves to demarcate the domain of moral action in a way which allows for the variability of morals, yet identifies a distinctive form of behaviour with its own specific nature and explanation. The distinctive feature of moral action is the role and relevance of moral reasons. From a practical point of view, of course, it is important that people do the right things for the right reasons, otherwise we cannot rely in their behaving morally in any systematic way. Accordingly moral education, moral training and practice, depends crucially on our ability to grasp moral reasons, to recognize when they apply and to act on them when they do. But it is also important that these reasons be the right reasons: from the practical point of view we are concerned with moral reasons in the evaluative, not merely a neutral, sense. But moral reasons are also important from the theoretical point of view. What is distinctive about moral action, I suggest, is the way in which moral reasons enter directly or indirectly, consciously or unconsciously, into its motivation and explanation. The important question, theoretically as well as practically, will be how such moral reasons develop or are acquired, how we conceive and recognize them, and how they are translated into action.

This means, however, that so far we have only replaced one problem with another: instead of a definition of moral action we now need a definition of moral reasons. For how are moral reasons, in an appropriately neutral sense, to be distinguished from other sorts of reason for action? Which beliefs are to count as specifically moral beliefs, and why? And this question becomes even more pressing when we move from a philosophical perspective to a psychological, especially a developmental, one. For although I have allowed that an agent may act, and act morally, without selfconsciously reflecting on the reasons for his action, I have nonetheless implicitly adopted the traditional philosophical model of man the rational agent who knows what he believes and why he acts, even if he does not always stop to think it over. But how explicit, and how precise, are most people's moral beliefs? Indeed the distinction on which this account of moral action must depend, the distinction between moral reasons, and hence moral beliefs, and reasons and beliefs of other sorts, is a distinction which most people may not draw, or even comprehend; it is a distinction about which the philosophers themselves are in considerable dispute. And if there is a problem about the ascription of specifically moral beliefs and reasons to adults, how much greater will it be for children?

Clearly the present account of moral action presupposes an account of moral reasons, and that account, moreover, will need to be a developmental one, allowing for the way in which an individual's repertoire and understanding of moral reasons may evolve and vary in the course of cognitive, social, and moral development. But given such an account of moral reasons, or of moral cognition more generally, the present definition of moral action will itself be a developmental one, in that what counts as moral action, so defined, will vary in the course of moral development, depending not only on which factors the individual regards as morally relevant, but also on his understanding of moral relevance. This is, however, a matter which calls for separate, and much more complex, discussion, so I shall not pursue it further here, except to remark that a typology of moral reasons, such as Kohlberg's, may provide us with the answer we are looking for. My intention, in this chapter, is only to bring moral reasons, and hence moral cognition, to the centre of the stage: to indicate that a conception of moral action as a subject for scientific investigation must begin from a conception of moral reasons.

There is a second complication to the argument which I will also mention but ignore, as too complex a matter to pursue further here. The emphasis on moral reasoning and moral behaviour in contemporary moral research can easily conceal the fact that we should be equally concerned with *im*moral behaviour: in seeking to explain and understand why people behave morally we also, and perhaps more urgently, need to explain and understand why they behave immorally. Moral behaviour, as a subject for scientific research, should also include immoral behaviour; we need to exclude only such behaviour as is morally neutral or indifferent. But this, yet again, the present definition does not do. We need an account of immoral action to supplement the account of moral action, and this proves more difficult than may at first appear.

To begin with, immoral action is not simply the opposite of moral action: behaviour does not qualify as immoral just because it fails to be moral. Not only are there actions which are neither moral nor immoral, but morally neutral, such as spreading marmalade on your breakfast toast, grotesque and distasteful though that seems to me, there are also actions which fail to be moral in our technical sense without thereby being either immoral or morally neutral: accidentally moral actions, for example. And just as there are actions which are moral only by accident, so there are actions which are immoral only by accident (e.g. where the agent cannot possibly know of the harm he is doing), and which are therefore not, strictly, moral, immoral, or even morally neutral!

Nor can immoral action be defined as action performed for, or explained by, 'immoral' reasons, i.e. factors which make an action immoral. Such moral perversity is possible, among children as well as among diabolists, but people are more likely to behave immorally not because it is immoral, but simply because they do not care whether it is or not. But neither can immoral action be defined a action performed contrary to moral reasons, i.e. despite there being moral reasons for not doing it, for that will include not only actions which are immoral in a strict sense, but also those actions which are only accidentally immoral.

But rather than discuss these issues further here, I would prefer to clarify the argument so far, and especially the category of unreflective moral action, by looking more closely at moral habits. Not that all unreflective action is habitual, or all habitual action unreflective: I can hardly follow my habit of writing to the various members of my family on their respective birthdays without having to think, both about the date and about what to say; and someone who, without stopping to think, leaps into a canal to save a drowning child need not make a habit of it. But habitual action, like unreflective action, may seem only doubt-fully moral, and for the same reason: how can behaviour be moral, in either an evaluative or a neutral sense, if the agent acts spontaneously or out of habit, without taking any account of its morality or immorality? And yet, as I shall argue, moral habits are an essential ingredient in the moral behaviour of human beings as we know them.

The Place of Moral Habits

By a habit here I mean such things as the habit of folding your morning news-paper in a certain way, or following a particular route to work, not habits in the narrower and more technical sense in which psychologists speak of motor habits for example. In particular there is no implication that habitual actions are automatic in the sense of occurring independently of any form of awareness or belief. I can hardly follow my habitual route to work, for example, unless in some sense and at some level I realize where I am and where I have to go next. Habitual actions are automatic, rather, in the sense that you do not have to consider consciously whether or not to perform them: the mark of a habit is that it is something you do so regularly that you don't stop to think about it, like putting on a seat-belt when you get into the car. This does not mean that the action is unavoidable or uncontrollable: habits allow of variation, even if they can be broken only with difficulty; a habit which could not be altered would not be a habit but a compulsion. But it is characteristic of habits that we require some special reason, or special care or attention, or even a special effort, before we can alter or abandon them. And often it can be desirable, morally desirable, to make an action habitual in just this way: better to make a habit of phoning your aged aunt every Saturday night, to check that she is all right, than to have to remind yourself to do it, and why.

Yet habits have their drawbacks too. It may be desirable that people act morally from habit, but it would hardly be desirable for them to act always or only from habit. Indeed it would not even be possible: a being that acted from habit alone would be some sort of automaton, not a person; and there will always be situations where habits have to be varied or over-ridden, or where they do not apply, where some new or relatively unfamiliar action is called for. But more importantly, moral habits, if we follow them blindly, can lead us into error: sooner or later there will come the situation where that particular action is no longer the right thing to do, yet we do it just the same, out of habit. It is morally desirable to do the right thing as a matter of course only so long as the right thing is a matter of course; but where the right course of action is no longer obvious, we will have to have recourse to reasons. So if we are to act morally we need to be aware that our habits may sometimes have to be altered or abandoned, and why, and to take those factors into account when they arise. In short, moral habits must not be blind habits; they need to be sensitive to moral reasons, so that when the reasons change they will change too.

Now this gives rise to both a theoretical and a practical problem. The practical problem is that someone who has to stop and think what to do and why may fail to do the right thing, because he thinks instead of acting, or may do it in a way which detracts from its morality, because it is calculated when it should be spontaneous. Yet someone who doesn't stop to think may also fail to do the right thing, because he fails to notice features which on this occasion make the usual response the wrong response. Either way we can get it wrong, and the only way of deciding in advance which we should do is by engaging in moral thinking—which automatically excludes acting from habit! The theoretical problem is that it seems that to the extent that actions are habitual they will be insensitive to moral reasons, occurring regardless of whether those reasons apply. Yet if they are insensitive to moral reasons they cannot be moral in the sense we have defined: those moral reasons cannot explain the action, since the action would occur even if the reasons did not apply. It begins to seem as if habitual actions cannot qualify as moral actions, in our technical sense, after all.

The solution to both problems lies in a closer examination of the way in which habitual action can depend on reasons. Insofar as an action is habitual the factors which explain that action, the reasons why the agent acts as he does, are unlikely to include the fact that it is the right thing to do: that would seem to require some explicit thought on his part. But they may include considerations which make the action moral. For example, I may have a habit of holding shop doors open for old ladies with heavy baskets. I do it automatically, without thinking, but I do it because they are old and their baskets heavy (though not, in this enlightened age, because they are ladies); if this were not so, I would not do it. So although I do it without thinking I do it for the very reasons which make my action moral, and my action is moral action in the technical sense.

Nevertheless, with habitual actions in particular, this is not always so; the reasons why I act in my habitual way may have nothing to do with the morality of the action. Suppose, for example, that I have a habit of mowing an elderly neighbour's lawn whenever I mow my own. Now the reason why I mow her lawn on some particular occasion is, in all probability, not that she is old, nor that this is of benefit to her, much less that it is a good neighbourly thing to do. Inasmuch as it has become a matter of habit I mow her lawn simply because I am mowing my own; the one follows the other as naturally and inevitably as the back lawn follows the front. So the reason why I act has nothing to do with the morality of my action: it is not because it is right, nor even for reasons which make it right, that I am now mowing her lawn. True, it is because it is right that I have developed this habit; I make a habit of mowing the lawn for her precisely because it is a good neighbourly thing to do. So, we might argue, I have acquired the habit for moral reasons, and I mow her lawn because I have acquired the habit; in that slightly roundabout way my action is still to be explained by moral reasons. But this, as we shall now see, is not by itself enough to make the action moral.

No doubt most moral habits are acquired or developed because they are moral. It is because such things are right or good that society, or our parents, or we ourselves, encourage in us habits of honesty, politeness, tolerance, and the rest. But habits can, so to speak, acquire a momentum of their own, so that we continue to behave in a certain way quite independently of the reasons for which the habit was originally acquired: a habit of wearing a tie to work, originally acquired because everyone else wore a tie, may continue even when ties have gone out of fashion. We might call this sheer habit, as opposed to those habits which survive only so long as the reasons for them remain: I habitually follow a certain route to work because I find it the most pleasant and convenient; if it ceases to be that I quickly change my habit, though for a time at least I may find myself following the old route, out of sheer habit. Now if my habit of mowing my neighbour's lawn has become sheer habit—if, for example, I would go on doing it out of habit even when she asked me not to, because my inexpert mowing digs large holes in the grass—then my action ceases to be moral in the technical sense. I do it because I have the habit, and the habit is explained by moral reasons, but the action as such is no longer explained by moral reasons, because I would continue to behave in that way even if those moral reasons no longer applied.

So if the action is to qualify as moral in our technical sense, the action itself, and not just the habit, must be explained by moral reasons: the reasons why the action is moral must explain why I act as I do, not just in general but on this particular occasion. And this means that my action must be sensitive to moral reasons, in that I would not act as I do if those reasons did not apply; otherwise those reasons would not explain my action. But this is what generated the problem: how can the action be sensitive to the reasons if it is unreflective or habitual; how can those reasons affect my action, if I act without even noticing whether they apply?

The answer to the puzzle is to notice that to say that a man acts in a certain situation without stopping to think is not to say that he would not stop to think if the situation were different. The fact that I do something from habit in one situation does not necessarily mean that I would still do it from habit in a different situation. I have this habit of holding shop doors open for old ladies with heavy baskets; I do it unreflectively, without thinking whether to or why. But it would make a difference if, instead of groceries, this particular basket contained the shop till. If that happened no doubt I would notice it, and noticing it I would not behave in the habitual way. Of course I might not notice it, even then, and to the extent that I do not notice relevant changes in the circumstances the habit is, as we put it, blind. But habits need not be blind habits, and to the extent that the agent would notice relevant changes in the circumstances, and modify or interrupt his habit accordingly, his habit is sensitive to moral reasons. And this is entirely compatible with his taking no account whatsoever of those circumstances, provided that they do remain as usual.

So if habitual action is to qualify as moral action in the technical sense, and if moral habits are not to lead us astray as well as aright, these actions must be sensitive to moral reasons, in that they would be different—would cease to be unreflective, would cease to be habitual—if the relevant reasons failed to apply. This is not to say that the agent notices, takes into account, or in any way bases his action upon the moral reasons when he acts habitually, unreflectively, in the usual situation. But it is to say that if the situation were not usual, in particular if the moral reasons were affected, then he would notice and take it into account. Moral cognition, the understanding and awareness of moral reason, has its role to play, even with moral habits.

Many of these points might be dramatized by supposing that we had some way of producing moral habits at will. Suppose we had a drug, which we can call Suggestine, which makes people inclined to behave in whatever ways are suggested to them when they take the drug. It doesn't make them act in those ways invariably, much less make them incapable of acting in any other way: there would be serious moral objections, both to its use and its effects, if it did. It merely makes them tend to behave in those ways, in the absence of special reasons not to. Suggestine produces habits which like other habits can be broken or modified—though perhaps only with some difficulty—not compulsions. In that case, I think, it is not open to the same objections. Of course such a drug could be extremely dangerous in the wrong hands, but its social utility and moral desirability is obvious. It would enable us to transform the behaviour of those who are persistently immoral or amoral; it would be more efficient and more effective than either punishment or persuasion. And it is not just society that would be better as a result, but those individuals themselves. Suggestine is, after all, only a simpler and more reliable way of achieving what we aim at as parents, when we try to train or condition our children into morally acceptable patterns of behaviour.

Suggestine has its limitations even so. In particular it makes people inclined to behave in various ways without, in itself, making them aware of why they should behave in those ways. The habits it produces are blind habits, and since the agent does not appreciate the reasons for acting in that way he is unlikely to notice when these reasons fail to apply and there is no reason why it should make any difference to him if he did. His behaviour cannot be sensitive to those reasons, because it is not based on those reasons. And even if the drug were supplemented with a course of moral education, its workings would be independent of the reasons why the agent should act in that way; even if he knows why the action is right he will do it not because of what makes it right, but because of the Suggestine and its accompanying suggestion. So although Suggestine might produce morally desirable habits, and morally desirable actions, it will not produce moral action in our technical sense. It may be because that sort of action is moral that it has been suggested, and hence it is because it is moral that the habit is acquired; but it is because of the Suggestine, and not because it is moral, that the habit is retained and the action performed. It will be sheer habit, like those habits we acquire as children and as adults find it almost impossible to rid ourselves of, even though we are no longer able to justify them.

Now we could try to overcome these difficulties by, so to speak, building the reasons into the suggestion. We might say, for example: henceforth you will hold shop doors open for old ladies with heavy baskets provided that (a) they are not carrying things which do not belong to them, (b) they are not walking into a blazing inferno, (c) holding the door open for them does not inconvenience even older ladies with heavier baskets, and so on. But the crux, of course, is that 'and so on'. The more qualifications we can include, the more reliable and adaptable our Suggestine patient will be, the more we can rely on him to do the right thing. But the list is open-ended; we can never ensure we have covered every eventuality. But that is not the important point: it wouldn't take much to get the Suggestine patient as sensitive to the situation as most of us are, at least when it comes to holding shop doors open. What is important here is that in trying to make him sensitive to the situation we are, in effect, trying to give him some understanding of the morally-relevant reasons; we are trying to affect not just his behaviour but also his understanding of the situation. Of course this will not entirely succeed, since we are trying to make the agent aware of the reasons without making him aware of why they are reasons; but at least to some extent we are dealing with cognition as well as with conduct.

What is essential to moral action, therefore, is not moral cogitation but moral cognition, not moral thinking but moral awareness and understanding. It is individual moral cognition which will explain moral action, in both theory and practice. It is moral cognition which will determine, in the individual case, which reasons qualify as moral reasons to begin with. It may even be moral cognition which bridges the gap between moral thought and moral action, a matter to be explored by Straughan and Wright in the chapters that follow. But the elucidation of moral cognition, and with it the elucidation of moral reasons, must remain a topic for another occasion.

Morality in the Making
Edited by H. Weinreich-Haste and D. Locke
© 1983, John Wiley & Sons, Ltd.

CHAPTER 7

From Moral Judgment to Moral Action

ROGER STRAUGHAN

Socrates' claim that to know the good was to do it was denied by Aristotle on the grounds that it clearly contradicted the facts. The nature of the relationship between moral judgment and moral action has since then been vigorously debated by generations of philosophers, who have by and large tended to align themselves behind one or other of the two original protagonists. More recently psychologists have also contributed to the discussion, presenting empirical investigations and theoretical explanations of the extent to which people's moral judgments are consistent with their actions.

Little or no attempt has yet been made, however, to set the philosophical and psychological approaches alongside each other, and to view the logical and empirical accounts from a common perspective. The aims of this chapter will therefore be:

1. to review and illustrate some disagreements which exist among both philosophers and psychologists within this area,
2. to examine possible interconnections between the logical and empirical work that has been done,
3. to explore a particular logical account of the judgment/action relationship and its empirical implications.

Philosophical Accounts: Internalism versus Externalism

Philosophical discussions of the logical relationship between moral judgment and moral action have ranged between two extreme and opposed positions, which may be labelled 'internalism' and 'externalism'. In a detailed examination of these positions, Frankena draws the distinction as follows:

'Roughly, the opposition in question is between those who regard motivation as external and those who regard it as internal to obligation . . . Many moral philosophers (the externalists) have said or implied that it is in some sense logically possible for an agent to have or see that he has an obligation even if he has no motivation, actual or dispositional, for doing the action in question; many others (the internalists) have said or implied that this is paradoxical and not logically possible . . . Internalists hold that motivation must be provided for because it is involved in the analysis of moral judgments and so is essential for an action's being or being shown to be obligatory. Externalists insist that motivation is not part of the analysis of moral judgments or of the justification of moral claims; for them motivation is an important problem, but only because it is necessary to persuade people to act in accordance with their obligations.'

(Frankena, 1958, pp. 40–1)

The significance of this distinction for our present purposes lies in the fact that internalism emphasizes the logical *tightness* of the relationship between moral judgment and moral action and minimizes the possibility of a gap or inconsistency between the two, whereas externalism does the reverse. Many versions of the two positions have been expounded, as Frankena illustrates in his article, and the opposition cannot be neatly expressed in terms of the various '. . . isms' of ethical theory. These complexities will not be entered into here; a brief review of some representative arguments from the rival camps will suffice to show how widely differing views of the logical relationshp between moral judgment and moral action can be held.

Extreme forms of internalism have gone so far as to assert the logical *impossibility* of a gap or inconsistency between judgment and action, so denying in effect that cases of 'weakness of will' can ever occur. Different versions of internalism base this denial on different grounds. Socrates, for example, in the *Protagoras*, employs a hedonistic argument which equates what is good with what is pleasant, and what is evil with what is painful; thus it becomes nonsense to say that a person fails to do what he knows is good because he is 'overcome by pleasure', for the best course of action is that which ultimately leads to the *greatest* pleasure and satisfaction. No one therefore willingly does what he knows to be evil (and painful), and all wrong-doing is explicable in terms not of moral weakness but of ignorance or miscalculation of the consequent pleasures and pains. Plato, in the later Dialogues, builds upon this argument, giving it a metaphysical dimension by linking it with his Theory of Ideas. Moral knowledge now becomes knowledge of the Idea of the Good, and a person whose education has enabled him to ascend to the mystical heights at which this Idea is apprehended will 'know the Good' in a way which makes it impossible for him not to act in accordance with that 'knowledge'.

These examples of internalist arguments also serve to illustrate the difficulty of distinguishing between logical and psychological claims at times, for it is not altogether clear whether Socrates and Plato are making strictly logical points here about *necessary* features of moral understanding or psychological points about how moral agents tend to behave. The Socratic argument in the *Protagoras*, for example, concludes, 'To make for what one believes to be evil, instead of making for the good, is not, it seems, *in human nature*' (358D, my italics), which looks on the face of it to be a highly dubious, empirical claim;

while Plato similarly seems to be referring to the emotive, *psychological* effect produced by the quasi-religious experience of apprehending the Idea of the Good. On the other hand, however, both accounts lean heavily upon a particular stipulative definition of 'knowledge', which distinguishes it sharply from mere 'belief' or 'opinion', and which logically requires that 'moral knowledge' leads to the appropriate action; in other words, the response of Socrates or Plato to an apparent case of a person failing to do what he knew was right would be simply to maintain, as a logical truth, 'Ah, but then he cannot *really* have known in the first place!' As we shall see later, this question of what is to count as 'moral knowledge' has become a crucial methodological one for psychologists also.

Emotivism provides further examples of internalist claims about the nature of moral judgments, where there is again difficulty in disentangling the logical from the psychological. Stevenson, for instance, has argued that ethical terms have a 'magnetism', which makes the characteristic purpose of moral discourse not to inform but to influence:

'A person who recognizes x to be good must *ipso facto* acquire a stronger tendency to act in its favour than he otherwise would have had.'

(Stevenson, 1937, p. 16)

Such emotivist theories seem partly to be describing the psychological effect of making moral judgments, but also to be making this alleged effect a logical component of moral discourse; part of what it *means* then for a person to make a moral judgment is that he acquires a stronger tendency to act upon that judgment.

A clearer example of a strictly logical, internalist thesis is that of Hare, who makes prescription the central function of moral discourse and proposes the following chain of logical entailments. If I make a value-judgment that I ought to do x, I am thereby addressing a first-person command to myself ('Let me do x!'), to which I must sincerely assent and upon which I must act or try to act. So I cannot fail to do or try to do what I think I ought to do, provided that I am using 'ought' in its central, evaluative, prescriptive sense (Hare, 1952). Hare's response to an apparent case of moral weakness would thus, like Socrates' and Plato's, be to point to an allegedly logical truth, 'Ah, but then he can't *really* have made a value-judgment in the first place!' The man who fails to act upon his value-judgment is being hypocritical, insincere, or self-deceiving in his misuse of 'ought'—or else is physically or psychologically unable to translate his value-judgment into action (Hare, 1963).

Extreme versions of internalism, then, refuse to allow any wedge to be driven between moral knowledge (or judgment) and moral action. By contrast, externalism sees the relationship to be not logically necessary, but purely contingent: to recognize that x is good or obligatory *may or may not* be associated with wanting, trying, or committing oneself to do x. This has been characterized as a 'So what?' view of motality, i.e. the agent's judgment of what is right or good need not logically carry with it any implications for how he will act.

Externalism as such has been less openly espoused by philosophers than internalism, and is consequently less easy to identify with particular proponents. Echoes of the theory, however, can be heard in intuitionist accounts (such as G. E. Moore's), which hold that moral terms like 'good' refer to properties of a particular logical type. To call some thing or action or state of affairs 'good', then, is to state a 'moral fact' and to convey 'moral information', and intuitionism provides no argument for why one should ever *do* anything about these facts, or *act* upon this information. Certainly no logical relationship between moral judgment and action is even hinted at, the implication being that the relationship is merely a contingent one.

A similar implication follows from views of morality which equate what is good with certain empirical or supernatural states of affairs. If I believe that what is good is definable in terms of, for example, (i) those customs and conventions which most members of my society approve of, or (ii) that which ensures the survival of my society or of myself, or (iii) that which produces the greatest happiness for my society or for myself, or (iv) that which the law prescribes, or (v) that which God or the Pope or the Sacred Texts or the Party lays down, then these definitions will again provide 'moral facts' which I accept as accurate and informative but not necessarily of direct, practical relevance to my conduct.

Externalist arguments are also to be found in critical commentaries upon some of the versions of internalism already described. The allegedly tight, logical bonds which some internalists claim to exist between moral judgment and action have predictably been challenged, usually on the Aristotelian grounds that such claims are counter-factual. Gardiner, for instance, objects that extreme forms of internalism deny the possibility of what are apparently common human experiences:

'We have a use for expressions like "doing what I believed to be wrong" or "acting contrary to my principles" when there is no obvious implication of insincerity or of change of mind . . .'

(Gardiner, 1954–5, p. 29)

Other writers have also used the notion of 'sincerity' to attempt to loosen the judgment/action bond, arguing that acting in conformity with a moral judgment is not the only possible criterion of the sincerity of that judgment. Remorse, guilt, shame and repentance have been proposed as alternative criteria, and Horsburgh goes so far as to claim:

'There are times when we attach more weight to remorse that we do to conformity in our judgments of relative fullness of assent . . . (and) attribute a higher degree of assent to a person after he has violated a moral rule than we did before.'

(Horsburgh, 1954, p. 349)

Finally and more generally, some have maintained that the notion of rational morality presupposes the existence of free moral agents who must, by definition, be able to act contrary to their principles if they so decide. As Cooper puts it:

'Between principles and practice, ideal and fulfilment, there will in any normal morality be a gap—this gappiness is an essential feature of the moral life and is made manifest in the tension which may exist prior to action between principle and desire . . . It is a necessary feature of any rational morality that it should leave some room for moral weakness.'

(Cooper, 1971, p. 225)

There is then among philosophers no agreement over the nature of the logical relationship (if any) between moral judgment and moral action. This prompts us to turn to the psychologists for some illumination of the corresponding empirical relationship, in the hope that this may throw further light upon the vexed logical questions. Empirical investigation is of course unnecessary when logical points are beyond dispute (e.g. statistical surveys are not required to establish what proportion of widows have lost their husbands), but where the conceptual boundaries are more hazy, empirical findings can sometimes suggest pointers to hitherto unexplored logical connections; some of Piaget's work, for example, on the stages of intellectual development has been criticized as merely enunciating logical truths for which empirical support is superfluous, yet it is significant that these allegedly logical features of development were not paid much philosophical attention *before* Piaget's empirical claims had revealed a potential seam for philosophers to work.

Psychological Accounts: Findings and Interpretations

Evidence concerning the empirical relationship between the making of moral judgments and the performing of moral actions might be expected to help in clarifying the dispute between internalism and externalism, as suggested above. Furthermore, such evidence merits the close attention of researchers into moral development, for questions about the 'sincerity' of a subject's verbal response (e.g. to a hypothetical dilemma), and the relationship between that response and the subject's behaviour in an actual situation, are frequently evaded or ignored (Straughan, 1975).

Unfortunately, however, empirical evidence in this area is still fairly scanty, due partly to the obvious methodological problems of gathering data and partly to one particular psychological tradition, which has attempted to study moral judgment in isolation from moral action—a tradition established and illustrated in the opening sentences of Piaget's influential work on '*The Moral Judgment of the Child*':

'Readers will find in this book no direct analysis of child morality as it is practised in home and school life, or in children's societies. It is the moral judgment that we propose to investigate, not moral behaviour or sentiments.'

(Piaget, 1932)

(This is not to say that Piaget *in fact* totally ignores 'moral behaviour'. Piaget's conception of the relationship between 'theoretical' and 'practical' morality is examined in detail in the following chapter. Nevertheless, Piaget has undeniably been closely identified by many with the 'judgmental' approach to moral development and moral education; though whether this identification is justified or not is a question beyond the scope of this chapter.) Moreover, what evidence there is appears *prima facie* to point in no particular direction, and interpretations of its significance are as disputed as we have seen the logical accounts to be. This will be demonstrated in the following brief review, which will take as its focus the work of Lawrence Kohlberg.

The pioneering studies of Hartshorne and May (1928–30), exemplify clearly this lack of consensus, for they have been subjected to a wide variety of scorings and interpretations during their fifty year history; a cautious and generalized conclusion, however, would be that they seem to show a low but positive correlation between children's 'moral knowledge' of conventional norms and their conduct in various situations which offer opportunities for stealing, cheating, and lying.

In contrast to these findings, however, Kohlberg summarizes the results of similar but more recent studies by declaring:

'Half a dozen studies show no positive correlation between high school or college students' verbal expression of the value of honesty or the badness of cheating, and the actual honesty in experimental situations.'

(Kohlberg, 1969, p. 394)

In another paper he states baldly:

'People's verbal moral values about honesty have nothing to do with how they act. People who cheat express as much or more moral disapproval of cheating as those who don't cheat.'

(Kohlberg, 1970, p. 64)

This apparent disparity between the findings of Hartshorne and May and of Kohlberg also throws into relief the all-important methodological question of what empirical researchers in this area should count as 'moral knowledge'. Kohlberg's contribution here has been to attempt to link this question with his own developmental theory of moral reasoning, claiming that when the subject's *stage* of moral thinking, rather than his mere verbal espousal of conventional moral values, is taken as the measure of 'moral knowledge', his research supports the Platonic view that 'virtue in action is knowledge of the good' and that 'true knowledge, knowledge of principles of justice, does predict virtuous action' (Kohlberg, 1970, p. 64). Using data obtained from a cheating test, from Milgram's studies of obedience and authority (Milgram, 1974), and from a students' sit-in, he shows that far higher percentages of Stage 5 and particularly

Stage 6 subjects translate their moral judgments into action, compared with those at the lower stages (Kohlberg, 1969, p. 395; 1970, pp. 78–9). (For the sake of consistency, throughout this chapter the numbered stages will refer to the 'old' Kohlbergian sequence, as described in the corresponding references, and not to the latest proposed scoring system developed by Kohlberg with Colby, Gibbs, Speicher-Dubin, and Power, 1977.)

Some support for Kohlberg's thesis is provided by studies of bystander intervention. Huston and Korte, for instance (1976, p. 277), cite McNamee's findings to the effect that the frequency of help given to an apparently distressed individual increased with each higher Kohlbergian level of moral development: subjects at Stage 2 helped 11% of the time, at Stage 3, 27%, at Stage 4, 38%, at Stage 5, 68%, and at Stage 6, 100%.

On the other hand, Burton (1976) in a review of empirical studies of honesty and dishonesty refers to the work of Podd (1972), who found no relationship between Kohlberg's moral judgment test and the level of shock administered to a 'victim' in Milgram's obedience test; and that of Krebs (1967), who found a slight positive relation between Kohlberg's scale of moral judgment and honest conduct if the moral judgment measure had been obtained *before* the conduct test, but a negative relation when the interview followed the test. Similarly, Mischel and Mischel argue, against Kohlberg, that the predictive validity for moral reasoning to moral behaviour is no more than 'modest'; referring to a study by Schwartz, Feldman, Brown, and Heingartner (1969), which was in fact cited by Kohlberg (1971) in *support* of the reasoning/action link, they conclude:

"Correlations of the type obtained so far suggest that, overall, knowledge of individuals' moral reasoning would permit one to predict no more than about 10% of the variance in their moral behaviour.'

(Mischel and Mischel, 1976, p. 101)

Some of these apparent disagreements can perhaps be partially resolved by noting a possible source of confusion between the notions of 'virtuous action' and 'consistent action'. Strictly speaking, it is studies only of the latter which can throw light upon the empirical relationship between moral judgment and action. For this purpose we need to know *not* whether subjects at Stage X act in ways which *we* (or 'society') deem to be morally desirable (e.g. by helping strangers in apparent distress), but whether subjects at Stage X actually translate into action what *they* judge is the right thing to do. Thus, the McNamee study cited above, for example, shows that assistance to apparent drug victims is progressively more likely to be offered as one proceeds up the Kohlbergian ladder (i.e. 'virtuous action'), not that higher stage subjects are necessarily more likely to act in accordance with their judgments than lower stage subjects (i.e. 'consistent action'); the subjects at Stage 2, who offered help least often, may have believed for various reasons that the right thing to do was *not* to help, and so may conceivably have shown *more* consistency between judgment and action than those at Stages 5 or 6 (some of whom might also for different reasons have judged that they ought not to offer help).

These complexities cannot be pursued at greater length in this brief review, the main purpose of which has been to show how Kohlberg's attempts to refine Hartshorne's and May's account of 'moral knowledge' and its relationship to moral behaviour have opened up further areas of dispute. It seems fair to conclude that at present there is not much more ageement over the empirical nature of that relationship than there is over its logical nature—a conclusion supported by Blasi in a recent and extensive review of the psychological literature. Arguing that the relationship between 'moral cognition' and moral action is an extremely intricate one and that generalizations are difficult to arrive at because empirical studies have concentrated upon different aspects and interpretations of that relationship, Blasi infers there to be 'considerable support for the hypothesis that moral reasoning and moral action are statistically related'; yet he goes on to warn that this statement needs careful qualification:

'Empirical support, in fact, varies from area to area: It is strongest for the hypothesis that moral reasoning differs between delinquents and nondelinquents, and that at higher stages of moral reasoning there is greater resistance to the pressure of conforming one's judgment to other' views. The support is clear but less strong for the hypothesis that higher moral stage individuals tend to be more honest and more altruistic. Finally, there is little support for the expectation that individuals of the postconventional level resist more than others the social pressure to conform in their moral action.'

(Blasi, 1980, p. 37)

The remainder of this chapter will try to erect a few speculative signposts in the hope that they may indicate a possible escape route from this interdisciplinary morass. Let us take as provisional premises two points of reasonable, though by no means unanimous, agreement—that the empirical relationship generally seems to be only a 'modest' one, but that a subject's *stage* of moral reasoning is a better predictor of his subsequent action than is his mere verbal espousal of, or acquiescence with, moral values and standards.

These two points, if accepted, raise four further key questions of both psychological and logical dimensions, upon which the final sections of this paper will concentrate. The questions are:

1. Why should there be any positive relationship at all between moral judgment and action?
2. Why should this relationship be a 'modest' one?
3. Why should the relationship be stronger when the subject's *stage* of moral reasoning is taken as the measure of his 'moral knowledge'?
4. Why do Kohlberg's own findings apparently fail to give complete support to his claim that 'true knowledge predicts virtuous action'?—i.e. why do even Stage 6 subjects still at times seem to act contrary to their moral judgments?

A Possible Resolution of the Logical Dispute

To investigate further the four questions just posed, we must return to the logical issue and see whether some reconciliation can be achieved between the extremes of externalism and internalism, both of which appear to embody serious weaknesses.

On the one hand, to hold that moral judgments are wholly 'external', and thereby only contingently related to moral action, is to ignore a central feature of moral concepts. Recognizing a moral obligation is not logically parallel with recognizing a face or a tune, for it is to *acknowledge* the weight and validity of non-prudential reasons and principles, which are seen as *justifying* a particular course of action. If, for example, I believe that I have an obligation not to light a bonfire in my garden when the wind will blow the smoke in the direction of my neighbour's washing on the line, I am acknowledging that the possible dirtying of my neighbour's washing is a *factor* relevant to the question whether I ought to light the bonfire or not—a factor which constitutes a valid reason why I ought *not* to light it, because I am accepting the justificatory principle that one ought not to cause avoidable annoyance to others. So I cannot truly be said to recognize the obligation which I believe to be upon me (or to make a moral judgment), unless I at the same time acknowledge the normative pressure and authority being brought to bear upon me by the reasons and principles whose justificatory force I show that I appreciate by *recognizing the obligation*. Recognizing a face or a tune carries with it no prescriptive cargo of the sort entailed in recognizing an obligation, yet externalism in effect draws no distinction between these two logically separate forms of 'recognition'.

Extreme versions of internalism, on the other hand, seem to make the logical connection between moral judgment and action far too tight, so denying the possibility of yielding to temptation. I can in all sincerity believe that I ought not to light my bonfire, yet be so eager to get rid of my ever-mounting pile of rubbish on the first fine day for weeks that I go ahead and act against my principles (perhaps further encouraged by the aversion I have towards my neighbour's barking dog). After the event the sincerity of my original judgment may be confirmed by a variety of indications (e.g. I may feel guilty, embarrassed, apologetic, over-defensive, etc.). Action in conformity with a moral judgment, then, is not the only possible criterion of the sincerity of that judgment. Indeed the conceptual geography of the word 'ought' suggests uncertainty as to whether or not the appropriate action will in fact ensue because of the likely presence of countervailing factors ('I know I really *ought* to do x, but . . .'). As Thalberg succinctly puts it, 'Ought implies might not' (Thalberg, 1971, p. 245).

Extreme versions of internalism and externalism, therefore, are equally unsatisfactory. Most of the problems can be resolved, however, by positing an internal connection *of sorts* between moral judgement and action, but not of strict logical entailment. To make a moral judgment, I have suggested, is to acknowledge that certain factors in a situation constitute reasons which justify on non-prudential grounds a certain course of action, by reference to a more general moral principle. But considerations which one sees as *justifying* the doing of *x* may not in practice *motivate* one to do *x*. Often justificatory considerations do coincide with and even help to provide motivational ones (e.g. I may want to do what I conceive to be my duty *because* I conceive it as such), but this is by no means always the case. As Edgley argues:

'There are, I think . . . reasons of a sort such that their being some particular person's reasons for doing something does not imply that he wants to do that thing. Moral reasons seem to me to be of this kind.'

(Edgley, 1969, p. 162)

On this view of moral reasoning, then, it is quite possible for me on the one hand to form a sincere moral judgment, which acknowledges that there are good, non-prudential reasons which justify my refraining from lighting my bonfire, yet on the other hand not to *want* to refrain from lighting it because there are countervailing factors in the situation which lead me to want to get rid of my rubbish more than I want to avoid inconveniencing my neighbour. This distinction between justifying and motivating considerations, which I have elaborated in much greater detail elsewhere (Straughan, 1982), suggests a loose, internal connection between moral judgment and action which might be partially expressed in the principle, 'Believing that one ought to do *x* is to do *x* in the absence of countervailing factors'—a principle which Griffiths describes as 'necessary to the explicability of the rational behaviour of men' (Griffiths, 1958, p. 299). According to this more moderate version of internalism, then, one does what one believes one ought to do unless one wants to do something else more, and the sincerity of one's beliefs is thus not necessarily wholly dependent upon one's acting in accordance with them.

Empirical Implications of this Logical Account

How does this loose, internal connection which has been proposed relate to empirical findings and interpretations? To see whether any points of possible contact and compatibility can be discerned, this final section will return to the four key questions raised in the review of empirical studies, and will consider them in the light of my suggested logical account of what can be labelled 'moderate internalism'.

1. Why Should There be a Positive Relationship at all Between Moral Judgment and Action?

A logical connection of the sort outlined above clearly gives us a warrant to expect *some* empirical, positive relationship to exist. Moderate internalism does not support the 'So what?' model of morality, implied in extreme versions of externalism, which would lead one to expect no consistent empirical relationship of any sort; rather it suggests a presumption in favour of a positive relationship, for it claims that, *other things being equal*, moral judgments will be translated into moral action (or, at least, attempted moral action).

2. Why Should the Relationship be a 'Modest' One?

Moderate internalism is again not in conflict with this relatively undisputed empirical conclusion. The type of test situation which empirical researchers normally use is characterized (even more than situations encountered in real life) by the presence of powerful countervailing factors, with the result that other things are decidedly *not equal* when the question of whether to act upon a moral judgment arises. Often the subject is given every opportunity to cheat, lie, steal, etc., and little motivational incentive is provided to support the translation into action of any judgment *not* to cheat, lie, steal, etc. As Blasi comments, 'The experimental situations for assessing honesty have some common characteristics: In all of them some incentives to cheat are offered, and the impression is conveyed that it is safe to cheat' (Blasi, 1980, p. 20). It is consequently not surprising if the motivational scales are often tipped against the implementation of the moral judgment, because the subject finds that situational factors are such that he wants to cheat, lie, steal, etc. more than he wants to do that which he sincerely believes he ought to do. If moderate internalism is right, therefore, a modest but positive link between moral judgment and action is just the kind of empirical relationship which test situations might be expected to produce.

3. Why Should the Relationship be Stronger When the Subject's Stage of Moral Reasoning is Taken as the Measure of His 'Moral Knowledge'?

Moderate internalism also sheds some light upon this question, although at first sight it appears rather puzzling why 'principled' moral judgments (i.e. Kohlberg's Stages 5 and 6) should be more likely than 'conventional' or 'preconventional' ones (i.e. Stages 1–4) to be acted upon. Are not the reasons which make a judgment 'principled' essentially justificatory rather than motivational, and if that is so why should one be more likely to act upon a principle than upon what Kohlberg calls a 'concrete rule of action' (Kohlberg, 1970, p. 69)? Should we not expect the very 'concreteness' of rules to exert a *more* direct motivational influence than less specific justificatory principles, when the chips are down and situational pressures are at work? Principles seem to possess what Cooper has called a 'cool-hour quality': ' . . . a man's moral principles are those of his principles of action which in a cool hour he is least prepared to abandon belief in, however much he may be tempted to deviate from them in the heat of the moment' (Cooper, 1968, p. 152). Yet it is in the heat of the moment that the decision has to be made whether or not to act upon our principles, and if they are indeed characterized by this cool-hour quality, this does not suggest a particularly close link between holding a principle and acting upon it.

However, if 'principled' moral judgments are in fact more likely to be acted upon than 'conventional' or 'pre-conventional' ones, as Kohlberg claims to have shown, there may perhaps be some other logical feature of 'principled' judgments which provides an explanatory basis for this phenomenon. The queries raised in the previous paragraph make it doubtful whether this feature could reside in the principle-versus-rule distinction itself, but that distinction when considered alongside the further distinction between justificatory and motivational considerations does offer possible logical support for Kohlberg's claim in the following way.

If I fail to do that which I sincerely believe I ought to do (while being fully able to do it), I am presumably not sufficiently motivated to do that which I consider to be justified. So what are the usual means by which motivation for moral behaviour is strengthened, and which are apparently lacking in such cases? These can be roughly classified as either 'self-directed' or 'other-directed' in type, corresponding to Piaget's autonomous and heteronomous levels. Praise, blame, encouragement, criticism, reward and punishment, for example, are all important forms of incentive or sanction which can be brought to bear upon the moral agent, *either* by external judges and teachers *or* by the internal verdicts of his own conscience. ('Conscience' is a notoriously ambiguous notion; it is used here and in what will follow to refer not to the causal process of experiencing guilt reactions, stemming from unexamined and unconscious sources, but to rational acts of judgment made by a moral agent about his own past, present and future conduct, based upon what he regards as justificatory reasons and obligatory principles.)

Gilligan, identifying other-directed morality as a 'shame ethic' and self-directed morality as a 'guilt ethic', argues that Kohlberg's data show that the motive for morality is to avoid either shame or guilt, and that the developmental trend described by Kohlberg is from an earlier, 'shame-motivated' morality to a later, 'guilt-motivated' one (Gilligan, 1976, p. 154). If this interpretation is correct, perhaps 'guilt', to which (according to Gilligan) one becomes increasingly sensitive as one goes up the developmental ladder, possesses certain logical features distinguishing it from 'shame', which constitutes the predominant form of motivation at the lower stages; and perhaps these features may explain why 'principled' judgments may be the most likely ones to be acted upon. Kohlberg himself comments on this motivational distinction between what Gilligan would call 'shame' and 'guilt', noting that 'intense fear of punishment does not predict to resistance to temptation, whereas self-critical guilt does' (Kohlberg, 1969, p. 392). However, he offers no explanation for this important finding beyond the generalized (and somewhat uninformative) statement that the difference between the two forms of motivation is a 'cognitive-structural' one, although 'in some sense, the feeling in the pit of one's stomach is the same whether it is dread of external events or dread of one's own self-judgment.'

But is there not a further, straightforward logical distinction to be drawn here (of such simplicity perhaps that it has been lost in the complexities of psychological theory), which may explain why 'principled' subjects act upon their judgments more often than other subjects? Other-directed sanctions are avoidable; self-directed ones are not. However attractive or unattractive the prospect of an externally derived reward or punishment may be to the agent, he knows that it will materialize only if his behaviour is witnessed by others or brought to their notice. The motives which characterize Kohlberg's lower stages are all of this sort: at Stage 1 the avoidance of punishment, at Stage 2 the obtaining of rewards, at Stage 3 the avoidance of disapproval and dislike, at Stage 4 the avoidance of censure by legitimate authorities, and even at Stage 5 the maintenance of respect from the community—all consequences which will accrue to the agent only if his action (or inaction) is publicly noted. But the feelings of guilt, remorse, anxiety and inadequacy which result from the agent's violation of his *own* self-accepted moral principles (on which Stage 6 judgments are based) cannot be escaped, and this is a logical 'cannot'. The principles are *his* principles, indicating obligations which *he* acknowledges as weighing upon him and justifying the doing of *x* rather than *y*. If he then goes ahead and does *y*, he knows that as long as he continues to accept the normative authority of those principles self-castigation is inevitable. 'I wouldn't be able to live with myself afterwards' is a typical response of Stage 6 subjects to Kohlberg's moral dilemmas.

However, it would be an over-simplification to draw too stark a contrast between the 'internal', 'self-directed', 'guilt-ethic' motivation of Stage 6, and the 'external', 'other-directed', 'shame-ethic' motivation of Stages 1–5. The shame/guilt distinction is most convincingly portrayed in terms of a continuum, for clearly Stages 1–5 are not all equally 'shame-based'; as Gilligan puts it, 'The middle stages . . . are mixed shame-and-guilt ethics which are transitional between the relatively pure and extreme shame ethic of Stage 1 and the guilt ethic of Stage 6' (Gilligan, 1976, p. 153). Similarly, there is often an 'internal' element in the forms of motivation which characterize the lower stages: the 'external' sanctions of reward, punishment, approval and disapproval may become 'internalized', and thereby operate as motives (and justifications) for action when no source of 'external' authority is present. The concept of 'internalization' is in any case a somewhat hazy one, and the 'internal/external' distinction is consequently of limited value for the purposes of the present discussion. Nevertheless, there is still an important sense in which the motivation for moral action at Stage 6 is more guilt-based and less dependent upon sanctions *originating* from 'outside' the agent than it is at the lower stages, and this feature of Stage 6 reasoning entitles us, for the reasons outlined in the previous paragraph, to expect a greater degree of consistency between judgment and action at that stage.

4. Why Do Kohlberg's Own Findings Fail to Give Complete Support to His Claim that 'True Knowledge of Principles Predicts Virtuous Action'?

Kohlberg's Platonic view of 'moral knowledge', when allied to the logical features of guilt demonstrated above, might lead one to expect Stage 6 subjects *always* to act in accordance with their 'principled' judgments. Yet Kohlberg's own data show that such subjects do at times act against their principles—for example, in continuing to administer increasingly severe electrical shocks to the 'victim' in Milgram's study (if this is admitted as an example of 'inconsistent' as well as 'immoral' action).

Again, moderate internalism offers a formal account of why it is not surprising that 'principled' judgments, though more likely to be acted upon than 'conventional' or 'pre-conventional' ones, are at times overridden in practice. The prospect of suffering guilt and self-castigation is by no means the only motivating influence upon human behaviour. I may know that guilt will be experienced as a result of a particular action which I believe I ought not to do, yet still for other reasons *want* to perform the action so much that the inevitable pangs of self-condemnation become outweighed or diminished in my estimation; I fail to do that which I believe I ought to do because of the strength of the countervailing factors. Thus, if the Stage 6 subjects who continued to administer shocks in the Milgram experiments were acting contrary to their 'principled' judgments, they must in practice have wanted to avoid self-condemnation *less* than they wanted something else (e.g. to avoid the embarrassment of open conflict with the experimenter). Such a decision may sometimes be deliberately and consciously made, but probably more often results from allowing one's attention to dwell upon the more immediate situational sanctions and incentives at the expense of the more remote, 'cool-hour', 'principled' considerations (Straughan, 1982, Chapter 6). In the Milgram experiments, for example, the subject is faced here and now with the experimenter's instructions, demands and apparent expectations, opposition to which will create immediate tension and antagonism, whereas the situation has to be *translated* and *re-interpreted* in terms of moral principles before reflective self-judgment and self-castigation can occur.

This view of 'weak-willed' Stage 6 subjects suggested by the logical features of moderate internalism is supported by some empirical studies which have found relationships between attention and self-control. The ability to attend closely to a task without being distracted has been shown to correlate positively with resistance to *moral* temptation (e.g. in a cheating test) (Grim, Kohlberg, and White, 1968). Other studies have indicated connections between being able to resist temptation and being able to delay the gratification of one's desires (e.g. in choosing a delayed, larger reward in preference to a smaller, immediate one (Mischel and Gilligan, 1964)). There are, then, both logical and psychological grounds for attributing 'weak-willed' behaviour at Stage 6 (and presumably at lower stages also) partly to a failure in attention and imagination which causes the subject to allow immediate motivational factors to override more remote justificatory ones, despite the fact that the latter are in accord with his 'cool-hour' principles. Whether or not a person will act upon his principles in a particular situation, therefore, will depend not only upon his level of moral reasoning but also upon the way in which he directs his attention and imagination to the morally relevant features of that situation.

In this chapter I have presented some conflicting accounts of the logical and empirical relationships between moral judgment and moral action. A form of moderate internalism was proposed as a way of resolving the philosophical dispute between extreme internalism and extreme externalism. Some empirical studies were then considered, resulting from which four key questions were formulated. Finally, these four questions were examined in the light of the explanatory framework offered by moderate internalism, and some answers were suggested which took note of both the logical and empirical dimensions of the issues at stake.

I hope that these tentative probings have not only highlighted the diverse problems surrounding the relationship between moral judgment and moral action, but have also shown that it is not impossible for philosophers and psychologists to explore a common problem jointly and fruitfully.

References

Blasi, A. (1980). Bridging Moral Cognition and Moral Action: A Critical Review of the Literature. *Psychological Bulletin*, **88**, 1–45.

Burton, R. V. (1976). Honesty and Dishonesty. In T. Lickona (Ed.), *Moral Development and Behaviour*, Holt, Rinehart, and Winston, New York.

Cooper, N. (1968). Oughts and Wants. *Proceedings of the Aristotelian Society*, **XLII**, 143–54.

Cooper, N. (1971). Further Thoughts on Oughts and Wants. In G. W. Mortimore (Ed.), *Weakness of Will*, Macmillan, London.

Edgley, R. (1969). *Reason in Theory and Practice*, Hutchinson, London.

Frankena, W. F. (1958). Obligation and Motivation in Recent Moral Philosophy. In A. I. Melden (Ed.), *Essays in Moral Philosophy*, University of Washington Press.

Gardiner, P. L. (1954–5). On Assenting to a Moral Principle. *Proceedings of the Aristotelian Society*, **LV**, 23–44.

Gilligan, J. (1976). Beyond Morality: psychoanalytic reflections on shame, guilt and love. In T. Lickona (Ed.), *Moral Development and Behaviour*, Holt, Rinehart, and Winston, New York.

Griffiths, A. P. (1958). Acting with Reason. *Philosophical Quarterly*, **VIII**, 289–99.

Grim, P. F., Kohlberg, L., and White, S. H. (1968). Some Relationships between Conscience and Attentional Processes. *Journal of Personality and Social Psychology*, **8**, 239–52.

Hare, R. M. (1952). *The Language of Morals*, Clarendon, Oxford.

Hare, R. M. (1963). *Freedom and Reason*, Clarendon, Oxford.

Hartshorne, H., and May, M. A. (1928–30). *Studies in the Nature of Character*, Macmillan, New York.

Horsburgh, H. J. N. (1954). The Criteria of Assent to a Moral Rule. *Mind*, **LXIII**, 345–58.

Huston, T. L., and Korte, C. (1976). The Responsive Bystander. In T. Lickona (Ed.), *Moral Development and Behaviour*, Holt, Rinehart, and Winston, New York.

Kohlberg, L. (1969). The Cognitive-Developmental Approach to Socialization. In D. A. Goslin (Ed.), *Handbook of Socialization Theory and Research*, Rand McNally, Chicago.

Kohlberg, L. (1970). Education for Justice: A Modern Statement of the Platonic View. In N. F. Sizer (Ed.), *Moral Education: Five Lectures*, Harvard University Press.

Kohlberg, L. (1971). From Is to Ought. In T. Mischel (Ed.), *Cognitive Development and Epistemology*, Academic Press, New York.

Kohlberg, L., Colby, A., Gibbs, J., Speicher-Dubin, B., and Power, C. (1977). *Assessing Moral Stages: A Manual*, Harvard University Press.

Krebs, R. L. (1967). Some Relations between Moral Judgment, Attention and Resistance to Temptation. Unpublished doctoral dissertation, University of Chicago.

Milgram, S. (1974). *Obedience to Authority*, Tavistock, London.

Mischel, W., and Gilligan, C. (1964). Delay of gratification, motivation for the prohibited gratification, and response to temptation. *Journal of Abnormal and Social Psychology*, **69**, 411–7.

Mischel, W., and Mischel, H. N. (1976). A Cognitive Social-Learning Approach to Morality and Self-Regulation. In T. Lickona (Ed.), *Moral Development and Behaviour*, Holt, Rinehart, and Winston, New York.

Piaget, J. (1932). *The Moral Judgement of the Child*, Routledge, London.

Podd, M. H. (1972). Ego identity Status and Morality: the relationship between two developmental constructs. *Developmental Psychology*, **6**, 497–507.

Schwartz, S., Feldman, K., Brown, M., and Heingartner, A. (1969). Some Personality Correlates of Conduct in Two Situations of Moral Conflict. *Journal of Personality*, **37**, 41–58.

Stevenson, C. S. (1937). The Emotive Meaning of Ethical Terms. *Mind*, **XLVI**, 14–31.

Straughan, R. (1975). Hypothetical Moral Situations. *Journal of Moral Education*, **4**, 183–9.

Straughan, R. (1982). *I Ought to But . . .: A Philosophical Approach to the Problem of Weakness of Will in Education*, NFER-Nelson, Windsor.

Thalberg, I. (1971). Acting Against One's Better Judgment. In G. W. Mortimore (Ed.), *Weakness of Will*, Macmillan, London.

Morality in the Making
Edited by H. Weinreich-Haste and D. Locke
© 1983, John Wiley & Sons, Ltd.

CHAPTER 8

'The Moral Judgment of the Child' Revisited

DEREK WRIGHT

Piaget's monograph, *The Moral Judgment of the Child*, has been around for a long time now, and is familiar to all students of moral development. Since it was published there have been many reviews of its content and numerous attempts to replicate in a more sophisticated manner most of the empirical conclusions reported in it. Predictably, these replications have supported some conclusions and heavily qualified others More important, over the last decade or so Kohlberg's work has begun to make its full impact and many people feel that he has superseded Piaget in this area, and reduced the latter's contribution to one of mainly historical interest.

However, close scrutiny of Kohlberg's work reveals its limitations. Despite its considerable significance it is clear that Kohlberg has dealt with only one aspect of moral development, namely the kind of reasoning the individual offers in defence of assertions about what hypothetical people ought or ought not to do in hypothetical dilemmas. This leaves out a great deal. Kohlberg's work is of course still developing. But in considering those aspects of moral development not yet satisfactorily assimilated into Kohlberg's scheme it is perhaps not untimely to return to Piaget's original monograph to consider again some of the ideas in it which have to some extent been forgotten.

In this paper I shall not be concerned, except incidentally, with his empirical claims but rather with his theoretical speculations. It would be altogether misleading to say he presented a theory of moral development. He offers a collection of ideas, many thrown out in passing, many intuitive, all of them expressed, characteristically, in concepts of teasing abstraction and imprecision. It is a relatively easy task to point out the obscurities, inconsistencies, and idiosyncracies in Piaget's thinking. It is these very qualities, though, that make his writing stimulating and provoke further speculations.

Piaget and Kohlberg

A convient starting point is to draw out some of the more obvious contrasts between Piaget's monograph and Kohlberg's subsequent contribution. It is commonly said that Piaget's monograph was the main stimulus for Kohlberg's investigations. There is obviously overlap. But though Kohlberg has remained faithfully within the mainstream cognitive-developmental tradition created by Piaget, he has clearly moved away from Piaget's original monograph and has, at least to some extent, been concerned with different problems.

To begin with it is worth pointing up certain differences in approach to empirical inquiry. Kohlberg's interview technique is focused upon hypothetical dilemmas in which two duties or obligations are in conflict. His aim is to find stage specific 'moral philosophies'. Piaget's interview procedure, though much less standardized and systematic, was a good deal more broadly based. He sampled many aspects of the subject's thought as it relates to morality, and the question 'What ought X to do and why?' which is central to Kohlberg's interview, appears little in his interrogations. His interpretive ideas, therefore, draw on a richer, if less reliable, empirical base.

There is a more fundamental difference. Both have been concerned with the development of moral thinking but Piaget has also addressed himself to a central problem which has been, so far, peripheral to Kohlberg's published work. One way of elaborating the point is as follows. Consider first the standard syllogism: 'All A's are B; C is an A; therefore C is B.' Once the premises are understood there is an inexorable compulsion about the conclusion (Piaget's phrase is 'acquired self-evidence'). Doubtless the logician can explain this in terms of the logic of classes. There remains the psychological question of how it comes about that people unsophisticated in logic nevertheless experience this compulsion. Among other things Piaget's mainstream work has been devoted to answering this question. Consider now a similar argument in the moral sphere: 'I ought not to steal; if I take this book it would be stealing; therefore I ought not to take this book.' The same logical self-evidence is present and the moral philosopher can explain it through analysis of the concepts involved. But this time the conclusion is concerned not with knowing but with acting, and possibly acting under conditions in which what I ought to do conflicts with what I want to do. For such an argument to be embedded in living, and not an exercise in thinking, the initial premiss must be expressive of what for convenience may be called a moral as distinct from a logical compulsion, It is then, I think, not too inaccurate to say that Kohlberg has been concerned with the development of logical self-evidence in moral thinking whereas Piaget has paid less attention to this but has also focused, like Freud and Durkheim before him, on the development of moral compulsion (in his term, *respect* for moral prescription).

Of course Kohlberg is aware of this. Indeed to an extent not true of Piaget his focus on the developing logic of moral thinking tends to sharpen the dichotomy between thought and action. Because of this he finds it necessary to invoke the concept of ego strength as a mediating factor. Two things can be said about this. If part of the definition of ego strength is a consistency between action and thought it has little explanatory value. Secondly, if moral obligation is subsumed under the more general notion of ego strength then the implication is that it is not the uniquely distinctive motivating force in human experience that many people believe it to be. In contrast, Piaget uses the subject's moral thinking in order to reach through it to an understanding of the origin of moral obligation. The thought-action problem, though still present, is less salient in his work. More important, his speculative explanation offer an account, at one and the same time, of the development of both moral thinking and moral obligation.

Since he was interested in moral reasoning rather than moral obligation, Kohlberg draws his explanatory theorizing, not from Piaget's work on moral judgment, but from his theory of general intellectual development. Hence his commitment to stage sequence, his search for stage structure, and his assertion that the primary stimulus to moral development is cognitive disequilibrium. The loose theoretical scheme Piaget offers for moral development is much more social psychological than it is cognitive developmental. This is inevitable enough since moral obligation is generated within relationships between people. True, Piaget believes that intellectual development is an important factor in moral development, and he draws certain parallels between, for example, intellectual egocentrism and moral realism. But he devotes far more space to his social psychological speculations. Moreover, though he distinguishes two kinds of morality and thinks that one tends to precede the other, he is for ever reiterating that these do not constitute stages in the ordinary sense but rather modes of thinking and experiencing, morally, that coexist from the earliest years, and that development, if it occurs, consists of a progressive shift in salience from one to the other.

Kohlberg is naturally aware of the importance of social context, but it features in his theory in a more limited way through the concept of social perspective. By this he means the way in which the subject intellectually construes his social environment. As such it is an aspect of the subject's own cognition, and constitutes the broader cognitive context within which his specifically moral reasoning is embedded, and from which it draws its support. Again it must be said that Kohlberg's position is still evolving, and one of its points of evolution is in the direction of establishing a social psychological dimension. Such a dimension will only be present when he is able to define independently those social conditions, structures, or processes which can be linked to moral reasoning as interactional determinants. When that point is reached, Kohlberg will be at least on the brink of providing an explanation of moral obligation. Piaget's theory is already a social psychological one in the sense that he postulates types of relationships between people which can be defined independently of the subject's construing of them and which are seen as determinants on the one hand of the individual's mode of moral thinking via his level of intellectual development, and on the other of his sense of moral obligation via the respect he feels within the relationships.

In short, Kohlberg's work has been less a development of Piaget's contribution to moral development than an original application of his mainstream work on intellectual development to moral reasoning. On the other hand Piaget, in his monograph, has raised issues and put forward ideas the elaboration of which may prove of value in supplementing Kohlberg's existing work and making it more comprehensive and convincing. Some of these ideas will now be discussed.

Practical and Theoretical Moral Thinking

It may be a useful preliminary to spell out the kinds of situations in which a moral issue (say the keeping of promises) arises. They will be placed along a rough and ready dimension of personal involvement or 'hypotheticalness' of the issue for the subject.

1. There is the coalface. The subject may have made a promise and suddenly be precipitated into a situation in which it is difficult for him to keep it. Personal involvement is high and thinking is likely to be dominated by a confusion of feeling. We may suppose that his conscious decision will be a function of the strength of the sense of obligation ('I must keep my promises') that surfaces in awareness and his instant assessment of the situation, and in particular his feeling-laden assessment of the possible consequences for himself and others.

2. The testing situation may lie in the future so that the subject has time to reflect upon what his action will be. Since the decision is not immediate there is already a sense in which it has a small element of the hypothetical. But though he may seek advice and can consider fully all aspects of the situation, personal involvement is high because the decision is his.

3. There is the post mortem reflection following whatever decision is made. Personal involvement is less and will take a different form because the original situation has passed and he is now in one of a different kind.

4. The problem may be the personal concern of a friend who approaches the subject for advice. For the subject the problem now has about it a clearly hypothetical quality. However empathic he may be he will not be able to see it entirely through his friend's eyes. There is clearly a strong element of personal involvement though. At stake will be the subject's readiness to put himself into his friend's shoes, his moral ideology and reasoning, and his concern for his friend's welfare.

5. The promise-keeping situation may be entirely hypothetical, unrelated to any decision the subject has to make, and largely stripped of contextual detail. In ordinary living this is probably not very common. But caught by a predatory experimenter the subject may find himself presented with the

dilemma and his reflections sought. Insofar as there is personal involvement it will be of a quite different order, depending upon his interest, his desire to please the experimenter or demonstrate how clever he is, and so on. We can couple with this situation the occasional debate on some controversial moral issue that happens on social occasions.

6. Finally there is the explicit meta-activity of the professional moral philosopher.

Piaget's concept of practical morality presumably encompasses situations 1–3, and in particular 1 and 2. It should be emphasized, though, that in speaking of his practical morality in these situations we are not referring to the subject's behaviour alone (whether he keeps his promise or not) but also to the cognitive activity, conscious and unconscious, that shapes the decision he makes. The concept of theoretical morality refers to situations 4–6, though it is effectively 5 that we are concerned with.

Clearly the study of the subject's theoretical morality is interesting in its own right. But its value is much diminished if we do not know how it relates to his practical morality. Obviously correlations between theoretical morality and observed behaviour will not give us the answer. What Piaget offers us is one particular conception of the relationship. It is speculative, imported from another context, and only supported in his text by some dubious observations of children playing games, anecdote, and 'common observation'. Nevertheless it is a plausible conception and worth serious consideration. It is his Law of Conscious Realization, adopted from Claparéde, and used extensively as a developmental principle in his work on intellectual development. He is characteristically imprecise about the definition of this 'law'. It is worth noting, however, that the concept carries the implication which Piaget has since made explicit that there is a cognitive unconscious, and indeed, as he says in his later statement, mechanisms of cognitive suppression and even repression.

There are broadly three different contexts in which Piaget has used the notion of conscious realization, and there appears to be a difference, and possibly even an inconsistency, in the functions attributed to it in these contexts. In order to clarify its function in moral development as such we will consider the other two contexts first.

Within the context of his theory of intellectual development, conscious realization appears to be an aspect of the mechanism of transition from one major stage to another, associated with vertical décalage. Thus formal operational thinking may be defined as the conscious realization of concrete operational thinking. By conscious realization, however, Piaget does not mean a passive process of becoming aware but an active one of construing and conceptualizing (or thinking about thinking). This understanding of conscious realization remains consistent in every context in which Piaget uses the notion. 'Conscious realization does not consist in the projection of an inner light which is limited to illuminating a perfected construction, but as we have seen, it presupposes a reconstruction which transcends, whilst integrating, the structure of the previous construction thus "reflected"' (Beth and Piaget, 1966, p. 190). It is through the process of being consciously realized that concrete operational structures are reintegrated and transformed into formal operational structures.

There are several points to be made about this. First the consciously realized reconstruction of concrete operations, though it transforms them, yet also by implication remains faithfully isomorphic to them. Secondly, conscious realization is developmentally progressive; it results in more effective knowing and understanding. As we shall see, in the area of action as commonly understood its progressive function is equivocal. Thirdly the conscious realization of one structural level involves the creation of a new structural level which is itself unconscious.

This last point suggests that the process of conscious realization need not stop with the acquisition of the capacity for formal operations, and Piaget clearly implies that it does not. He suggests, for example, that the history of mathematical discovery has been at least partly one of successive conscious realization of existing mathematical activities, or, we might say, the creation of second order reconstructions at a higher level or generality of logical processes already part of the mathematician's repertoire of skills. At the level of discovery Piaget is talking about, the processes thus reconstructed must presumably already be a manifestation of formal operations. Yet he does not allow any further qualitative development beyond formal structures. It follows that we must credit formal structure with the reflexive capacity continuously to take itself as the object of its own functioning and thereby perpetually creating further operations to be consciously realized.

After using the concept as an explanatory device for many years, Piaget has recently made some attempt to study the process of conscious realization directly (*The Grasp of Consciousness*, 1976); only now he uses a new term for it, cognizance, and the context is only tangentially related to intellectual development. In this recent monograph he attempts to trace how the child comes to reconstruct as conscious knowledge a coordinated skill such as using a catapult, or a more intellectual operation such as seriation, which are, so to speak, already 'unconsciously' known (i.e. how he comes to 'know' his 'know-how', to use Piaget's words). Though Piaget's interest is in the mechanisms of cognizance rather than its function, the implication is that in this context it is not an agent of stage transition. On the contrary, it does itself manifest horizontal décalage and is constrained by the limitations of the intellectual stage the child's thinking has reached.

The general conclusion Piaget draws is that cognizance proceeds from the periphery to the centre. Action is goal directed, 'hence the first two observable features, which can be termed peripheral because they are linked to the triggering of the action and to the point of its application: consciousness of what the goal is—in other words, awareness of the general direction of the action needed to attain it (intention)—and cognizance of its result, either success or failure.'

The means employed in the action constitute its 'central region'. Cognizance of the means (and simultaneously of the knowledge of the object upon which the action is directed) is stimulated by two factors. The first is failure to attain the goal, or non-adaptation. 'In the case of failure the reason must be sought and this leads to cognizance of more central regions of the action' in order that the subject can correct the means. The second is the generalization and consequent differentiation of assimilatory schemes. In attempting the same goal in different situations, problems inevitably arise which lead to conscious comparison of the two situations and therefore also of the differences in means needed.

Cognizance, the subject's conceptual construction of his own action whether overt or interiorized, involves self observation, the coordination of such observation, and reflection that goes beyond it. It is similar to the construction of knowledge of an object, and 'is as laborious as if it corresponded to nothing already known by the subject himself.' In the early stages subjects were found to import preformed beliefs about their own actions, to suppress observations which they were aware of in isolation, and thereby disrupt the smooth process of conscious realization. In conceptualizing their actions they would 'put out of mind' elements they were already aware of.

Piaget says little about the effects of cognizance upon the actions themselves. He implies that the intervention within an action of 'thought-out' choices can make it more effective but some of his tasks (such as crawling on all fours) are such that it is difficult to see how they could ever be improved by any amount of cognizance.

With regard, them, to the concept of conscious realization this monograph confirms the use of the concept in the intellectual sphere by showing that it is an active, constructive process, that it follows the effective performance of an action only after an appreciable time lag, that it is stimulated by the problematic, and that its goal is to become isomorphic with the original action. It differs from the previous usage in that it does not necessarily bring about stage change or even more effective functioning (though it may), and is vulnerable to distortion by beliefs already held. What is added is the notion that the process is one of movement from the periphery to the centre. (Further, more esoteric refinements of the process are described but these will be left for the reader to explore himself.)

In the light of Piaget's use of the notion in other contexts we can now turn to his assertion that theoretical morality is the conscious realization of practical morality. The fact that it is a reconstruction and that there is a time lag between the two still apply. But plainly what is here being realized is distinctively different from a general structure of intellectual functioning or a skilled action or mental operation. In the moral sphere we are concerned with the realization not of logic but of reasons for acting in relation to others, not with particular actions but with rules which inform the decision to act, and not with the experience of success and failure as such but with the experience of obligation and value.

Piaget does not spell out in any detail what he means by practical morality. He talks of the child's 'true thought' which in contrast to his verbal beliefs 'lies much deeper, somewhere below the level of formulation.' Thus it is cognitive and mainly unconscious. And of course it is in some sense structured for it has a certain coherence and stability over time. The nature of the child's practical morality is, for Piaget, a function of the nature of his dominant personal relationships insofar as he assimilates them. This structured and mainly unconscious practical morality, or 'true thought', must embody the child's experience of relationship insofar as it relates to morality. Its conscious realization is therefore to a considerable extent the realization of relationship.

The conscious realization of practical morality is inevitably more vulnerable to distortion and inhibition than is the same process in the other areas described. Central to human interaction is the exchange of thought. The child's theoretical morality is influenced by the moral teaching he receives from adults, and indeed he is likely throughout his life to be under pressure to share the theoretical morality of the groups to which he belongs. Expressing an immoral thought can itself become a quasi-immoral act. The importation of beliefs foreign to his practical morality with the consequent suppression of elements true to it will reduce the degree of isomorphism between the two. Nevertheless we may suppose that the continuing experience of salient relationships will set limits to this distortion.

There are some obvious implications of Piaget's law of conscious realization in moral development. First, as just mentioned, theoretical morality is unlikely ever to be more than partially isomorphic with practical morality. 'For the child's moral realism is certainly far more systematic on the plane of theory than on that of action, so that we would seem to be dealing here with something in the nature of a new and different phenomenon.' Second, it follows that accounts of moral development based on theoretical morality will be systematically misleading as indices of practical moral development, though they will not be wholly misleading. Third, it is difficult to see how theoretical morality can exercise an influence on practical morality, though since conscious realization does have consequences for functioning in other contexts the issue must remain open. Fourth, education in theoretical morality can only be a living and relevant experience for the child if it enables him to consciously realize his practical morality. Fifth, if education in theoretical morality takes the child beyond the level of his practical morality it will become increasingly divorced from obligation.

This last point is important. Piaget's account of intellectual development would imply a natural developmental tendency to divorce practical and theoretical morality, especially at the formal operational level. It is true that the evidence indicates that a relatively small proportion of people become firmly established at the formal stage. But formal operational thinking is characterized by an awareness, even a preoccupation, with the possible and the hypothetical, the abstract and the general. A diet of discussion of hypothetical and general moral issues may be expected to attract students at this level but will also strengthen the dissociation between practical and theoretical morality.

It follows that if any moral education intervention is to bite, especially for the intellectually mature student, it must occur when he is at his own moral coalface, in effect at situation 2 and perhaps 3 above. Moreover its goal must be to counter cognitive suppression and aid the fullest possible articulation of the situation and its moral implications.

Moral Obligation and Thinking

The feature which distinguishes practical morality (situations 1 and 2) from theoretical is that at the practical level thinking and obligation (what I must do) are indissolubly wedded. Empirically this means studying obligation and thinking as one phenomenon, as obligation-charged thinking or as cognitively structured obligation. This has barely begun. Our present concern, however, is theoretical, and with Piaget's speculations in particular.

He distinguishes four factors which contribute to practical moral development.

The first is intellectual stage, and perhaps especially the shift from egocentric to decentred thinking. Little need be said about it here. It determines the nature and limitations of the way the subject construes his practical social situations and subsequently his conscious realization of his actions in them.

The second is habit. Piaget deals with this under the label of the 'motor rule', which precedes understanding of rules proper, and which does not itself constitute obligation. The function of habit in moral development has been neglected. The sensori-motor habits of which Piaget speaks can be regarded as a special case of more general regularities in the physical and social world of the individual. Indeed for the young child perception of social regularity in others and the development of habits of social interaction in himself is likely to be more salient in his experiences than either his perception of physical regularity or his awareness of his own motor habits. It is interesting that in his study of the perception of physical regularity, Piaget found that the young child's interpretations were quasi-moral, quasi-causal, as if the distinction between moral and causal had not yet differentiated.

We may speculate that as this differentiation progressively occurs, so the young child *experiences* the regularities of social interactions as obligatory and later consciously realizes them in terms of 'I must' or 'I ought'. It is as if he says 'because everyone acts towards others in this kind of way, therefore they, and I, ought to'—a formulation which at least in implicit form appears sometimes to linger on into adulthood.

But this still leaves unexplained why the child does not just become a social psychologist, understanding social regularities in causal rather than moral terms. Piaget's answer lies in the fact that the child does not only observe and participate in social regularities, but for him these regularities occur within significant personal relationships. It is the nature of these relationships which determines the nature of his experience of obligation and the way he cognitively structures it, first in his practical and later in his theoretical morality.

Piaget distinguishes two kinds of relationship, one of heteronomy, unilateral respect and constraint, and the other of autonomy, mutual respect and cooperation. He does little to spell out in detail the meaning of these concepts. But he clearly recognized that they are idealized abstractions, and that neither is found in its pure form. A relationship is by definition a continuing bond within which a rhythm is established encompassing a variety of kinds of interaction. In conceiving relationships along a single dimension we are necessarily referring to general tendencies and excluding from consideration many other ways in which they might differ.

The first kind of relationship experienced by the child is one of unilateral respect for adults in particular but also older childern. This is inevitable given the huge asymmetry of the two parties in skill, understanding, and power.

It is unclear whether Piaget regarded such relationships as a necessary condition for the emergence of obligation (as Durkheim did) but he conceded its inevitability and acknowledged that it is this kind of relationship which determines the child's first experience of obligation and which subsequently determined his first consciously realized theoretical morality. It is the adult who imposes regularity on the child and formulates prescriptive rules for him. The obligation the child feels is not to the rule as such but to its origin. His feeling of obligation to keep the rule, whether he does or not, derives from the respect he feels for the adult. And this respect, Piaget says, is compounded of quasi-physical fear and love.

An important, indeed crucial, question is which of the two elements, fear and love, is the more significant for the sense of obligation. It may be assumed that both are always present; for the most loving adult caretakers can hardly avoid being the cause of fear, and however unloving the adult may be the evidence suggests that young children will always form some measure of attachment to them. Piaget is silent on this, though it is consistent with his account of relationships of mutual respect to suppose that affection is the more relevant factor. Evidence from studies of delinquents and children raised in institutions might be adduced in support. To take these speculations further we might hazard the guess that fear alerts the child to the causal mechanisms in human relationships and love generates obligation. Perhaps in these early stages love is obligation.

If it is the case that love or affection is the primary root of the sense of obligation, then it raises a further intriguing issue. For the practical morality of the young child in whom obligation is strong would, if truly realized at the conscious level, be formulated in some such way as 'I ought to act like this because I love my parents and they say I should.' Yet studies of the first consciously realized theoretical moralities of children seldom involve love as a reason for moral prescription, whereas fear-motivated reasoning (this is wrong because you are punished for it) is much more common. This may reflect the greater difficulty for the child (and boys in particular?) in consciously realizing the significance of his attachment (in Piaget's language it is most central and furthest from the periphery), or, as Piaget hints, it may reflect the difference between the situation of personal involvement in practical morality and the relatively impersonal and generalized nature of theoretical morality. As Piaget says, when the child 'simply has stories told to him, he will be led to make judgments devoid of pity and lacking in psychological insight, testifying therefore to a more or less systematic moral realism, whereas in real life he would undoubtedly sympathize with those whom from after he regards as the greatest sinners.' We must remember, too, that his theoretical morality will be much influenced by what adults say.

In relationships of unilateral respect, then, obligation takes the form of obedience to what is recognized as authority and moral rules are maintained because their source is this authority, and at the same time moral thinking has about it the features that Piaget calls moral realism. For Freud and Durkheim, unilateral respect relationships are the only source of moral obligation and thinking. In Freud's theory the objects of unilateral respect are internalized through the processes of identification with the aggressor and anaclitic identification with the consequent formation of the conscience and ego-ideal components of the super-ego. Durkheim, on the other hand, sees moral obligation as dependent throughout life upon a continuing relationship of unilateral respect to an external authority. This authority begins as the parents, extends to other adults, and then to impersonal social authorities, and finally either to God or to the concept of society as some kind of superordinate being superior to its individual members, and commanding their allegiance.

The difficulties with Freud's account are, first, that if we take it seriously we become embroiled in his unconvincing metatheory of the economics of aggressive energy turned inwards in countercathexis, and the cathexis of libidinal energy, and second, he allows little room for development after the age of five. Piaget has mounted his own critique of Durkheim and it need not be rehearsed here. His main point is that Durkheim (and we might add Freud) failed to see the great importance for moral experience of relationship very different from those of unilateral respect. 'The fundamental difficulty of Durkheimism seems to us to be the illegitimate identification of constraint and cooperation,' and 'he actually comes to identify the two most antithetical conceptions of obligation— the heteronomous submission of reason to the "higher authority" and the necessity residing within reason herself.' If the individual submits to an external authority as the source of morality so that moral obligation is an expression of allegiance to that authority, then either he must abjure autonomous reasoning in this area, or if he engages in it, risks the separation of his moral thinking from obligation.

Piaget allows that many people may remain in the morality of unilateral respect and constraint for the whole of their lives, though it is not clear whether he was referring to practical or to theoretical morality or both. At the adult level, relationships of unilateral respect may be embodied in the social system through some elaborate hierarchical role structure. The more this is so the more we would expect people living in such a society to manifest, at least at the theoretical level but also to some extent the practical level, the corresponding morality. But as Piaget says, whether in the history of societies or in the development of the child, relationships of unilateral respect are inherently unstable. The child grows up, and however hierarchical society may be, relationships of mutual respect will spontaneously occur among both child and adults. These form the basis for the realization that authorities are as fallibly human as everyone else. 'The unilateral respect belonging to constraint is not a stable system, and the equilibrium towards which it tends is no other than mutual respect.'

In turning now to consider relationships of mutual respect it is important to remember that Piaget is idealizing the conception; actual relationships approach more or less closely to it. Moreover he is concerned only with the features of such relationships that relate to morality.

Mutual respect relationships are symmetrical, same-level relationships between equals who relate to each other in a state of equilibrium. Within the continuing rhythmn of exchange within the relationship each is as much as the other a leader, teacher, authority, and source of opinion, judgment, and pre-scription. Piaget claims that such relations can exist from an early age, and even suggests that adults can enter into them with young children. But it is plain that this can only be true in a very limited and attenuated sense for as Piaget elaborates the nature of these relationships, it becomes plain that to sustain them demands a high measure of social and intellectual maturity. Moreover we need to distinguish, though Piaget does not, except tangentially, between mutual respect relations and the phenomena of groups. Clearly many of the processes generated within groups, such as role differentiation, conformity to norms, deindividuation and diffusion of responsibility, and dependence upon the group as such, are antithetical to the full emergence of mutual respect relations; though groups may nurture such relationships within them in a less developed form. It seems that mutual respect relationships are only likely to be fully functional 'when two or three are gathered together'. 'Either respect is directed to the group and results from the pressure exercised by the group upon the individual or else it is directed to individuals and is the outcome of relations of individuals amongst themselves.'

The mutual respect relationship 'implies personalities that are both conscious of themselves and able to submit their point of view to the laws of reciprocity and universality.' The subject is both aware of himself as separate and individual, and also as related. There is a kind of equilibrium between the two; and obviously the awareness of both can progressively deepen. Because each sees the other as having equal status and value, each can reason autonomously, and each affirms and supports that autonomy in the other. Neither subject can, or tries to, impose solutions to problems; instead each cooperates with the other to find *the* solutions. 'The great difference between constraint and cooperation or between unilateral respect and mutual respect, is that the first imposes beliefs or rules that are ready made and to be accepted *en bloc*, while the second only suggests a method—a method of verification and reciprocal control in the intellectual field, of justification and discussion in the domain of morals.' Moral rules are both inherent in the structure of mutual respect relationships and also their functional outcome. 'So-called moral rules can, generally speaking, be divided into constituted rules dependent upon mutual consent, and constitutive rules or functional principles which render cooperation and reciprocity possible.' To enlarge on what Piaget says, we may suppose that when the subject initially enters into and practises cooperative relationships the constitutive rules or fundamental principles that make such cooperation possible are unconscious. One of the functions of such relationships is, however, to create constituted rules by mutual consent. As problems arise in this process, so the subject is stimulated into a conscious realization of the constitutive principles which make the relationship possible.

We can take two illustrations of this from Piaget. Truth-telling is, so to speak, an emergent property of mutual respect relationships, one of its constitutive rules. 'One must have felt a real desire to exchange thoughts with others in order to discover all that a lie can involve.' In the subject's consciousness at the level of practical morality we might say that telling the truth is self-evidently what one ought to do. Understanding why one should tell the truth, and under what conditions, involves the conscious realization of the whole fabric of constitutive rules that necessarily sustain such relationships. The second emergent property of mutual respect relationships is a sense of fairness and justice that transcends authority. For the child dominated by unilateral respect, 'Justice is identified with formulated rules—as it is in the opinion of a great many adults, of all, namely, who have not succeeded in setting autonomy of conscience above social prejudice and the written law.' Indeed Piaget would argue that what we ordinarily understand by a sense of justice is ultimately based on a sense of the equal value of persons, and can only evolve through relations of mutual respect, at first at the practical, and later at the theoretical, levels.

As far as obligation is concerned it depends upon the nature of the respect which, in these relationships, is mutual. Piaget does say in passing that respect in this context is probably a very different phenomenon from respect in unilateral relationships, but he does not explore the point. It is, one may presume, initially tied up with the subject's investment in such relationships, and presumably they may be characterized by the increased salience of affection over fear. At the affectional level there is a kind of equilibrium between approach and avoidance. 'The play of sympathy and antipathy is a sufficient cause for practical reason to become conscious of reciprocity.' The point is, however, that whatever the forces which sustain the relationship and keep it alive, within it the perception, however intuitive, that, for example, telling the truth is self-evidently important and desirable, is itself charged with a sense of moral obligation.

Concluding Remarks

Practical morality, or moral judgment charged with obligation, is, then, an emergent property of the child's relationships with others. There is, however, a certain confusion in Piaget's account of the relationships which make this possible. He tends to use the same terms, such as obligation, respect, obedience, and duty, for both the child's conformity to adult prescription within unilateral respect relatedness, and for the autonomous commitment of the child to his own moral prescriptions within mutual respect relatedness. Yet he is emphatic that these two kinds of relationship are so qualitatively different as to be incompatible in their consequences for the child. Moreover, in regard to two fundamental aspects of morality, truthfulness, and fairness, he explicitly denies that adult prescription has any significant influence. The confusion seems to stem from the fact that, though he recognizes that these relationships can never exist in their idealized forms, he nevertheless tends to talk about them as if they did.

To some extent the confusion can be removed if we retain the concepts of relationship in their idealized forms and understand that their application to actual relationships must always be partial. The essence of the unilateral component in a relationship is the assertion of power and control by one party over the other through rewards and punishments. Compliance by the other is therefore motivated by fear of punishment or the desire for approval. To act from either of these motives is not to act out of moral obligation. It follows that the stronger the unilateral repect component the less the relationship will generate moral obligation in the child, though of course it may induce behavioural conformity. This does not mean that parent-child relationships do not foster moral obligation in the child but that they only do so to the extent to which the mutual respect component is present. Piaget strongly encourages parents to develop the mutual respect component in their relationships with their children as much as they can.

The mutual respect component is held to be the optimal condition for the development of the child's personality, self esteem, and reasoning capacity. It is therefore experienced by the child as good, though not, initially, consciously recognized as such. The child's obligation to maintain the constitutive rules of such relationships is a function of this experience.

It has to be said again that Piaget's speculations represent at best a tentative prolegomena to a theory of practical morality. It nevertheless enables us to see Kohlberg's stages in a somewhat different light. Instead of these stages being taken as indicative of cognitive structures which determine moral decisions they can be understood as steps in the progressive conscious realization of a practical morality the child has been living all along. Kohlberg's stage five might be defined as the final conscious realization and generalization of the constitutive rules of those mutual respect relationships which were first experienced in early childhood.

References

Beth, E. W., and Piaget, J. (1966). In D. Reidel (Ed.), *Mathematical Epistemology and Psychology*, Dordrecht, Holland.
Piaget, J. (1932). *The Moral Judgment of the Child*, Routledge and Kegan Paul, London.
Piaget, J. (1976). *The Grasp of Consciousness*, Routledge and Kegan Paul, London.

Morality in the Making
Edited by H. Weinreich-Haste and D. Locke
© 1983, John Wiley & Sons, Ltd.

CHAPTER 9

Theory and Practice in Thought and Action

Don Locke

It must seem surprising to many that so much contemporary moral research is concerned with judgment and reasoning rather than with moral conduct, given the obvious and familiar difference between what a person may say, or even think, he ought to do and what he actually does. Of course it is only natural that cognitive developmentalists, in particular, will focus on moral thinking, just as behaviourists, in the widest sense, can be expected to concentrate on moral behaviour. There are, moreover, good reasons why the empirical researcher should prefer to deal with the former. It is not just, as Piaget points out, that 'you cannot make a child act in a laboratory in order to dissect his moral conduct' (1932, p. 108), or as Kohlberg repeatedly insists, that moral action cannot be defined in terms of behaviour but has to take account of the agent's reasons as well. It is also because it is possible to identify moral judgments and reasons neutrally, without taking a stand on questions of substantive morality, by the key role played by such words as 'good', 'bad', 'right', 'wrong', and 'ought' which the context will indicate as having a specifically moral force, whereas identifying conduct, either inside or outside the laboratory, as moral or immoral seems to presuppose some personal decision from the researcher as to which things are right and which wrong. Indeed I have argued above (Chapter 6) that this problem can be avoided only, once again, by taking accounts of reasons.

Yet obviously any adequate account of moral development must include both areas, and elucidate the interaction between the two. And it is here that the apparent gap between thought and action becomes a major problem: the problem of whether, how far, and why a person's moral opinions, especially those expressed about situations which are so far wholly hypothetical, will relate to his actual conduct. There are, moreover, two separate issues here, each discussed in the two preceding chapters. Because the first is more likely to present itself to a philosopher and the second to a psychologist, it is tempting to call them the philosophers' problem and the psychologists' problem, or, more personally, Straughan's problem and Wright's problem, or even Kohlberg's problem and Piaget's problem, though whereas one is a problem *for* Kohlberg, the other—also, as it happens, a problem for Kohlberg—is rather a problem raised *by* Piaget. But instead, to indicate both the connection and the difference between the two, I shall label them the Thought/Action problem and the Action/Thought problem. In this paper I want to explore both issues further in the light of their discussion by Straughan and Wright, to assess their interrelation and their implications for the study of moral development.

The Thought/Action Problem

When a philosopher approaches the problem of thought and action he is likely to operate, explicitly or implicitly, with some such model as this. On the one hand we have the moral agent, with some fairly explicit and coherent set of moral beliefs, and on the other the concrete situation which calls for some specific action on his part. He applies his beliefs to the situation and so arrives at a decision as to what, in these circumstances he ought or ought not do. But this decision, so far, is still only a judgment, albeit a concrete, practical one. The question then arises whether or not he will act on that judgment, whether or not he will do as he believes that he ought. And so far this seems an entirely open question: it seems perfectly possible for the agent to recognize that morality, even his own morality, requires him to act in a certain way in the particular situation, and yet not act in that way, because it happens not to be to his personal advantage, because he does not want to do it, or simply because he cannot be bothered.

Thus arises the traditional philosophical problem of 'weakness of will', the failure to translate thought into action. But as Straughan points out, the problem is also psychological: if, as is all too evident, moral thinking does not lead directly or inevitably to moral action, then we need to examine those other factors—a sense of duty, obligation, or conscience, 'ego strength', or whatever they may be—which combine to determine how the individual will actually behave. And even if it is shown empirically that there is, for example, a connection between a person's stage of moral reasoning, i.e. the form rather than the content of his moral judgments, and the likelihood of his acting as he believes he ought, this is something which itself demands a theoretical explanation.

However this philosophical picture is grossly over-simplified. For a start the developmental psychologist will scarcely even recognize it. It can hardly apply to children, who are still in the process of evolving not only their moral beliefs but their understanding of what morality is in the first place—and are we not all children here, to some extent? Moreover, as the philosophers themselves have recognized, the moral situations we confront may also shape and alter our moral convictions. But in any case moral thought and moral action cannot be separated as cleanly as this picture suggests. The prescriptivity of moral judgments consists precisely in the fact that they are, and are recognized as being, action-guiding, so that to believe that you ought to do something is ipso facto to recognize that you have good—though perhaps not overriding—reason to act in that way. Hence the fact that moral thought leads to action, ceteris paribus, is not something that calls for special explanation; it follows simply from the fact that it is *moral* thought.

Indeed at the extreme Hare believes that it is of the essence of moral judgment that it actually determines our actions, provided they are actions we are capable of. So the fact that someone fails to act in a way that he could have is itself sufficient to demonstrate that he did not really believe that he ought to do it. A more moderate position might allow that someone could fail to do as he genuinely and sincerely believed that he ought if, while he recognized that he had good reason to act in that way, there nevertheless were for him at that time other, stronger reasons for not doing it. This is the 'moderate internalism' for which Straughan argues above. As it stands, however, this formulation, like Straughan's, seems tautological, or at least unfalsifiable: any course of action will be compatible with believing that you ought to do x; if you do y instead that simply means that you had stronger reasons for doing y. The problem is to state this moderate internalism, without reducing it to the triviality that people will do one thing unless they want to do something else more.

An answer might be found by returning to Straughan's distinction between justification and motivation. If I believe that a certain course of action is morally correct in the circumstances then, it follows of necessity, I regard that course of action as justified. But does it follow that I will be motivated to act in that way? The extreme externalist says not: believing it right is one thing; wanting to do it is quite another. The extreme internalist disagrees: if you do not actually do it, that shows that you did not consider the action to be fully justified after all. The moderate internalist attempts to moderate: insofar as you do regard the action as justified then to that extent you will be motivated towards doing it; but there may be other reasons and wants to be taken into account, and these may override both the motivation and the justification.

However this belief that our behaviour is justified can be revealed in other ways than by the behaviour itself. This is the mistake of the extreme internalist: to think that behaviour is the only test of our beliefs. But if someone does do something which we regard as unjustified, or fails to do something which he believes was justified, then we might expect some degree of reproach or remorse, guilt or shame. If none of these occur either, then we might well conclude that he does not really believe that he ought to have done something else instead. Thus moderate internalism might be stated as the doctrine that if you believe you ought to do something, then to that extent you will be motivated to do it, and hence will do it other things—and in particular other wants—being equal. But if you do not do it, then to that extent you will regard your action as criticizable, and yourself as at fault.

Of course this philosophical account leaves the psychological questions quite open. In particular the question of whether a specific individual will or will not do as he believes that he ought will depend not only on his other wants, but also on the motivating force of such factors as guilt and shame, integrity and self-respect. This is what I am calling the Thought/Action problem: the problem at once philosophical and psychological, of explicating the relationship between what a person says he ought to do, or even what he thinks he ought to do, and what he actually does. Without some such explication the relation between moral judgment, as investigated by the cognitive developmentalists, and moral conduct, as investigated by the more behaviouristically-minded, remains entirely problematic.

It has, however, been argued that there can be no such problem:

'In actuality, there can never be a split between judgment and conduct or between thought and action. These are inseparable activities, since every human social inter-action by necessity involves both judgment and conduct, both thought and action. It is not possible to imagine, for example, a person engaging in a social action without some corollary mental process which we would call "thought".'

(Damon, 1977, p. 17)

Instead, Damon argues, the question at issue is 'the connection between theoretical-hypothetical knowledge on the one hand and active real-life knowledge on the other' (p. 19). But this argument reveals a serious misunderstanding of the problem, which in turn affects Damon's research programme. First of all it is not the case that social interactions necessarily involve thought or judgment. It might perhaps be argued that intentional action must, by definition, involve thought in some sense, since intending is itself a form of thinking— though even this is not as obvious as it seems, since it is clearly possible to perform familiar actions intentionally, like opening a closed door or turning on a light in a dark room, without any explicit or conscious thought or judgment. But social interactions can also be unintentional, even accidental, and can certainly occur without the agent being aware of what he is doing: to take a homely example, parents constantly shape and control their children's behaviour, and even answer their questions with an absent-minded 'yes', 'no', or 'maybe', without knowing they are doing so. Indeed sociology and social psychology are often primarily concerned precisely with such 'unconscious' actions.

But this is not the major point at issue. Even if it were impossible to act without thinking, it is possible to make many different, conflicting judgments about the action in hand. What concerns us here is not what the agent thinks he is doing, but what he thinks he ought to be doing, and clearly the two may differ. Accordingly Damon's conception of 'real-life (or practical) knowledge' as 'an active kind of judgment that is manifested both in a person's real-life reasoning and in his real-life conduct' (p. 101), like Wright's notion of practical morality, fails to take account of the fact that what a person preaches, even for the concrete situation in which he finds himself, may not be what he practises. If, after his subjects had arrived at an agreed decision as to how their sweets should be shared out, Damon had then got each child to carry out a division without the supervision of the others, he would not only have had incontrovertible evidence of the gap between moral thought and action, but also have been able to illuminate the relationship between this gap and the child's level of justice reasoning. But the opportunity was missed, because Damon perversely identifies 'moral conduct' with the child's *decision* as to how the sweets ought to be shared!

This mean, however, that instead of one gap between thought and action, we now have two: first the gap between theoretical-hypothetical moral reasoning (Wright's 'theoretical morality') and active real-life moral reasoning (Wright's 'practical morality'); and second the gap between this practical morality and actual practice. And this in turn means that there are particular difficulties for the Kohlbergian approach to moral development, insofar as the dilemmas which he uses are wholly hypothetical ones. It is extremely unlikely that many respondents have ever been, or will ever be, in a position even analogous to that of Heinz for example. (It would be of great interest, especially for the Action/ Thought problem, to know whether there are systematic differences between performance on the Heinz dilemma and performance on those other hypothetical dilemmas utilized by Kohlberg, which connect more directly with the subject's own experience, e.g. the breaking of promises. But here, as with so much one wants to know, the data are not available.) It is likely, therefore, that the subject's responses will be more a matter of what he thinks he ought to say than authentic moral beliefs, and his further explanations will be more in the nature of rationalizations. True, a study even of this, no matter how removed from actual practice, may tell us much about the child's level of moral understanding. But it will tell us little about his moral behaviour.

The Action/Thought Problem

It is now well recognized, thanks to Piaget, that to a quite remarkable extent a child's ability to perform even quite complex and sophisticated actions precedes its conscious understanding of what it is doing and how. If the data contained in *The Grasp of Consciousness* (1976), for example, fail to astonish us, it is only because Piaget's earlier work has made us familiar with the point. The psychologist, therefore, is likely to approach the relation between thought and action from the other end: the question is not how thought gets translated into action, but how action gets taken up into thought. For Piaget, however, it is not simply that there tends to be a time-lag between the child's acquisition of some skill and its 'cognizance' of what it is doing;[1] it is only because the child is first

---

[1] In *The Grasp of Consciousness* Piaget refers separately to consciousness, cognizance, conceptualization, and understanding, without ever explaining their connections. Cognizance, it seems, is a form of conceptualization, whereas understanding is possible without either (the so-called 'cognitive unconscious'?). But whether conceptualization is possible without cognizance, whether cognizance simply is conceptualized understanding, and whether conceptualized understanding is identical with conscious understanding, is not made clear.

able to do something at the level of action that it is then able to conceptualize and become conscious of it. 'The child's verbal thinking consists of a progressive coming into consciousness, or conscious realization of schemas that have been built up by action' (1932, p. 112); cognizance must come after active practice, because it is the latter which makes the former possible. This, I take it, is the Law of Conscious Realization.

Piaget himself has been primarily concerned with the child's dawning realization of what it is doing and how. Only in *The Moral Judgment of the Child* does he address himself to the question, more important for our purposes, of *why*, of what its reasons and motivations might be. But here too, apparently, the Law of Conscious Realization should apply: the child will act for reasons before it can become conscious of those reasons as reasons. Thus a child may react to its parents' approval and disapproval, for example, long before it is aware of them as approval or disapproval, and hence before it can react to them as such. At a more sophisticated level it has been shown that people's choice of behaviour will gradually adjust to the outcome probabilities of a situation, even though the vast majority are not only unable to state the relevant probability rules, but frequently entertain quite erroneous hypotheses (Goodnow and Postman, 1955). And Piaget himself gives several examples of how the child's 'theoretical reflections' may be 'a year or two behind his life reactions, that is to say, his effective moral feelings' (1932, p. 273, cf. pp. 78–9, 113, 115).

However the Law of Conscious Realization does not simply assert a time-lag between practice and reflection; it also attempts to explain this time-lag by asserting that motivational considerations, for example, can be utilized in conscious reflection only after they have been utilized in actual practice. Thus the common picture of the psychopath as someone who cares nothing for the needs and feelings of others and so ignores them in his behaviour, actually has it back to front. Instead it will be because his behaviour take no account of the needs and feelings of others that the psychopath is unable to recognize, at a conscious level, that these provide reasons for action. More generally, morality can enter our thought only after it has already entered our actions.

Now this, as Wright points out, has important consequences for the study of moral development. There is first his point that if conscious reflection must inevitably lag behind actual practice, verbal moral reasoning will be systematically inaccurate as a measure of practical moral development. But secondly, and more importantly, any attempt to understand, or influence, moral development via conscious moral reasoning must be to start at the wrong end. Kohlberg and his associates have suggested, for example, that it is cognitive conflict, and the attainment of an equilibrium at a higher stage of reasoning, which accounts for the movement from one stage to another. But if the Law of Conscious Realization holds true here, then any such cognitive conflict must occur first at the level of action, at a pre-conscious level, before it can be taken up into conscious reflection by the process of conscious realization. Any attempt to affect moral reasoning by the discussion of wholly hypothetical dilemmas will therefore be misguided; patterns of thought evolved in the course of classroom discussion cannot be incorporated into the subject's moral understanding unless and until he has already utilized them in his own conduct. Which means that to the extent that such programmes of moral education do seem to have some effect they must impinge on the subject's practical concerns after all—or, alternatively, the Law of Conscious Realization is not entirely valid, a point to which we shall return.

None of these problems, however, amounts to what I have dubbed the Action/Thought problem, which, as I understand it, is the problem of how action gives rise to moral thought specifically. Curiously Piaget himself is not so much concerned with the conscious realization of those factors which have been shaping the child's conduct pre-consciously as with the passage from 'effective moral thought . . . which leads him to form such moral judgments as will guide him in each particular case as it comes his way and enable him to evaluate other people's actions when these concern him more or less directly' to the 'theoretical or verbal moral thought' which 'appears whenever the child is called upon to judge other people's actions that do not interest him directly or to give voice to general principles regarding his own conduct independently of his actual deeds' (1932, p. 171), i.e. from Wright's 'practical morality' to his 'theoretical morality'. Like Damon, and like Wright, Piaget seems not to distinguish practical morality in this sense from actual practice. This is surprising because this practical morality, of course, already operates at a conscious level: if the Law of Conscious Realization is correct practical morality must itself be the conscious realization of factors which motivated the agent before he became consciously aware of them as such.

We seem, therefore, to be dealing with a three-stage hierarchy, similar to that discussed in the final chapter of *The Grasp of Consciousness*. Here Piaget distinguishes first the material action without conceptualization, then the conceptualization or cognizance of that action, and finally a 'reflected abstraction' or theorizing about that action. Similarly in the moral domain we seem to have first the behaviour itself and its motivation, then the conscious realization of that motivation, and finally, through a second-order conscious realization, theorizing about that motivation and its application to unfamiliar or wholly hypothetical situations.

Now I do not myself think that the step from concrete moral judgments to moral theorizing, from practical to theoretical morality, is best illuminated by talk of a second-order conscious realization—the process seems altogether different—but clearly the important step is the prior one from active practice to practical morality, for it is there that moral conceptions will first occur. Now it may seem that this is the problem to which Piaget addresses himself in the first chapter of the *Moral Judgment of the Child*, concerning the rules of the game of marbles. But it too is concerned with a step analogous to that between practical and theoretical morality, rather than the step from practice to an initial conscious realization. Piaget does detail a developmental progression in both the child's practice or application of rules and in its consciousness of them, the former consisting, roughly, in a gradual recognition and codification of the rules which apply, the latter in a movement from heteronomy to autonomy, from regarding the rules as imposed from outside and therefore unalterable, to regarding them as dependent on mutual consent and accordingly alterable by consent. But first it is hard to see how these two progressions can be related by the Law of Conscious Realization since, with their quite different contents, the one cannot follow simply in the steps of the other. And secondly, what Piaget terms the child's consciousness of rules clearly corresponds to theoretical morality (it represents the child's theorizing about those rules which it has consciously recognized) while what he terms the practice or application of rules corresponds to practical morality (it represents the child's developing awareness of what rules there are). The prior step, from the child's obeying rules in its play to its conscious recognition of those rules, is left largely undiscussed, though it is here, most of all, that you would expect the Law of Conscious Realization to apply. This, it seems to me, is the major missing link in Piaget's theoretical speculations, the failure to discuss how distinctively moral conceptions enter consciousness in the first place.

There is, moreover, a major problem here, which has never received the attention it deserves, from either psychologists or philosophers. It is, in one form, the problem raised but avoided in Chapter 6, the problem of defining moral reasons specifically. For practical morality is not merely the conscious realization of factors which already motivate behaviour; it also involves according those factors a specifically moral force and status. That is, they must be recognized not merely as reasons for action, but as reasons why one ought to act, or is entitled to act, in that way. At whatever primitive level the child must be capable of some such distinction, between the moral and the non-moral, between obligation in the widest sense and mere inclination, if it is to be said to have a practical morality, effective or concrete moral thought, at all. But how, exactly, do these conceptions arise, where do they come from? To be sure Piaget gives us some useful pointers, in his discussions of adult constraint and mutual cooperation. But the details are not worked out, Piaget being more concerned to argue for the psychological and moral superiority of cooperation over constraint than to explain how such considerations may give rise to our first moral conceptions, our first conceptions of morality. And it is at least as plausible to suggest that distinctively moral notions must come from outside, from the teachings of others, and especially from the teaching of such moral terms as 'good', 'right', and 'ought', as to insist that they must be developed by the child for itself, by reflecting on its own practice, as the Law of Conscious Realization implies.

This, then, is the Action/Thought problem: the problem of how the child can evolve, from its own practical experience, distinctively moral notions—not necessarily the moral notions of the philosopher, or even those of the psychologists, but notions which have, for it, the force of ought and ought not, right and wrong. And this is a problem which cannot be solved if, like Piaget and Kohlberg, we start from moral judgment rather than from moral conduct.

The Problems Combined

Thus we have two problems for the study of moral development in general through the study of moral reasoning in particular. One is the question of how moral thought gets translated into action, the other the question of how action gets transformed into moral thought. But to the extent that these problems work, as it were, in opposite directions it may seem that they must cancel each other out, that the one will provide the solution to the other. In particular, if Piaget's Law of Conscious Realization is correct it will seem that what I have termed the Thought/Action problem cannot arise. For it rests on the assumption that moral reasoning can get ahead of moral behaviour, that our deeds can lag behind our beliefs. And that is precisely what the Law of Conscious Realization denies.

Yet it can hardly be denied that the Thought/Action problem exists: it is too familiar a phenomenon of everyday moral experience for that. As Cooper (quoted by Straughan, p. 129 above) says, 'this gappiness is an essential feature of the moral life': it is precisely because we do not always do what is right that we have a need for moral principles and moral judgments; as Kant says, a being who would invariably do his duty would have no use for the notion of 'ought'. So if the Law of Conscious Realization implies that there is no such gap between thought and action, it must itself be suspect. We must look more closely at Piaget's 'Law'.

The empirical evidence to date is scrappy and inconclusive and, like Piaget himself, concentrates on the connection between practical and theoretical morality, rather than the more crucial connection between practical morality and actual practice. Piaget's own evidence is barely even anecdotal, and is directly challenged by the finding of Havinghurst and Neugarten (cited in Hoffman, 1970) that almost three-quarters of Navajo children believed that the rules of white American games could be altered at will, while only 1 in 28 believed this of their own Navajo games. Havinghurst and Neugarten suggest that this is because they learn the white games by formal instruction, and see them modified to suit local conditions, while their own games are not taught but observed and absorbed until they feel able to join in, and moreover have important links with Navajo culture and religion. But whatever the explanation, this is a clear example of a heteronomous orientation towards those games of which they have most practical experiences, and an autonomous orientation towards those of which they have less, and not the other way round as Piaget's theory would imply.

However, studies using Kohlberg's six stages of moral reasoning present a more complex picture. When Haan (1975) assessed student's level of reasoning both on the Kohlberg hypothetical dilemmas and on the issue of the Berkeley

Free Speech Movement sit-in, in which those students had been actively involved, she found that 46% reasoned at higher levels on the latter 'real-life' issue, 34% reasoned at the same level, and only 20% reasoned at a lower level—though curiously, those reasoning at a higher level about the sit-in were concentrated at Kohlberg's Stages 2 and 3, where this was the dominant trend, and the higher the stage the greater the tendency to reason at lower levels for the real-life situation! A similar tendency, for higher-stage reasoners to reason at lower levels as regards real-life situation while lower-stage reasoners reasoned at higher levels, is also reported by Arndt (1976), though in this case the more general tendency was the opposite of Haan's, towards lower-level reasoning on the real-life issue. Haan also cites a finding by Blatt that black adolescents used lower stages in reasoning about society than in reasoning about interpersonal relations, which seems to support Piaget, as well as a finding by Kohlberg that prisoners used lower stages in their reasoning about prisons, which seems to point in the opposite direction—though this lower-level reasoning may simply reflect a realistic appraisal of the situation (and the institution) in which the prisoners found themselves!

Results very similar to Haan's are also reported by Gilligan and Belenky (1980): of 21 women making abortion decisions, 9 reasoned at a higher level on their own real-life problem, 7 reasoned at the same level, and only 4 at a lower level. Interestingly, both groups who showed a disparity between real-life and hypothetical reasoning proved much more likely to have moved to a higher level of hypothetical reasoning a year later, and another study by Gilligan and Murphy (1979) provides useful evidence of the crucial role of real-life problems in promoting changes in moral thinking.

So far the general trend of the Kohlbergian evidence is to support Piaget, though the presence of even a handful of exceptions would be enough to show that the Law of Conscious Realization is not strictly a law, but at best a general tendency. Moreover Damon (1977), like Arndt, reports the opposite tendency. In a study of children's level of reasoning about positive justice in both hypothetical and real-life situations, 50% reasoned at the same level in both cases, 27% were scored one level higher in the hypothetical situation, 10% at two levels higher, while only 13% were scored higher, and by only one level, in the real-life situation. Damon attempts to explain this by the greater element of self-interest in his real-life situation, which involved children sharing sweets, than in the cases studied by Piaget. But however it is explained, it provides a clear instance of theoretical morality being in advance of practical morality. A second study, dealing with the child's understanding of authority relations, proved inconclusive, finding no significant difference in reasoning between a hypothetical example and a real-life situation.

The trouble with all such findings, finally, is that it can never be clear whether apparent evidence against the Law of Conscious Realization might not rather be evidence against the postulated developmental progression: what appears to be lower-level reasoning in the real-life situation might in fact be higher-level reasoning which the particular theory does not recognize as such. Thus Levine's finding, cited by Vine (p. 64 above), that subjects dropped from Stage 4 to Stage 3 when reasoning about close friends or relatives, suggests that in a setting of close personal affection, Stage 3 is more appropriate, and more adequate, than Stage 4 (Levine, 1976). This may also explain the regression found especially among higher-stage reasoners by both Haan and Arndt.

But whatever else is obscure, at least it is clear that Piaget's Law cannot be taken for granted. And in one respect at least it seems clearly inadequate. For as Wright points out, 'The child's theoretical morality is influenced by the moral teaching he receives from adults, and indeed is likely throughout his life to be under pressure to share the theoretical morality of the groups to which he belongs' (p. 148). Indeed I suggested earlier that specifically moral conceptions and considerations are as likely to be imposed on the child from outside as to be developed from within its own experience. Certainly it will meet such notions as right and wrong, ought and ought not, in the judgments of others long before it is capable of forming any such judgments for itself. Moreover, a major contributory factor in moral development is the extent to which adults instruct children in moral reasons, not merely presenting them with moral demands and prohibitions but also explaining them (Hoffman, 1970), something which Piaget seems not to take into account. It may be difficult to see, in terms of Piaget's theory, how theoretical morality can exercise an influence on practical morality, but there can be no question that it does.

Thus the child's practical morality is, as it were, under pressure from two directions at once: from the moral judgments and moral teaching of others, and from its conscious realization of its own practice. And it will be this double pressure, with the possibility of a divergence between them, which gives rise to the Thought/Action problem, the possibility of a gap between what the agent thinks he ought to do—or, we might even say, what he thinks he ought to think he ought to do!—and the considerations which will actually motivate his conduct.

The tables now seem to have turned. The Thought/Action problem is with us still, but it appears that we can dispose of the Action/Thought problem instead. For if a person's moral judgments can stem from the example and teaching of others, rather than from a conscious realization of his own practice, then there is no need to explain how action gives rise to moral thought specifically, nor will it be a misconception to approach moral development through the study of moral reasoning. There are, however, signs in Piaget of an answer to these objections, which serves also to present his theory as more cognitive-developmental and less social-psychological than Wright suggests. First of all, conscious realization is not simply a faithful representation of what occurs at the level of action; it is 'a reconstruction and consequently a new and original construction super-imposed upon the constructions already formed by action'

(1932, pp. 173–4). Moreover 'the individual is not capable of achieving this conscious realization by himself' (p. 407). Hence such factors as adult constraint or the need for mutual cooperation, which originally shape the child's conduct in a wholly non-moral way, may later be apprehended consciously, under the guidance of parents and others, in specifically moral terms, as providing not just reasons for action but moral obligations.

Even more important is Piaget's claim that moral judgment which is not the conscious realization of actual practice will be merely verbal, or as he—or his translator—also terms it, 'mere psittacism'. Piaget even seems to offer this as an argument for the Law of Conscious Realization, though as such it is circular, since the claim that such judgments must be empty verbalisms itself depends on the Law's being true. Piaget assumes, in effect, that either moral judgments must consist in the conscious realization of 'truly spontaneous thought' i.e. thought in action, or they will sustain no relations with it whatever (p. 109ff.); he is not prepared even to consider the possibility that moral judgments might affect action without being derived from it.

Nevertheless if Piaget is right about this, then to the extent that the child's judgments and reasoning do go beyond a conscious realization of actual practice, they will be mere mouthings: the child will not properly understand what it is saying. We must distinguish, therefore, between the judgments the child expresses and its comprehension of them. The content of its moral opinions may be independent of personal experience and practice, Piaget would seem to imply, but its understanding is not: it may preach what it does not practice, but it will not understand it. Thus one's understanding of such values as life and law, for example, must be limited to considerations which have actually been taken into account in one's own conduct. The 'sanctity of human life' will be an empty verbalism unless and until one's behaviour has been shaped by a respect for other individuals simply as individuals in their own right; someone whose behaviour is based solely on a fear of punishment or unpleasant consequences, or a desire for the approval of others, may speak of the sanctity of human life, but will not comprehend it for what it is, will make sense of it only in the terms which he operates within his own conduct.

There is, finally, the point on which Wright insists, that to the extent that the child's moral judgments do represent a conscious realization of actual practice, obligation and thought will be fused into one phenomenon: obligation-charged thinking, cognitively-structured obligation. Since the child already adopts those reasons in its action they will be seen not merely as reasons why it should behave in a certain way but, more concretely, as reasons to behave in that way. The moral judgments it acquires from others, on the other hand, will not have this feature: they will be reasons why, morally, it ought to act in a certain way; but why, the child may ask, subconsciously if not consciously, should I do as I ought? The Thought/Action problem will then arise precisely to the extent that moral thought is not the conscious realization of practice, but is instead the result of teaching, training—or even of cognitive conflict.

Some Implications

I have not argued that Piaget's Law of Conscious Realization is correct: we lack clear data either way, though there is evidence (Jordan, 1972) that it can hardly be a universal law of human development. Instead I have been concerned with the twin problems of how moral thought gets translated into action, and of how moral thought arises in the first place, in particular how far it is itself the product of moral action. These problems cannot be resolved, or Piaget's Law evaluated, unless the study of moral development extends beyond the study of moral reasoning to the independent study of moral action. And for this, rather surprisingly, we already have a tool in Kohlberg's typology of moral stages, provided that these are understood not merely as modes of reasoning but as type of reason, which can apply to action even at a pre-conscious level. Once it is recognized, as I argue above (Chapter 6), that moral reasons need not involve moral reasoning, and that moral reasons can apply to action even in the absence of conscious thought, then Kohlberg's typology can provide us with a classification not merely of moral judgment, but also of moral conduct. People might, for example, act out of concern for the opinion of others before they begin to reason, morally, in those terms. Indeed if Piaget is right, this must be what happens: Kohlberg's stages must be utilized in action before they can be utilized in thought.

The role of reasons in moral action, as distinct from moral reasoning, is something which has so far been sadly neglected by those in the cognitive-developmental camp, though there have been some first attempts by Damon (1977), Gilligan (1977), and Haan (1978). The explanation, of course, is the formidable methodological difficulties: it proves difficult to apply the moral stages classification directly to action, to test whether there is indeed a time-lag between the application of reasons in action and their adoption in conscious thought, and so on, simply because it is difficult to assess the agent's reasons except by asking him; and the agent will be able to formulate his reasons adequately only to the extent that they have already passed from the level of action into conscious realization. Thus an earlier study by Haan (1975) was still concerned to assess what subjects said their reasons were, which is not necessarily the same as why they actually did it, and it is not clear how far the later study avoids the same difficulty. Similarly Damon, as we have seen, identifies moral conduct with the subject's verbal decision as to how he ought to act—and then, ironically, worries whether this invalidates his evidence against Piaget's Law (p. 109), without noticing that Piaget too had, of necessity, to appeal to what children say about real-life situations.

We end, therefore, where we began, with the point that among the reasons for concentrating on moral judgment and reasoning rather than moral action is that the former is easier to assess than the latter. But as the Thought/Action problem and the Action/Thought problem combine to demonstrate, this is only part of the story, and perhaps the wrong part. So far from moral thought providing the key to moral action, moral action will—if Piaget is right—provide the key to moral thought.

References

Arndt, A. W. (1976). Maturity of moral reasoning about hypothetical dilemmas and behaviour in an actual setting. *Dissertation Abstracts International*, **37**, 435-B.

Damon, W. (1977). *The Social World of the Child*, Jossey-Bass, San Francisco.

Gilligan, C. (1977). In different voice: women's conceptions of self and of morality. *Harvard Eduation Review*, **47**, 481–517.

Gilligan, C., and Murphy, J. M. (1979). The Philosopher and the dilemma of the fact: Evidence for continuing development from adolescence to adulthood. In D. Kuhn (Ed.), *Intellectual Development Beyond Childhood*, New Directions for Child Development, No 5, Jossey-Bass, San Francisco.

Gilligan, C., and Belenky, M. F. (1980). A naturalistic study of abortion decisions. In R. L. Selman and R. Yando (Eds), *Clinical Developmental Psychology*, New Directions for Child Development, No. 7, Jossey-Bass, San Francisco.

Goodnow, J. J., and Postman, L. (1955). Probability learning in a problem-solving situation. *Journal of Experimental Psychology*, **49**, 16–22.

Haan, N. (1975). Hypothetical and actual moral reasoning in a situation of civil disobedience. *Journal of Personality and Social Psychology*, **32**, 255–269.

Haan, N. (1978). Two moralities in action contexts: relationships to thought, ego regulation, and development. *Journal of Personality and Social Psychology*, **36**, 286–305.

Hoffman, M. L. (1970). Moral Development. In P. H. Mussen (Ed.), *Carmichael's Manual of Child Psychology*, Vol. 2, 3rd ed. Wiley, New York. pp. 261–359.

Jordan, N. (1972). Is there an Achilles heel in Piaget's theorizing? *Human Development*, **15**, 379–382.

Levine, C. (1976). Role-taking standpoint and adolescent usage of Kohlberg's conventional stage of moral reasoning. *Journal of Personality and Social Psychology*, **34**, 41–46.

Piaget, J. (1932). *The Moral Judgment of the Child*, Routledge and Kegan Paul, London.

Piaget, J. (1976). *The Grasp of Consciousness*, Routledge and Kegan Paul, London.

SECTION III

The Moral Context—The Individual and Society

In Section I of this volume, the contributors engaged in a series of critiques of the currently dominant theory of moral development. They questioned some of the assumptions which Kohlberg makes about the nature and origin of morality. They paid some attention to social-psychological issues in moral reasoning and development on the grounds that, in assuming the universality of one form of morality, and placing emphasis almost exclusively upon individual processes in the development of morality, Kohlberg ignores social processes and the social context. In Section II the contributors addressed the relationship between thought and action. This, again, is essentially an individualistic question, whether it is defined in terms of 'will' or in terms of the individual reflecting upon action *post hoc*.

In this third Section, the contributors directly address a number of social psychological issues, from different perspectives. Each starts off from the assumption that the individual is in some sense a product of the social environment, and that 'morality' emerges from the individual's interaction with that. Social-psychological processes contribute to the development of individual morality but the contributors also remind us that morality serves other functions, such as the maintenance of social norms, and that it reflects the dominant belief system of the culture in which the individual grows up. In other words, as individuals we acquire and perpetuate the morality which serves our individual, group, and societal needs, and our explanations of morality, as social scientists, are likely to reflect similar assumptions.

Elsewhere in this volume it has been pointed out more than once that despite superficial resemblances to Kohlberg's approach, Piaget's work on moral development was in fact less about individual stages of moral growth, and more about the social psychological factors involved in the transmission of morality across generations. Piaget addressed the questions of early parent-child authority relations, the heteronomous morality which arose from this, and the later egalitarian peer relations which create the conditions under which a morality of

171

mutual, rather than unilateral, respect, can develop. In Chapter 10 Peter Kutnick explores the very early conditions of constraint and cooperation which are an essential aspect of parent-infant relations, and in particular the extent to which the recent research on attachment can contribute to Piaget's theoretical position.

In Chapter 11, Nicholas Emler looks at a different question, and a different aspect of explanations of morality. Commonsense notions of morality have always held that character and reputation are central to one's public self, and that we need to be able to take predictability of behaviour for granted in order to function effectively as social beings. Much of the research on the consistency of moral traits and the predictability of behaviour across different situations has failed to confirm this commonsense notion—a situation which, incidentally, contributed greatly to the decline in research on morality for many years. Emler argues that much of the experimental work on which these conclusions were based is essentially trivial. In his chapter he carefully examines both methodology and data, and concludes that neither a personality trait nor a situational explanation is adequate. He proposes instead a social-psychological interpretation which argues that we present an appropriate social self to others, and that we negotiate our reputation both in order to define ourselves and to make ourselves comprehensible in the social world.

In Chapter 12, Tom Kitwood pursues the argument that morality is part of personal identity, part of the search for coherence and definition of the self. But Kitwood goes further, and explores the implications of this for the normative theory of ethics within the culture. In particular, he criticizes the dominant utilitarianism of industrial society on the grounds that it focuses upon the universal, the social, and the public, and has no place for personal experience, and therefore no place for the personal identity and personal integrity which, Kitwood argues, must be the roots of individual morality. His view is that we must take into account social-psychological realities in formulating an ideal ethical system. Utilitarianism is a product of industrial society and reflects the needs of an economic system, but it is of necessity *psychologically* unsound as an account of individual morality.

In the final chapter, Glynis Breakwell extends the social psychological analysis to the group. She looks at the way that moral rhetoric functions to define ingroup and outgroup, and to maintain power relationships between and within social groups. The individual uses moral rhetoric to establish and maintain social identity, and Breakwell explores the way in which a group will modify moral rhetoric, and modify who the rhetoric applies to, as a means of exerting power, legitimating its own existence and defining the status of individuals. These four chapters echo in many ways the criticisms of unitary and ethical realist models of morality made in the first Section. They demonstrate the social origins of moral codes, the necessity of locating morality in the social environment, and the need for the individual to define him or herself at least in part by the expression of a 'moral' self. Thus they also underline the dangers, pointed out in the first Section, of accepting too glibly any one theory of morality as having a claim to particular psychological validity.

Morality in the Making
Edited by H. Weinreich-Haste and D. Locke
© 1983, John Wiley & Sons, Ltd.

CHAPTER 10

Moral Incursions into Constraint

PETER KUTNICK

The psychology of moral development is currently full of ambiguities and incon-sistencies. This chapter will attempt to eliminate some of the confusion in the field by drawing out aspects of cognitive development theory which have not been extensively explored in relation to moral development. It will focus on the first relationships of the child. The first relationship provides the initial social experiences and interactions which are a significant factor in moral develop-ment. The first relationship introduces the child into a system of authority. The child interacts with authority and comes to an understanding of it. I will describe stages of authority realization and examine parallel developments in social and intellectual life. Finally, I will pose a stage-developmental analysis of social authority which is intended to integrate the above areas of research and sets the background for moral development.

Recent research in childhood and adolescent moral development has shown that intellectual development (Kohlberg, 1976) and social-cognitive develop-ment (Selman, 1976) are prerequisites for the development of moral reasoning. Other chapters in this volume have considered the implications of this. It is curious, however, that little work has been done on the earliest foundation of moral development; the relationship between early experience, early cognitive development, and the foundation of morality. In the past, infancy has been researched in terms of the transition from oral to anal stages, the sensory-motor stage, and the formation of attachment bonds. In this chapter, I will use a cognitive-developmental perspective to explore the child's perception and understanding of moral and authority relations.

Extensive research in the Piagetian paradigm on the infant's general sensory, cognitive, and social abilities demonstrates that the child is *active* in his or her environment. What has often been forgotten in this research, as Denzin (1977) reminds us, is that development takes place within a particular context, often a social context. So, although the child actively interacts with the world, the context imposes constraints. Some of these constraints are physical, most are social; the individual is required to comply with moral and social codes. Early on, therefore, the child learns that the world is both constraining and contradictory. Development is the process of making cognitive sense of this contradictory world. This process is mediated by age, stage, and the cultural characteristics of the environment.

It is in early social development that the child learns to come to terms with the constraints imposed by parents and peers, and begins to generate the basis of an understanding of rules, sanctions, and normative patterns of interpersonal behaviour. The constraints are the foundation of moral development. In the earliest years, the constraints upon the child—by virtue of its weakness, its lack of muscle control, and its dependence upon adults and older siblings—are inevitably in the form of authority relationships.

Moral Development: Insights from Piaget

The most influential work in this field has been Piaget's *Moral Judgment of the Child*, and it is in this work that authority relations were fully explored. In observing and questioning children as they played marbles, Piaget initially noted: (1) that children practise the use of rules differently according to their age; and (2) that children have different realizations or consciousness of rules at different ages. The practice of rules followed the stages of: (a) motor and individual character (from birth), (b) egocentric (2–5 years), (c) incipient cooperation (starting at 7–8 years), and (d) codification of rules (starting at 11–12 years). Consciousness of rules followed a similar sequence: (a) motor rules (0 to 4 years), (b) rules regarded as sacred (4 to 9–10 years), and (c) mutual consent as a basis for rule-making.

In explaining the consciousness of rules Piaget noted that from the earliest years everything 'conspired' to impress upon the infant the notion of regularity.

'Certain physical events are repeated with sufficient accuracy to produce an awareness of 'law' or at any rate to favour the appearance of motor schemes of prevision. The parents, moreover, impose upon the baby a certain number of moral obligations, the source of future regularities.'

(Piaget, 1965, pp. 51–52)

The baby was 'bathed' in an atmosphere of rules and ritual acts; he/she was constrained by the social environment.

A central concept of Piaget's system is the Law of Conscious Realization—through repeated practice the individual comes eventually to an awareness of rules. Motor intelligence contains the 'germs' of 'completed reason'. But, motor rules must first merge into habit, regularity, and consciousness of regularity. A 'feeling of repetition' arises out of ritualization of schemes of motor adaptation. Motor rules are more general than the marble playing suggested above, and are found in interpersonal behaviours simultaneously. Piaget described the earliest months of life as a period of feeding, cradle, and dispositional habits, dominated by a coercive relationship with the mother. Motor adaptation is based upon assimilation of the environment such that 'rules come into existence—as a balance between adaptation and assimilation, the course of conduct adopted becomes crystallized and ritualized' (p. 88).

In this one-sided environment the child receives a sense of duty; the individual receives commands from another and must accept them. The sense of duty provides a basis for Piaget's 'moral realism'. Moral realism was characterized by objective responsibility, and hierarchical authority—the 'morality of constraint'. As the child develops interaction through games and communications between children provides the basis for equality or reciprocity of actions. The practical realization of mutuality lay the groundwork for a 'morality of cooperation', which is explored in interviews on retributive and distributive justice. Mutuality, or cooperation, is based upon an equal share of authority and responsibility found initially amongst a non-hierarchical peer group. Upon the realization of the practical moralities of constraint and cooperation, the child should be able to make autonomous judgments concerning moral situations.

Important features to be extracted from the *Moral Judgment of the Child* include:

1. Stages in moral development were noted as: autistic, heteronomous, autonomous.
2. Moral relations had a necessary, but not sufficient, basis in authority relationships, which formed a cognitive basis for Piaget's stages (i.e. the hierarchy of constraint, the equality of cooperation).
3. The roots of constraint lay in the unilateral respect given to parents by the infant. More particularly, the roots of constraint lay in sensory-motor intelligence and sympathetic and affective reactions.
4. Piaget argued that sensory motor schemes were the roots of constraint, and that logical-mathematical schemes are an integral part in the further development of heteronomy and autonomy. For example, practice of cooperative behaviours preceded knowledge of cooperation in games (a pre-operative scheme).
5. The above points demonstrate an interaction between the individual, the environment, cognitive, and social structures.

Further Moral Development Research: the Establishment of Authority Relations

Virtually all research in moral development endorses Hogan's (1973) assertion that 'man is a social, rule-making and rule-following animal'. Peters (1974) takes the point one step further in stating that morality is learned through reason and that reason is learned through habit. Not all writers, however, accept such a narrow definition of morality as Piaget did. Other writers have focused more attention on the dynamics of moral development, which effectively illustrate many facets of the early authority relations central to Piaget's theory. While moral stages and sequences of learning have been noted for content, structure, and situational aspects by other authors (Kohlberg, 1976; Lickona, 1976; and others), the underlying dynamics of moral development remain the most coherent way of drawing this information together. Such research includes work on: authority relationships between the child, adults, and other children; practices of early upbringing and socialization; moral knowledge (specifically of constraint and cooperation) and the ability to use it; and reciprocity—its development and role in determining moral character and judgments.

Recent writing by Hoffman (1976) has postulated that the roots of altruism (and hence morality) lie in early caring and holding interactions between caretaker and infant. The infant becomes 'somatically' aware of the caretaker's bodily states of distress and other emotive moods. The infant is classically conditioned to empathetic distress, leading to the ability to experience empathy, sympathy, and altruism. Despite his greater emphasis on the role of conditioning, there are two important parallels between Hoffman and Piaget: (1) the roots of morality are to be found in the sensory-motor period; and (2) the sensory-motor period is one of active assimilation by the child, in which schemes are not limited to mere physical and object contact and repetition— they also include social contacts and repetitions, and somatic contacts and repetitions. According to Hoffman, the dynamics of early moral development include much more than simple logical relations.

The early roots of morality are established in the power/authority, yet caring, relationship of parent and child. The child's understanding and acceptance of the relationship is mediated by intellectual and social abilities. Interaction with peers becomes more important with age. Peers help to promote intellectual and social development. The equal power relationship amongst peers is essential for cooperation. In this vein, Garbarino and Bronfenbrenner (1976) have cited parental and peer power relations as the basis of a broader theory of the socialization of morality. Leaving aside the role of the peer group, they focused on the importance of the early attachment relationship of child and parent in establishing the power/authority concept in the child.

Attachment has been widely researched in the context of the development of the child–adult bonding relationship. I want to argue that attachment can be interpreted in part as an authority relationship. The research evidence on attachment and bonding (see Ainsworth, Bell, and Stayton, 1974; Bernal, 1974): (1) emphasizes the affective (secure and dependent) nature of the initial authority relationship of constraint; (2) demonstrates obedience of the child to the authority figure from as early as the third-quarter of the first year of life (Stayton, Hogan, and Ainsworth, 1971); and (3) is universal: virtually all children establish a bond of this sort with one or multiple individuals (a further discussion of attachment follows).

Obedience is a fundamental aspect of the morality of constraint. It has two components: the authority relationship of dominance and submissiveness (hierarchical), and acceptance of it by the child. The acceptance of obedience by the child demonstrates that both child and parent are involved and committed to the relationship. Youniss (1976) found stages of obedience in older children, showing a growing sophistication in the child's concepts of obedience; i.e. from demand to offering to perform services. The sophistication demonstrated a hierarchical relationship of the child to constraining authority. The child was obliged to accept the relationship. Yet the child felt secure and natural in the relationship. The child initially (and passively) acknowledged authority. He/she was able to cope with the realization of being less powerful and thereby submissive to adults.

Obedience or compliance to authority demonstrates an acceptance of the relationship. Acceptance may be taken further than the attachment relationship described above. Acceptance may be one of two types: (1) based upon the affective state of the relationship; and (2) lack of viable alternatives. Characteristic affective statements include: 'I won't go to bed because I don't like you' or 'I'll do it (because I love you).' Affective statements show a realization of the individual's position within the confines of an authority relationship. Acceptance based on affect is more often found amongst young children: they have little or no alternative.

On the other hand, non-compliance may derive from the ability to draw upon an alternate authority to challenge the original, e.g. adult vs. peer. The ability to use an alternative requires a cognitive advance by the individual in the realization of an equitable and reciprocal peer relation. Peers help to denote the limitations and extent of parental power. The peer relationship derives from interactions amongst equals and the necessity of jointly 'sorting out' of problems. Research suggests that peer relations are not normally attributed to childern until 5 to 8 years of age. But several writers have suggested that the age levels may only be an artefact of Western cultural and social lifestyles (Lewis and Rosenblum, 1975).

A summary of the above points indicates that: (1) authority relationships of parent and peer are the root of cognitive-moral stages of constraint and cooperation; (2) the child is in a position of awareness, acceptance, and involvement in both moral stages; and (3) socialization procedures start earlier than has been normally considered, i.e. constraint has roots in sensory-motor stage.

The above material does help to illuminate some of the ambiguities posed in the review of Piaget's moral development; it also indicates gaps and available evidence. First, an understanding of sensory-motor schemes must include information about empathy and paradigms of child learning abilities. But research in this area so far has only explored somatic factors in development, and sensory-motor intelligence remains to be further explored. Second, why do parental and constraining relations appear as a necessary but not sufficient condition for the development of peer and cooperative relations? Why does compliance remain a dominant mode of response in later life? The gaps emphasize the inadequacy of present cognitive-developmental theory in providing a holistic approach to development.

Intellectual Development: The Sensory-motor Stage

Research on older children and adolescents indicates a rough parallel between stages of moral judgment and intellectual development. Certain schemes or patterns of action are minimally necessary to arrive at stages of moral judgment and intellectual development. These action schemes are characteristic of intellectual as well as moral stages and may be decribed briefly as: (1) pre-operatonal, in which initially behavioural, and later symbolic, actions are repeated again and again until cognitively realized; (2) concrete operational—in which actions and realization may take place simultaneously; and (3) formal operation, in which reasoning is no longer tied to external actions. Action schemes are built-up by adaptive interaction between the individual and the environment. Of primary importance in this adaptive sequence are the processes of assimilation and accommodation. As posed in stage theory, the action schemes of intellectual and moral development are based upon the schemes of the sensory-motor stage.

The sensory-motor stage, curiously, is underexplored except in the most blatant cognitive terms. Piaget's six sensory-motor substages describe the infant's developmental progress culminating in the ability to use symbolic thought. The earliest substage, neonetal reflexes, shows the range of perceptual and sensory mechanisms available to the child. The primary and secondary circular reactions are strongly 'assimilative'. The infant is aware of and acknowledges events in the surrounding environment. The events affect the infant, either by actual physical sensation (characteristic of the primary circular reactions) or by perceptual and sensory involvement (characteristic of the secondary circular reaction). For the events to be assimilated, they must be repeated multiple times. Most often, the control of the events and their repetitions is undertaken by parents in their caretaking and upbringing functions. In *Play, Dreams and Imitation* Piaget (1951) stated that the early assimilation was dependent on a willing acceptance of the state of the environment; an environment controlled outside the realm of the infant. Tertiary circular reaction and symbolic sub-stages are a major advance for the infant. Control, manipulation, and experimentation of the environment are within the grasp of the child. The child is no longer dependent on people and events. These final substages are mainly 'accommodative'.

Most research on the sensory-motor period has explored cognitive relations (as in object permanence) or social-cognitive relations (as in memory of attachment figure), but leaves affective schemes unexplored. The affective schemes are important for Piaget (1951) in that:

'There is an exact correspondence in the case of the relationships which determine unconscious symbolism. Affective life, like intellectual life, is a continual adaptation, and the two are not only parallel but interdependent, since feelings express the interest and the value given to actions of which intelligence provides the structure. Since affective life is adaptation, it also implies continual assimilation of present situations to earlier ones—assimilation which gives rise to affective schemes or relatively stable modes of feeling or reacting—and continual accommodation of these schemes to the present situation.'

(Piaget, 1951, pp. 205–206)

Affect then parallels and is interdependent with cognitive schemes of the sensory-motor period. Affect has strong social qualities. It has been studied for its relationship to attachment. Attachment requires that the infant be at the secondary circular reaction substage. Actions affecting the infant can be assimilated. While not being in control of the social environment, the child's intellectual capacity allows for the realization of parental constraining relations. But, unlike cognitive schemes, affect does not generalize according to Piaget. The child is able to apply symbolic understanding of objects and concepts to other (similar) objects and concepts. The relationship between child and parent is different. Many individuals can provide stimulation and events to promote cognitive advancement. But caretaking/comforting (necessitating the repetition of caring physical contacts) are usually limited to child and parent. These caring physical contacts are the responsibility of parents, and thereby differentiate the qualities of parent from others. They are the affective root of regularity, emotion, and rules.

The contradiction between the fact that there is an unequal power relationship between caretaker and child and, at the same time, affective 'love' for caretaker is established by the secondary circular reaction. The child now maintains physical, sensory, social, and affective schemes with certain individuals, as well as the physical-cognitive and simpler sensory and social schemes of action during the sensory-motor period. Through interaction with the environment, the child develops cognitively, socially, and emotionally. Schemes of action/realization that have, up to now, been explored mainly in the intellectual realm are also found in the social and affective realm. Early actions and schemes are assimilated by the child and repetitions of these schemes form the basis for rules and operational development. There are strong similarities between physical and social relations. The infant's touching and caring relationship (affective) with the caretaker sets that relationship apart from other interactions with the environment.

Drawing together the diverse points of this section: (a) in the early sub-stages of sensory-motor development the child is the recipient of actions initiated and controlled by the caregiver; (b) these actions are repeated and ritualized; and (c) the affective closeness between child and caregiver establish a specific authority-oriented bond which lies at the root of constraint. Sensory-motor actions lie at the root of moral, as well as intellectual, development. The realization of actions by the child demonstrate an action-thought causal linkage in early stages of moral development; and this development limits type and quality of social and intellectual activities of the child.

Social Development

Like moral development, most information on social development concerns the verbal child, leaving the sensory-motor roots vague. Reviewers such as Lee (1975) discuss the similarity of physical and social schemes, noting in detail the growing complexity of emotions, roles, settings, etc. for the child; yet the behavioural origins are not made explicit. Undoubtedly, there are biological predispositions for the infant to act socially. Realization of action and control is built up in a sequence of social interactions. Initial constraints on the child are biological, but the actors quickly develop modes and rules for communication, etc., through interactions. Interactors here are the infant and parents. Social development takes place, most often, in a secure and loving atmosphere.

Characteristic of developing social relationships are power and understanding, with affective elements that underlie both. Parents' ability to control resources, stimulation, and attention dominate the first months and years of the infant's life. It would be naive to suggest that the baby does not and can not control certain adult behaviours (for example, crying brings a concerned reaction, the baby may initiate a peek-a-boo sequence, etc.). In fact, the neonate is endowed with biological capacities to promote communication. But, the child must still depend on a caretaker for a response. Dubin and Dubin (1965) reviewed studies showing a developmental sequence of behavioural control and authority inception by parents. In charting an age-ordered sequence of authority development, they showed the child evolving from a dependent relationship in feeding and weaning, to regulation of social control in the presence of others. The sequence is rather one-sided in its view of authority inception, the child being dominated by parents. The steps of authority expectation and realization sound remarkably similar to recent work on early stages of social and moral development (see Selman, 1976; Damon, 1977; and others). This relationship of power lays a structural basis for future interpersonal relationships. The question next to be asked is not why, but how, the authority relationship comes to exist.

These dyadic or triadic relationships of authority and power are most deeply explored in the attachment relationship. Attachment is a loaded word and perhaps an outmoded concept; but it is indicative of a bonding between the infant and a caretaker. The formation of a bond involves close interaction with a limited number of individuals, and the ability to stimulate one another.

Studies by Ainsworth and her colleagues add insight into this process of attachment. Ainsworth and Bell (1970) provided a useful two-part definition as: (1) a cognitive/affective tie to someone or thing; and (2) attachment behaviour as actions used to promote proximity of that person. The attachment relationship has been shown to be one of trust and dependence/security between the child and certain persons. Attachment becomes evident in the last half of the child's first year. Research cited by Ainsworth, Bell, and Stayton shows that the *more* sensitive the mother was in the first few months of life the *more* secure and exploratory the infant would be in the last half of that year. The attachment relationship is dependent on cognitive processes such as object recognition and permanence, which becomes applied to the person as object. Once the attachment bond takes place, Stayton, Hogan, and Ainsworth found that children show a 'disposition toward obedience' emerging in relation to the attachment figure.

Clearly there is a large cognitive element in attachment. Yarrow (1972) noted that attachment was an organizing concept for a wide range of behaviours. Attachment depends upon a realization of the external environment, and upon differentiation of the self from the environment. Attachment parallels the perceptual discrimination and memory stability of object permanence characteristic of the child at the stage of secondary circular reactions. The child is able to perceive and realize actions of its own body and the surrounding environment (physical and interpersonal), but that child is dependent on randomized and habitualized behaviours for realization. Most interpersonal behaviours, however, take place in a context where the child is in a less powerful position in relation to the caretaker; therefore, schemes of the secondary circular reactions operate to form the child's first realization of constraint. Cognitive development is necessary for attachment, but there is also an affective component.

Within the sensory-motor schemes, Stern (1977) pointed out that there was a strong interpersonal, expressive and emotional element. Defining affect is notoriously difficult, but several studies demonstrate the significance of affect in cognitive processes. Let us consider three studies which suggest possible lines of inquiry concerning the qualities of affect. The first study was undertaken in the attempt to promote the well-being (weight gain, feeding, etc.) of premature neonates in hospital. White (1976) found that kinesthetic and tactile stimulation for only a few minutes per day in the first ten days after birth promoted greater weight-gain and formula intake than normally treated premature neonates. Another study, by Nass (1964), found that a group of congenitally deaf children between 8 and 12 years old resident in their school during the week had more advanced peer-oriented morality than normal hearing children of the same ages. Nass speculated that 'common experiences' may promote the authority-independence attitude of the deaf children. The experiences included tactile contacts and the development of non-verbal communication skills. A further study, undertaken by the author (Kutnick and Brees, 1982), showed that sensitivity training experiences promoting trust among 4-year-olds increased their ability to perform on cognitive tasks and make mature moral (peer oriented, self-initiated) judgments.

The conclusion from these studies and research on attachment is that physical contact encourages a *comforting* and *trusting* state among individuals—a process well known to lovers and those engaged in sensitivity training. The tactile contacts promote cognitive and moral development in the spontaneous interactions between child and parent and in experimental sessions of the laboratory. Once initial child-adult relationships are looked at in this way, one can consider the role of sensory-motor affective schemes and interactions of interpersonal relations in the generation of early social-affective cognitive stages. Early child-caretaker interactions demonstrate an unequal, or constraining, power/authority relationship. The child's acceptance of this relationship is not simply based on its realization. The child derives security and dependence, a trust in this relationship also. The existence and trust in the relationship combine in the formation of constraint. Cooperation, one can speculate, may have similar roots in a trust/dependence relationship—but found amongst childhood peers.

Constraint and cooperation may then be looked upon as 'archetypical' authority relationship patterns; the underlying elements upon which power, obedience, and, later, morality are based. If a series of cognitive-structural stages can be extracted from the above review of the child's social development, it would include cognitive, behavioural, and affective elements and would follow in this order:

1. Reflex behaviour and neonatal capacities—drawing the infant into close physical contact with caretakers.
2. Sensory-motor-affective schemes—incorporating primary and secondary circular reactions:
   (a) realization of sensory schemes;
   (b) recognition of caretaker;
   (c) trust/dependence of caretaker.
3. Development of dependent relationship while realizing self is different from environment; behavioural interactions with peers.
4. Early rule/authority application and reflective egocentric understanding.
5. Concrete and rational rule/authority application, with self-reflective questioning of the rule basis.
6. Involvement and stages of reflective mutual social development.
7. Reflective ability to balance and apply constraining and/or cooperative principles (in moral judgment, friendship, affiliation, political development, etc.).

Ages are not ascribed to these (hypothetical) stages, but they roughly coincide with intellectual moral developmental stages as

Stages 1 and 2	— Sensory-motor	— autistic
Stages 3 and 4	— Pre-operational	— heteronomous
Stages 5 and 6	— Concrete operational	
Stage 7	— Formal operational	— autonomous

Summary and Implications

This chapter has presented a view into the generation of the child's initial authority relationship and the cognitive and environmental factors that promote that relationship. In tracing the roots of authority and attempting to fit the various findings into a coherent perspective, aspects of early moral, social, and intellectual development have been reviewed. Gaps in particular areas were filled by citing research from other areas. The statements presented here can only be held up to the internal logic of the paper—more, precise, empirical work is needed to support or deny the arguments.

The authority relationship is focused upon as it underlies the primary relationship between child and caretaker. Authority characterizes the child's first social relationship. Authority forms a basis for interaction between the child and other adults, and the child and other children. Aside from the early social relationships, authority is also at the root of moral, political, and other social development. The type or quality of the relationship, though, is rooted in the pre-logical sequence (schemes) of behaviour of the primary and secondary circular reactions. A contradiction characteristic of these sub-stages is the adaptation process. Adaptation has been labelled as the most free and dialectical process (Piaget, 1971; Riegel, 1975) of development, but it is restricted in type and quality by parental interaction. After the initial dominance-submissive (hierarchical) relationship is realized (though positive justice, obedience, etc.) the child must then sort out the contradictions of mutuality and cooperation.

To illuminate why and how the authority relationship develops three basic aspects of cognitive social developmental theory were drawn upon. First was the understanding that the child constructs active schemes to assimilate social and physical relations. The schemes could, in the early sensory-motor sub-stages, be controlled by the child or by events external to (but involving) the child. Second, the development of the authority relationship with caretaker is generated through security, trust, and dependence schemes built through tactile, kinesthetic, and more general care and loving physical contacts; characterized in this paper by the attachment relationship. The type and quality of interpersonal contacts necessitate the expansion of our understanding of the sensory-motor period to a sensory-motor-affective period. Third, there is a parallel between stages of intellectual, social, and affective development; each of which may provide necessary but not sufficient conditions in the child's advancement. Active repetition within the sensory-motor and pre-operational stages precedes ritualization, habits, and general intellectual and social rules. Operational thought in the concrete and formal periods allows the individual to extend, generalize, and qualify previous schemes. Operational thought also allows the individual to reflect upon one's personal position in the cognitive, social, or affective relationship.

What has been laboriously drawn out in this chapter is, simply, the roots of constraint. Neonatal and early infant interactions with the caretaker inevitably lead to the realization of this power/authority relationship. The development of this realization is a complicated process involving sensory, motor, and affective schemes, and stages. To bring this theoretical account into the real world requires more empirical work and a discussion of its implications for social/authority relations. The young child (and in fact all of us) lives in a contradiction. The child is free to develop within the bounds that the environment offers. Parents may try to promote the child's freedom, but their social relationship with the child only serves to limit it. Upon realizing such a relationship the child may submit, reject, or seek alternatives. But, where may the alternatives arise from? The two most viable answers are the play-group and the school. These, too, embody the same adult-child contradiction. Organized play-groups and schools emphasize that both the child and the peer group are under the adult's constraining influence. Such an analysis provides a background for children taking on dominance based relationships amongst themselves, and peer group relations simply replicating an adult-based hierarchy.

Development of the cooperative morality/authority must take place outside the confines of constraining relations, a principle which: (1) seeks to promote greater sensitivity and affective relations amongst children themselves (something that may be found in residential creches and some radical kibbutzim); and (2) questions the existence and structure of moral education curricula in schools today.

References

Ainsworth, M., and Bell, S. (1970). Attachment, Exploration and Separation: illustrated by the behaviour of one-year-olds in a strange situation. *Child Development*, **41**, 49–67.

Ainsworth, M., Bell, S., and Stayton, D. (1974). Infant-Mother Attachment and Social Development: 'Socialisation' as a product of reciprocal responses to signals. In M. Richards (Ed.), *The Integration of a Child Into a Social World*, Cambridge University Press, London.

Bernal, J. (1974). Attachment: Some Problems and Possibilities. In M. Richards (Ed.), *The Integration of a Child Into a Social World*, Cambridge University Press, London.

Damon, W. (1977). *The Social World of the Child*, Jossey-Bass, San Francisco.

Denzin, N. (1977). *Childhood Socialisation*, Jossey-Bass, San Francisco.

Dubin, E., and Dubin, R. (1965). The Authority Inception Period in Socialisation. *Child Development*, **34**, 885–898.

Garbarino, J., and Bronfenbrenner, U. (1976). The Socialisation of Moral Judgement and Behaviour in Cross-Cultural Perspective. In T. Lickona (Ed.), *Moral Development and Behaviour: Theory, Research and Social Issues*, Holt, Rinehart, and Winston, New York.

Hoffman, M. (1976). Empathy, Role-Taking, Guilt and Development of Altruistic Motives. In T. Lickona (Ed.), *Moral Development and Behaviour: Theory, Research and Social Issues*, Holt, Rinehart, and Winston, New York.

Hogan, R. (1973). Moral Conduct and Moral Character: A Psychological Perspective. *Psychological Bulletin*, **79**, 217–232.

Kohlberg, L. (1976). Moral Stages and Moralization: The Cognitive and Developmental

Approach. In T. Lickona (Ed.), *Moral Development and Behaviour: Theory, Research and Social Issues*, Holt, Rinehart, and Winston, New York.

Kutnick, P., and Brees, P. (1982). The Development of Cooperative Understanding; Explorations in Cognitive and Moral Competence, and Social Authority. *Brit. J. Educational Psychology* (in press).

Lee, L. (1975). Toward a Cognitive Theory of Interpersonal Development: Importance of Peers. In M. Lewis and L. Rosenblum (Eds), *Friendship and Peer Relations*, Wiley, New York.

Lewis, M., and Rosenblum, L. (Eds) (1975). *Friendship and Peer Relations*, Wiley, New York.

Lickona, T. (1976). Research on Piaget's Theory of Moral Development. In T. Lickona (Ed.), *Moral Development and Behaviour: Theory, Research and Social Issues*, Holt, Rinehart, and Winston, New York.

Nass, M. (1964). The Development of Conscience: A Comparison of the Moral Judgement of Deaf and Hearing Children. *Child Development*, **35**, 1073–1080.

Peters, R. (1974). Moral Development and Moral Learning. *The Monist*, **58**.

Piaget, J. (1951). *Play, Dreams and Imitation in Childhood*, Routledge and Kegan Paul, London.

Piaget, J. (1965). *The Moral Judgment of the Child*, The Free Press, New York.

Piaget, J. (1971). *Science of Education and the Psychology of the Child*, Viking, New York.

Riegel, K. (1975). Dialectic Operations: The Final Period of Cognitive Development. *Human Development*, **16**, 346–370.

Selman, R. (1976). Social-Cognitive Understanding: A Guide to Educational and Clinical Practice. In T. Lickona (Ed.), *Moral Development and Behaviour: Theory, Research and Social Issues*, Holt, Rinehart, and Winston, New York.

Stayton, D., Hogan, R., and Ainsworth, M. (1971). Infant Obedience and Maternal Behaviour: The Origins of Socialization. *Child Development*, **42**, 1057–1067.

Stern, D. (1977). *The First Relationship: Infant and Mother*, Fontana/Open Books, Glasgow.

White, J. (1976). The Effects of Tactile and Kinesthetic Stimulation on Neonate Development. *Developmental Psychobiology*, **9**, 569–577.

Yarrow, L. (1972). Attachment and Dependency: A Developmental Perspective. In J. L. Aronfreed (Ed.), *Attachment and Dependency*, Winston, Washington, D.C.

Youniss, J. (1976). Affirmation. Unpublished manuscript, Catholic University of America, as cited in Damon, W. (1977). *The Social World of the Child*, Jossey-Bass, San Francisco.

Morality in the Making
Edited by H. Weinreich-Haste and D. Locke
© 1983, John Wiley & Sons, Ltd.

CHAPTER 11

Moral Character

NICHOLAS EMLER

Introduction

It is time for psychology to take another look at the concept of moral character. I shall argue in this chapter that we have abandoned it without a fair hearing and if the merits of the case are reconsidered have done so unjustifiably. In the contemporary psychology of moral development the concept of moral character is considered an anachronism, at best a point of departure for better informed theories, at worst a reflection of precisely what is not true of human nature. To talk of moral character implies a consistency, predictability, and stability to people's conduct and it has been held that moral conduct simply does not possess these qualities; the behaviour of any individual person is inconsistent, shows little stability from one occasion to another, and is more obviously determined by the situations in which the person finds him or herself than anything that might be called character. The conviction of those inclined to this view draws support from virtually identical criticisms which have been directed at the more general concept of personality. The idea that personality differences can explain anything about social behaviour is now so widely disputed that this critical view has achieved the status of a textbook heading.

I shall argue that contrary to prevailing opinion in the discipline, consistencies in conduct do exist, that they are predictable and relatively stable. That so many authorities have been convinced otherwise has more to do with theoretical taste and with the prestige of experimental research than with the weight of evidence. Although, as I hope to show, there are reliable individual differences in moral conduct there remains, however, the more serious conceptual question of deciding what these mean and how they are to be explained. The position I shall advance here is that individual consistency in moral conduct is such that it is reasonable for us to talk of differences in moral character, but that moral character should not be interpreted individualistically as purely a psychological property or quality of the person. Rather, moral character is something created

187

and sustained through social processes. It involves not only an individual actor but also an audience and the relationships between the actor and this audience. I shall argue that moral conduct can be interpreted in terms of the contingencies of self-presentation and reputation-management. But let us first consider the position of the critics; what objections do they raise, what alternatives do they propose, and how convincing are their arguments?

Moral Character: The Case Against and For

The Critics' Five Arguments Identified

There appear to be five main kinds of claim by critics which apply both to the particular idea of moral character and to the more general concept of personality traits. The first and most common objection is that there is no intra-personal consistency in conduct; those who are for instance the more dishonest in one situation are not necessarily the more dishonest in another. The second follows from this. Since behaviour is inconsistent it is unreasonable to expect that it could be reliably predicted from other measurable personality characteristics. A third argument is that situational factors have a far larger impact on behaviour than personal qualities. This being so it makes little sense to ask how personality affects behaviour and far more to ask how situations affect behaviour. A fourth argument, a variant of the third, is that interactions between personal factors and situational factors account for much more of the observed variance in behaviour than either situational factors or personal factors considered separately. From this alleged empirical fact it is concluded that personality traits must be trivial factors in accounting for behaviour. Fifth and finally there is the claim that consistency cannot be found at the level of overt, publicly observable conduct; it exists only at the level of the psychological structure that underlies conduct. Each of these arguments will be considered in turn and for each counter-arguments and evidence will be offered.

Is Behaviour Consistent?

Many writers, and they have certainly not all been of the same theoretical persuasion, have pointed to the inconsistency of moral conduct as grounds for rejecting any account of moral development as the acquisition of moral traits or virtues. They have included cognitive developmentalists like Kohlberg (1964, 1971a,b) and also social learning theorists like Mischel (1968, 1969). Social learning theorists have argued that moral development must involve the acquisition of specific response tendencies to specific situations rather than any generalized tendencies, for instance, to behave honestly whatever the situation.
    Mischel (1968) also faces the question of why anyone should have imagined that people do display stable traits of character if the evidence is clear that they do not. Mischel's answer is that consistency exists only in the eye of the

beholder. We have such strong needs for a predictable world, he argues, that we perceive consistencies that are not actually there. Psychologists who try to measure this consistency are therefore merely compounding the error of naive observers. Mischel (e.g. 1973) does allow that consistency exists in cognitive functioning; performances on different intellectual tasks tend to be respectably correlated. But consistency in the domain of interpersonal or social behaviour is too limited to justify talk of personality differences.

Adopting a quite different perspective Kohlberg accounts for moral development in terms of changes in the cognitive structures assumed to underlie conduct. Kohlberg has asserted that 'you cannot divide the world into honest and dishonest people! Almost everyone cheats some of the time. Cheating is distributed in a bell-curve around a level of moderate cheating' (1971a, p. 277). The second and third of these claims are unexceptionable and possibly true but the first is quite a different matter. Indeed, the bracketing of such claims as if they all referred to the same point has been one of the main obstacles in discussions of the consistency issue.

Kohlberg supports his claim about the inconsistency of moral conduct, as so many others have done, with reference to the work of Hartshorne and May (1928) and Hartshorne, May, and Shuttleworth (1930), and their doctrine of specificity. Hartshorne and May concluded from their extensive study of the moral conduct of school children that whether or not a child is, for example, honest depends more on the specific situation than on any identifiable characteristic of the child. They concluded there was no generalized tendency for some children to be more, and others less, honest irrespective of the situation. Their conclusions were based on the responses of school children to a number of tests, each of which was intended to create conditions under which they might be tempted to cheat. The correlations between the various tests were positive but low—on average, little over 0.2—suggesting that a child who cheated on one test was no more or less likely than any other to cheat on any other test. Behaviour in one situation, it seemed, could not be taken as a reliable guide to what a child would do in other situations.

Although it has been widely accepted that Hartshorne, May, and Shuttleworth's evidence clearly demonstrates the inconsistency of individual conduct, there are features of their studies which make it likely that they overestimate this in consistency. One is that the subjects were children and part of what it means to be childlike is to be inconsistent. Hartshorne, May, and Shuttleworth themselves demonstrate that, although people do not in general become more honest as they grow older, they do become more consistent (1930, p. 326). Another is that the tests, for all the control and standardization they provide, may not be very good measures of moral conduct. A point that Kohlberg has made is that measures of this sort are 'Mickey Mouse'; the forms of dishonesty they allow are trivial (Kohlberg, 1971a, p. 229). The very fact that an adult gives a test in which cheating is apparently so easy tells the child that this adult cares little whether cheating occurs or not. Such tests also involve a serious moral ambiguity in that the test giver must lie and cheat in order to catch out the test taker lying and cheating.

These comments apply with equal force to subsequent research which has relied upon experimental measures of resistance to temptation. The criterion of consistency has become somewhat more refined, however. Currently, critics assess evidence in terms of the 'rank order stability' criterion (e.g. Endler & Magnusson, 1976), arguing that consistency is demonstrated only if the rank order of individuals on some dimension—e.g. honesty—in one situation correlates with their rank order on that dimension in another. They point out that the rank-order stability evident with respect to honesty in Hartshorne, May, and Shuttleworth's data is characteristically low. A more recent study by Nelsen, Grinder, and Biaggio (1969) reports correlations in the ranges .06 to .55 and −.08 to .77 between measures of honesty, depending on the scoring used. In a recent review, Rushton (1976) concludes that the average correlation between various measures of children's altruism is around .3. Both sources have been cited in support of the specificity doctrine.

By psychometric standards, that is, standards for the construction of measures of psychological attributes, the kind of evidence which has impressed the critics is of doubtful value. Consider what these standards involve. In the construction of any psychological measure, good psychometric practice would require first that a pool of items be developed. Each item is, in effect, a sample of what is believed to be a relevant piece of behaviour. If the test were of mathematical ability, one might expect each item to be some mathematical problem. If the test were a measure of attitudes to the police, each item might be some statement about the police. And if the test is to measure honesty, each item could involve a sample of a person's honesty in some situation. The second stage would involve examination of the correlations between individual items and the overall score. It would not be expected that all the items in this pool will correlate positively and highly with the overall score, and those that do not would be eliminated. At this stage some new items may be added to the remainder and the process repeated until a satisfactory set of items has been identified.

It is likely that had such a procedure been applied to the items used by Hartshorne, May, and Shuttleworth to assess honesty, at least some of them would have been eliminated on these grounds. One cannot assume that because something appears to assess honesty it does indeed do so. Similarly, Golding (1975) remarks with respect to Nelsen et al.'s (1969) findings that the 'interpretation of these data is based on the rather tenuous assumption that all six measures are alternative definitions of the construct' (p. 287). In effect, Hartshorne, May, and Shuttleworth aborted the test-construction process almost before it had properly begun. They noted the low correlations between their various 'tests' which were in effect a pool of items from which a test or measure might eventually have emerged, and stopped there. They and subsequent researchers considered only the correlations between individual items.

In what is perhaps the most long-established and sophisticated area of psychological measurement, intelligence testing, it is not anticipated that the correlation between any two items on a test will be particularly high, and this is true even though the items concerned have met other criteria for inclusion in the test. In these terms, the low inter-item correlations reported by Hartshorne, May, and later by others, are hardly surprising, especially as those items had not met such criteria.

A good example of a test-construction approach to the measurement of social behaviour is the work of Fishbein and Ajzen (1974) on the measurement of religious behaviour. They developed a pool of items decribing various forms of religious observance and non-observance, and these were presented to a sample of students in the format of a self-report inventory. That is, for each item the students were asked to indicate whether they had or had not engaged in the activity described. Responses to these items were tested against the three principal scaling procedures devised for the construction of attitude scales, Thurstone, Likert, and Guttman. It is worth reporting that a majority of the items was *rejected* by the criteria of all three procedures. To anticipate the argument a little, many actions simply do not carry any unambiguous information about the actor.

In the assessment of moral conduct, very few measures have been based on more than one item, Hartshorne and May (twenty-five items) and Nelsen *et al.* (six items) being among the exceptions. In none of the studies based on experimental measures has there been any attempt to submit these to the criteria of any scaling procedure. Given Fishbein and Ajzen's findings, it is possible that a high proportion of the measures used would not meet these criteria.

Fishbein and Ajzen (1974) found however that it was possible to develop a satisfactory behavioural measure through item selection which also correlated at respectable levels with conventional measures of religious attitudes. There is a parallel to Fishbein and Ajzen's approach in research on delinquency based on self-report inventories of criminal and anti-social behaviour. Strangely, research of this type has never been cited in reviews of the specificity-consistency issue yet it seems less vulnerable to some of the criticisms raised against Hartshorne and May's evidence; the samples have been somewhat older and the items and measures deal with non-trivial forms of misconduct. Moreover, individual differences here prove to be more marked with respect to more serious misconduct.

Self-report inventories of delinquent and anti-social behaviour have not yet been the object of any systematic programme of test development. Nonetheless, there is evidence concerning item-whole correlations, which are essentially the basis of the Likert scaling procedure, and Fishbein and Ajzen showed that items which best meet Likert criteria are those most likely to possess reliability and validity. Hindelang (1972) found a typical item-whole correlation of .4 for a set of items referring to various kinds of criminal offence. Unpublished evidence collected by Emler and Heather, with an inventory of forty-nine items describing various forms of delinquency and misconduct, provided item-whole correlations in the range .28 to .72. For a more restricted sample of twenty items the range was .51 to .79, which compares favourably with Fishbein and Ajzen's results for their scale of religious behaviour. These preliminary explorations indicate that anti-social behaviour is a measurable dimension. Given appropriate measures, one can identify considerable consistency in this aspect of moral conduct. Moreover, the measures are reliable (Singh, 1979).

Further evidence of consistency is provided by factor analyses of self-report data. Gibson (1971) found that the first component of such an analysis accounted for 20% of the total variance. Allsopp and Feldman (1976) found that the forty-eight items on their anti-social behaviour questionnaire had loadings between .28 and .62 on the first component of a principal components analysis and that this component accounted for 22.6% of the total variance. Shapland (1978) reported that the first principal component accounted for 25% of the variance in her self-report data. Our own research has given figures in the range 22% to 32% with varying sets of items and samples. Although in none of these studies were the items in the inventories selected on the basis of any scaling criterion there is nonetheless clear evidence for consistency.

However, caution is necessary in the interpretation of evidence based on self-reports. First, there is a sense in which the items in a self-report inventory are not independent measures of separate events. Responses to the items are given on the same occasion, in the same format, and in the same social context, and this is likely to inflate the degree to which an individual will react to different items in the same way. Not all of the common variance can be explained away in this manner, though. The contingencies of the testing situation could not account for the differing degrees to which items relate to one another and to the whole; some item-whole correlations are near to zero.

A second possible objection is that such inventories are vulnerable to social desirability effects; some people will wish to appear in a socially desirable light and will bias their responses accordingly whereas others less concerned about social desirability will answer more candidly. If this were the case it would introduce a systematic bias inflating the apparent consistency of behaviour. It has been shown that self-reported delinquency measures correlate significantly with lie scales (e.g. Allsop and Feldman, 1976; Powell, 1977; Emler and Ross, 1980). However, it only follows from this that self-reported delinquency measures are *biased* by social desirability effects if one also accepts that lie scales measure the degree to which respondents tell the truth about themselves. It is equally plausible that one person gets a high score on a lie scale because he has not done any of the things described in the scale while another gets a low score because he indicates with equal candour that he has done them all.

A third objection is that self-report inventories that have been refined by item selection procedures will give *more* rather than less biased estimates of the consistency of conduct, because the purpose of such procedures is to identify items determined by any general factor to an unusual degree. It is certainly true that items which correlate most highly with a general factor will provide the most economical measures of an individual's position on that factor. Whether, however, such procedures can be said to inflate estimates of consistency depends upon the question one wishes to answer. If, for instance, the question is one of the generality of criminal behaviour—i.e. to what extent do individuals who engage in one form of activity within the (legally defined) domain of criminal behaviour engage in other forms of such activity—the conclusion must be that such procedures do inflate apparent generality because they effectively restrict the domain in a systematic way. If, instead, the question concerns the scope of consistency then such procedures are, in effect, merely ways of establishing what this scope is, if any. It does not follow that, because there is a legally definable domain of criminal behaviour, this will correspond in any precise way with any form of consistency in individual conduct. The degree of correspondence that actually exists is a largely unanswered empirical question.

The most serious question mark over self-report studies must concern validity: are the data from self-report inventories valid measures of the behaviour they describe? It seems that almost all adolescents will admit to some of the criminal activities described in self-reported delinquency inventories, but those who have been convicted admit to much more frequent and more serious offending. Emler *et al.* (1978) found that borstal inmates admitted to more serious offences at a rate of about four to one when compared with an unconvicted group. Likewise, West and Farrington (1973) have found a strong relationship between officially recorded delinquency and adolescents' scores on a self-report scale. Allsopp and Feldman (1976) also reported that their self-report measure of anti-social behaviour related to an 'objective' measure of misbehaviour based on the number of school punishments received. Blackmore (1974) examined the relationship between self-reported delinquency and official convictions among adolescent boys and found that 75% of known offences were admitted on the self-report scale. Similar evidence has been reported by Farrington (1973) and by Hardt and Peterson-Hardt (1977).

One of the most thorough investigations of the validity of self-reported delinquency data has been made by Gold (1966) who concluded that fully three-quarters of the sample investigated had given truthful responses on the self-report inventory. However, as Box (1971) rightly observes, this means that the data from a quarter of the subjects are of questionable value and this minority poses a problem because it is unclear how their responses might bias the results.

Despite this difficulty, and despite other questions about the interpretation of self-report data which shall be raised later in the chapter, I believe that the weight of evidence is such as to suggest that a considerable degree of consistency may exist in moral conduct; some people are consistently more dishonest, more anti-social, or more likely to commit criminal offences than others. This view is further supported by the predictability of moral conduct (see below).

The fact that there exist such consistencies in behaviour, that there are relatively stable differences between individuals, says nothing about how such differences are to be explained. Among critics of differential psychology there seems to prevail an endemic confusion of description and explanation. It is widely assumed that traits are always used as explanatory concepts. While it is true that a few personality theorists have employed traits as explanations, most use trait terms only to describe consistencies or regularities in behaviour, and moreover accept that such regularities constitute the phenomena to be explained (cf. Hogan, De Soto, and Solano, 1977). From the observation that some people are frequently dishonest while others only occasionally transgress it does not follow that their behaviour is to be explained in terms of differences in some underlying psychological trait of honesty or criminality. The issue of explanation will be taken up in the latter part of this chapter.

Can Moral Conduct be Predicted?

Another argument that moral conduct does not reflect a stable characteristic of the individual is based on the claim that such behaviour cannot be predicted from other personal qualities or from behaviour at some earlier point in time. Kohlberg (1971b) provides a more specific version of this argument when he observes that 'People's verbal moral values about honesty have nothing to do with how they act. People who cheat express as much or more moral disapproval of cheating as those who do not cheat' (1971b, p. 75). Much of the available evidence supports Kohlberg's view but again one is entitled to ask about the quality of the evidence.

Kohlberg's observation is reminiscent of criticisms of the attitude concept to the effect that verbally expressed attitudes relate poorly, if at all, to actual behaviour. There is a considerable body of evidence consistent with this claim (see Wicker, 1969) but Fishbein and Ajzen (1974) point out that the fault may not be in the concept of attitude or even in its measurement but in the way that behaviour is assessed. Most research on the attitude-behaviour link has relied on a single-act criterion as a measure of the behaviour in question, i.e. a single item test. Fishbein and Ajzen show that a multiple-act (or multiple item) measure of behaviour (in their case, religious behaviour) does correlate positively and substantially with conventional measures of verbally expressed attitudes. They also show that only those individual items meeting the criteria of Likert scaling correlate with verbal attitude scales. In studies of the relation between verbal moral attitudes and moral behaviour we can have no confidence that the single act measures of behaviour typically used would have met such criteria.

Interestingly, in one study (Brown, 1974) it was found that verbal opinions could predict moral conduct. Brown found that a self-report measure of moral behaviour was significantly related to verbal attitudes among a sample of eleven to fifteen year olds, towards the law in general, policemen, and courts. Again similar evidence has been reported by Clark and Wenninger (1964) and by Gibson (1967).

Kohlberg (1976) has shown that moral reasoning is a measurable psychological characteristic on which there are individual differences, and according to Kohlberg it is a more stable characteristic than verbal moral attitudes. It might therefore be expected that if moral conduct can be predicted from anything it will be from moral reasoning.[1] Emler *et al.* (1978) found that Rest's (1975) measure of moral reasoning, modelled on Kohlberg's theory, was quite unrelated to moral conduct as assessed by a self-report inventory of delinquency. It would seem, then, that not all measurable moral attributes are related to moral conduct in the same way. (See also Jurkovic, 1980.)

Conventional personality measures, however, have been found to be particularly predictive of the anti-social behaviour/delinquency dimension of moral conduct. In America, Gough (1965) has shown that delinquency is reliably related to scores on the socialization scale of the California Psychological Inventory. Gough obtained a point-biserial correlation of .73 between a delinquent-nondelinquent criterion and scores on this scale. Hindelang (1972) has reported significant correlations between self-reported delinquency and scales of both the CPI and MMPI.

In Britain, Allsopp and Feldman (1976) found that scores on their anti-social behaviour self-report scale were related to responses on several items of the Psychoticism, Extraversion, and Neuroticism scales of Eysenck's (1975) Junior Personality Questionnaire, for samples of eleven to sixteen year olds. Powell (1977) found that correlations with a modified version of the Allsopp and Feldman Scale ranged from .13 to .57 for Psychoticism, with samples of eight to fifteen year old boys and girls. The average correlation was .45, the averages for Extraversion and Neuroticism being .16 and .23 respectively. Finally, Emler and Ross (1980) obtained a correlation of .78 between Psychoticism and a self-report inventory of delinquent activity; the correlations obtained for Extraversion and Neuroticism were, however, far lower. My purpose is not to make out a case for Eysenck's theory of criminality nor to decide here on the meaning of the various correlations reported but merely to point out that moral conduct can be predicted from conventional measures of individual differences.

With respect to predictability and stability over time, there is also no dearth of positive evidence. West and Farrington (1973) cite numerous studies in which teachers were shown to make much better than chance predictions of future delinquency among their pupils. West's own research shows that a large number of personal characteristics are significantly related to future delinquency, whether delinquency is assessed by official records or by self-report. Among the most effective predictors at age eight for delinquency at age fourteen were teachers' and peers' ratings of troublesomeness (West and Farrington, 1973).

---

[1] It is unlikely that Kohlberg would be entirely happy with the relevance of such a 'test' of his theory, however (see pp. 199–200).

Are Situational Factors More Potent than Personal Factors?

One of the most frequently heard objections to the use of personality concepts in social psychology is that social behaviour is largely situationally determined, and beside the impact of the situation, individual differences are trivial. Kohlberg (1971a) illustrates what he calls the battle of conscience with data from two studies of cheating. In one, 80% of the children tested cheated while in the other only 15% did so. The differences could, Kohlberg believes, plausibly be attributed to differences in the appearance of the apparatus used in the respective studies; i.e. to situational factors.

This example illustrates another meaning of the claim that there is no generality to honesty: some situations encourage honesty in almost everyone, some in almost no one. There are numerous other examples of this kind which imply that situational influences overwhelm any differences in the strength of personal dispositions to behave honestly or dishonestly. In another area, Milgram (1965) demonstrated that an overwhelming majority of people would follow instructions to give painful electric shocks to a helpless victim, despite the expectation that this action would violate the moral scruples of many of them. Mixon (1972) has made a further study of this particular case and shown that manipulation of the instructions can produce on the one hand 100% obedience, and on the other 0% obedience. In other words, it is possible to specify those situational conditions which will have the same effect on everyone's behaviour. But it does not therefore follow that there is no person-based consistency in behaviour, that the idea of moral traits is worthless.

One thing that it means for a test item to meet Likert criteria is that it discriminates. Not everyone responds to it in the same way. A test of intelligence that everyone passes or everyone fails might tell us something about the limits of human intelligence but it would be singularly unhelpful as a measure of individual *differences* in intelligence. The point is that there are many situations in which everyone does *not* respond in the same way. Moreover, even in the circumstances in which everyone does behave in similar fashion, differences in individual dispositions remain. If you put up a 'No Smoking' sign, no one may smoke in its vicinity but this does not eliminate individual differences in smoking tendencies among those who read the sign (and some may leave the vicinity).

Some research on attribution processes has shown that people attribute personal characteristics to another on the basis of his overt behaviour only when the situation is one in which not everyone would have been expected to act in the same way (e.g. Jones, Davis, and Gergen, 1961). That is why not every action can carry unambiguous information about the personal characteristics of the actor. When we say that someone is honest we mean he will act honestly in circumstances where perhaps 50% of the population could be expected to act dishonestly, not that he will act honestly in situations where everyone would do so.

The fact that there is variation in response from one individual to another in many situations still does not, of course, rule out the specificity option. Put another way, if a situation produces differential reactions this does not mean that it is automatically a good indicator of any generalized individual differences. The differential reaction found in one situation and on one occasion must also correlate with that found in the same situation on another occasion and with those found in other situations. If such effects could not be replicated in these ways one would have to conclude that they were indeed specific to a situation and occasion. The purpose of test construction procedures is to identify and select those situations (= items) for which differential reactions can be replicated.

Personality theorists like Mischel (1968) have argued that the specificity hypothesis has been so widely confirmed that it is appropriate to base research on a situationalist model of behaviour. An individual's reactions, Mischel suggests, are unique to situations and learning theory can account for this specificity: individuals learn responses to specific situations, not to general classes of situation. The advocates of situationism have tied their model of behaviour to an experimental methodology and in doing so have created a potential confusion about the respective aims of experimental psychology and the psychology of tests and measurements. Without making any assumptions about the ultimate theoretical objectives of each, it is clear that their immediate aims are different but certainly not incompatible. Test construction is a form of research programme in which the aim is to discover psychological differences between people, e.g. in intelligence, abilities, interests, or personality. Experimental psychology is a programme whose aim is to discover ways in which situations differ in their impact on behaviour, e.g. the effects of physical stimuli in the situation on some aspect of human performance. These different preoccupations lead to different forms of sampling but they do not, as Mischel and others seem to think, lead to mutually exclusive models of personality functioning—one in which behaviour is determined exclusively by the situation and one in which it is determined exclusively by individual psychological characteristics.[2]

Arguments for 'situationism' which appeal to the relative proportions of variance in behaviour accounted for respectively by differences between persons and differences between situations attract similar objections: it depends on what your theoretical interests are and what you choose to sample as a result. Whether persons or situations account for more observed variance is not theoretically a decisive question. But there is one further objection to the situationalist's experimental programme as applied to social behaviour. It requires a return to the positivist position that social situations can be objectively classified.

---

[2] If Mischel were correct then it would be pointless for experimentalists to employ repeated measures designs in their research; the correlations of rank-orders of individuals across conditions, exploited in such designs in order to reduce error variance, would not exist.

Are Interaction Effects More Important than Individual Differences?

A recent development in personality psychology has been the emergence of an interactionist view of personality functioning (e.g. Argyle and Little, 1972; Bowers, 1973; Endler and Magnusson, 1976). The substance of the 'interactionists'' claim seems to be as follows: interaction effects in analysis of variance designs, where 'persons' and 'situations' constitute the main effects, account for more variance than either main effect by itself. To make this the basis for a personality theory seems as naive as deciding theoretical priorities on the basis of the relative sizes of 'person' and 'situation' effects. But there are other objections.

First, Endler and Magnusson (1976), currently the foremost spokesmen for the interactionist position, urge that the strong interaction effects they find refute the implication of trait models of personality that there is rank order stability of persons across situations. Golding (1975) has shown quite clearly that the evidence on which Endler and Magnusson's case rests has no bearing on the rank order stability question.[3] Second, the interaction effects in some of the studies cited by Endler and Magnusson (1976) and by Bowers (1973), e.g. Argyle and Little (1972), Nelson, Grinder, and Mutterer (1969), are confounded with error variance; i.e. they are non-replicated interactions.

Third, and most damaging for their case, in those studies cited where error variance and interaction variance can be computed separately, the average variance in behaviour attributable to person x situation intereactions is 9%, hardly very substantial and certainly no greater than that which, according to Endler and Magnusson, can on average be attributed to persons. Overall the proportion of variance attributable to person x situation interactions is so unstable as to make any generalizations foolhardy. Endler and Magnusson (1976) do obtain higher figures for interaction effects—around 30%—but do so by summing variance from three different kinds of interaction, person x situation, person x mode of response, and situation x mode of response, and then contrasting that total with 'person' variance which is, to say the least, a little bit misleading.

Like the situationists, the interactionists have implied that only a small proportion of the variance that exists in human social behaviour can be attributed to the differences between individual people, but that other predictable sources of variance exist which account for much higher proportions. In the case of the interactionists these sources are the interactions between persons and situations. But this claim has proved unfounded; not only do such interaction effects account for very litle variance but also these interactions are not predictable because there is no theory from which they could be predicted.

---

[3] Endler and Magnusson refer to evidence from multidimensional variance components analysis. The omega-squared ratios on which variance components estimates are based (Endler and Hunt, 1968) are neither logically nor empirically related to generalizability coefficients which provide a more appropriate estimate of trait stability or consistency.

Is There Consistency in Underlying Structure Rather Than Overt Behaviour?

One account of moral development, that of Lawrence Kohlberg (1976), involves the claim that consistency exists at the level of cognitive structure rather than overt behaviour; individuals are consistent in the structure of their moral reasoning although their overt moral conduct may not appear objectively consistent.

In his initial work Kohlberg had predicted that younger children would prefer authority-serving solutions to moral dilemmas whereas older ones would prefer need-serving solutions. His findings failed to confirm this and Kohlberg concluded that the content of such moral preferences is not predictable; the choices made by different individuals do not conform to any coherent pattern. He argued, however, that the structure of the underlying reasoning on which such preferences or choices are based is predictable and shows a consistent pattern that is related to age.

Kohlberg has developed this idea in two ways that are relevant to this discussion. First, he has suggested that an individual's moral reasoning will conform to one of six structural types, these types having the properties of developmental stages. At any specific point in an individual's development, therefore, a common cognitive structure will underlie his reasoning about diverse issues (see Weinreich-Haste, Chapter 5). Second, Kohlberg has argued that behaviours which are overtly identical can arise from different types of reasoning; two individuals reasoning at different stages could nonetheless behave overtly in the same manner on some occasions. Conversely, two individuals reasoning at the same stage could nonetheless behave overtly in quite different ways on some occasions. Hence there is no point in simply looking at overt behaviour; one must look at the reasoning underlying behaviour (e.g. Turiel, 1969; Kohlberg, 1971a).

At other points Kohlberg has been less certain about the relation between the structure of reasoning and overt behaviour, and has been inclined to leave the question open: 'From the point of view of cognitive-developmental theory, the relation of the development of judgment to action is something to be studied and theoretically conceptualized' (Kohlberg, 1976, p. 46). But he has also said, 'Moral stage development predicts maturity of moral behaviour better than Hartshorne and May's measures' (1976, p. 46), and 'moral stage is a good predictor of action in various experimental and natural settings' (1976, p. 32). But how are we to define or identify 'mature moral conduct' if not in terms of some overt and consistent form of individual differences in moral conduct? What, furthermore, is there in action for moral stage to predict if not overt and stable differences between individuals in the way that they act?

Perhaps the interpretation most congruent with the spirit of Kohlberg's theory is that there will be a pattern to moral conduct which reflects underlying structure, rather than an overt similarity or covariation between one action and another. The closest researchers have come to specifying a structure underlying conduct is in the idea of norms of justice underlying people's allocation of resources to others. In a recent review, Hook and Cook (1979) identify various such norms which appear to underlie different patterns of resource allocation. They suggest the evidence supports the hypothesis of a link between levels of intellectual development—structurally defined—and the norms that children and adults practise. It remains, however, to be demonstrated that such structural consistencies exist in other areas of moral conduct or that they are related to the structural quality of moral reasoning stages.

Whatever the case, there has been no shortage of attempts to show that relations exist between moral reasoning and action or conduct, e.g. Mac-Namee's (1978) demonstration of a relation between level of moral reasoning and degree of helpfulness. Insofar as Kohlberg accepts that evidence of this kind is relevant (see Kohlberg, 1969, 1971a, b, 1976; also Broughton, 1978) he must also accept that there are consistent, stable, and reliable individual differences in conduct for otherwise there would be no relation to find. Kohlberg's (1971a) suggestion that a moderator variable, ego strength, may affect the relation between reasoning and action does not alter this conclusion.

The Interpretation of Behavioural Consistency

Alternative Explanations

If it is accepted that there are individual differences in moral conduct, there remains the problem of how these are to be explained and the related issue of what meaning, if any, can be attached to the concept of moral character. The evidence adduced here for such differences comes mainly from self-report studies of moral conduct. Therefore the question of interpretation of these differences is closely linked to the meaning that is given to the self-report responses. Some pointers are provided by classical test theory, and by its critics.

The classical view of item responses is that they are second-best sources of information about a person's actual behaviour, or perceptions, or feelings, appropriate because direct assessment would be difficult if not impossible (Meehl, 1945). Consistency in self-report responses is taken to reflect consistency in actual behaviour and consistency in behaviour exists because the behaviour arises from some underlying neuro-psychic structure. In this view behaviour is consistent insofar as an individual's separate actions have similar underlying dynamics. For the psychoanalytically inclined these dynamics might be unconscious motives or defence mechanisms. Adorno *et al.* (1950) interpreted high scores on the F-scale (a particular pattern of item responses) in terms of the operation of unconscious psychological defences formed in early childhood. For a more biologically oriented theorist like Eysenck, behavioural consistency arises from neurological factors.

Three criticisms of the classical view are worth considering. First, item responses as indirect measures of actual behaviour are distorted by the imperfections of human memory. Gold (1966) has admitted that even if responses to self-report inventories of delinquency are totally honest, one cannot assume that they will also be totally valid. Studies of retrospective reporting of child-rearing practices have shown that the degree of error in recall of own behaviour can be quite considerable (e.g. Yarrow, Campbell, and Burton, 1964, 1968). The crucial question, though, is whether errors in recall would produce any systematic bias. Could patterns of individual differences in self-reported conduct be attributed simply to systematic individual differences in rates of recall? One can only say that it does not seem plausible.

Second, the classical position requires that all individuals interpret test items in the same way for responses of different individuals to be comparable. There is what might be called a cognitive position according to which items may mean different things to different individuals. This position does allow that behaviour can be consistent but only in the sense that different actions can have the same meaning for the actor. The consistency derives from some privately held interpretation of the situations encountered. It is likely to be a unique con-sistency, therefore, and not necessarily apparent to the untrained observer. Consistency of this kind cannot be revealed by the conventional self-report measure because of the idiosyncracies of individual interpretations of test items. Instead, such procedures as the Role Repertory Grid and the Moral Judgment Interview have been developed to uncover the way that each indi-vidual interprets events. The fact is that one can nonetheless find consistent and stable patterns of individual differences in responses to conventional test items and it is difficult for the cognitive position to explain this.

The third criticism is that such patterns are test artefacts; they reflect response sets of, for instance, social desirability or acquiescence. It has been argued that self-report inventories are vulnerable to faking and that correlations between lie scale scores and self-reported delinquency indicate some individuals are more inclined to fake their responses in a socially desirable direction. I have already argued that this is not the only possible interpretation of such correla-tions (p. 192). What is of interest in this criticism is the implication that people will attempt to manage the impression that is created by the responses they give. In other words, contrary to the classical view in which item responses are treated as signs of unconscious dynamics given off by the test taker, they are to be treated as consciously intended communications by the test taker to the test giver.

I believe that item responses can be usefully treated as self-presentations, the dynamics of which are no different from those underlying other facets of social behaviour (see also Johnson, 1981). On this view, behavioural consistency is interpreted as reflecting consistency of social or interpersonal meaning; an individual's behaviour is consistent if his various actions are understood by both himself and his audience to mean the same thing.[4] The empirical covariation of

---

[4] It does not follow, of course, that meanings are universal. On the contrary, it is more likely that many will be shared only by members of the same society, social group, or community and some may be restricted to specific relationships or occasions.

actions or item responses would indicate that the covariates have similar social meanings. With respect to self-report inventories, items meeting Likert criteria are those that have, for the population responding to or judging them, similar and unambiguous meanings. This view of consistency suggests a self-presentational analysis of moral conduct and the possibilities of such an analysis will be considered.

Self Presentation and Moral Conduct

The interpretation of social behaviour as self presentation (cf. Goffman, 1959) is based on the idea that one of the major problems the individual faces is to make himself understood. The problem is one of controlling a process of communication, making explicit to others one's intentions, feelings, desires, and above all the kind of person one is or wishes to be taken for.

The cognitive position, referred to above, implies that these problems belong exclusively to the audience as problems of perception; it is for the audience to infer the character and attitudes of the individual from his actions. But given a situation in which, as Kohlberg suggests, there is consistency in the cognitive structure that underlies behaviour but not in the overt behaviour itself, the moral significance of an individual's actions would remain obscure to any audience not professionally equipped to analyse such structure. Goffman believes that the interpretation of action is a problem for the actor and not just for the audience. The actor will not be unaware that others will interpret his actions and he will want to influence that interpretation. Every public action is potentially a communication by the actor to others about himself. If others are to form the impression he desires then it is necessary for him to manage that impression by exploiting a set of shared meanings.

Since among other things an audience might be inclined to draw conclusions about an individual's moral qualities—his trustworthiness, honesty, reliability, loyalty, fairmindedness, and so on—we would expect that the individual would also wish to influence these conclusions and usually in a positive direction. Goffman's interpretation indicates that actually being in some objective sense moral is of less consequence than success in seeming to be moral; appearance, if not everything, is certainly a great deal. In this sense, character converges with reputation.

The significance of moral reputation is not a new discovery. We find Hartshorne, May, and Shuttleworth (1930) saying:

'When enough opinions (about the character of a subject) can be gathered with reasonable care and from contrasting sources—as from pupils, teachers, and parents—the resulting score becomes a fair substitute for an elaborate and expensive program of objective testing.'

(Hartshorne, May, and Shuttleworth, 1930, p. 369)

In a later study of moral development, Havighurst and Taba (1949) based their index of character on ratings of reputations by acquaintances of the research sample. In both cases, however, moral reputation is considered from the point of view of an observer. The self-presentational approach treats moral reputation as something that must be actively and to some extent consciously influenced, if not managed, by the person to whom it refers.

This view has some interesting implications. For example, Goffman suggests that certain qualities of character can present considerable problems of dramatic realization. If an individual wishes to appear courageous he may find that there are few opportunities to act in such a way that his audience will accept it as unambiguous evidence of courage (Goffman, 1967). On the other hand, many situations put at risk such reputations as the individual has built and are therefore to be avoided. As Goffman puts it, 'there is much to be gained from venturing nothing' (1955, p. 43).

Critics may feel this view also has some rather obvious flaws. One such is that it places all the emphasis on public behaviour. Traditionally psychologists seem to have accepted that to act morally means above all to act in accordance with rule, law, or principle precisely when one's actions are not open to public appraisal. 'Conscience strength' has accordingly been operationalized in terms of resistance to temptation under conditions of anonymity. Most theories of moral development are based on this view for they are concerned with the development of internalized, autonomous moral controls which will operate in the absence of public supervision or external sanction.

This, I believe, gives an inappropriate emphasis to the private and covert side of moral misconduct. People do commonly take account of the likelihood that their actions will be observed or detected, and what they do will depend on how they assess the repercussions. I do not claim that conduct is exclusively determined by estimates of the probability of detection, though this factor is important (cf. Rettig and Rawson, 1963). My point is rather that conduct which transgresses conventional standards, rules, or laws, is often overt and unconcealed; there is an audience, though not necessarily one that can or will deliver penal sanctions. From research it appears that most delinquent acts are committed in the company of others (Hood and Sparks, 1970; Emler and Ross, 1980). Moreover, many delinquent acts are witnessed by the victims. Assault is one obvious example and it represents a major component of the criminal statistics. The extent of crime that is witnessed by the victim is such that victim reports have provided a new methodology in the study of crime and delinquency (e.g. Hindelang, 1978). It also appears that the culprits are often known to their victims. Furthermore, commission of this overt form of moral misconduct is highly correlated with what are normally considered the more covert forms such as theft (Emler and Ross, 1980).

Even if there is no immediate audience it is quite possible that an individual will recall his misdeeds when there is an audience present. In a series of studies, Emler and Fisher (1981) found that when people meet acquaintances they exchange a great deal of personal information. The largest proportion of this information relates to their own past and current activities. It would seem that people are strongly disposed to make their acquaintances indirect witnesses of their own doings. If this pattern is normal then it would be difficult grossly to mislead one's acquaintances about one's past conduct because it would either require quite sophisticated fabrication of imaginary doings or keeping silent which would itself be a suspicious departure from the norm.

Ratings of reputation by peers, teachers, and other acquaintances have been used with considerable success in the prediction of future delinquency. This suggests that there must be distinctive qualities to the deliquent's behaviour that are quite apparent to anyone acquainted with him. Finally, self-report inventories, as we have seen, provide a reliable guide to conduct and this suggests that most adolescents are willing at least to make the researcher a witness to their past behaviour. Moreover, guarantees of anonymity seem to have little impact on what is admitted (Kulik, Stein, and Sarbin, 1968b).

It is not hard to understand why psychology would have been vulnerable to the idea that morality is concerned with conduct in secret. First, given its individualistic bias and consequent failure to notice that people interact with each other, the concept of the moral domain tended to leave out what people do to each other face to face, and confined itself to what they do behind each other's backs. Second, not having discovered, for the same reasons, that people in their everyday lives belong to small, face-to-face communities of mutual acquaintances, and that they spend much of their time in the mutual exchange of personal information within these communities (cf. Emler and Fisher, 1981), this psychology did not appreciate that there is very little of importance that is quite private, that has no audience apart from the self.

Sources of Individual Differences in Self Presentation

We have yet to consider why there should be individual differences in self presentation, why some individuals should wish to be taken for one kind of person while others wish to be taken for something quite different. In particular, why should some consistently act so as to appear law abiding and others do the reverse? This could lead us back to explanations in terms of deep-seated personality dynamics. We have already seen that anti-social or delinquent behaviour is correlated with several conventional personality measures. However, causal interpretations of these relations would be premature. Item responses and test scores of personality inventories are potentially just as much self-presentations as are responses to self-report inventories of behaviour (e.g. Wiggins, 1966; Mills and Hogan, 1978). A careful examination of the items composing the Psychoticism and Lie scales of the JEPQ, both correlated with self-report delinquency, reveals that they are in effect self-reports of the same kinds of behaviour as delinquency measures. They correlate simply because they sample the same things.

Instead of seeking explanations for moral conduct in terms of personality traits, let us first see how far it is possible to get by treating moral character as a response to immediate interpersonal and social relations. Given that an individual's relationship can change, the manifest character of the individual is not necessarily something irrevocably fixed. Impressions are managed with respect to particular other people—those with whom one associates regularly—rather than with respect to people in general. For most of us most of the time it matters little what strangers or the abstract general public think of us; we are concerned with the reputation we have within our own immediate community. And this suggests reasons why there may be variations in moral conduct or the self-presentation of moral character.

Box (1971), in a discussion of 'control theory', gives a clue to some of the more modifiable influences on moral conduct. The first of these Box calls commitments. Being discovered in a misdemeanour will mean different things to different individuals by virtue of what they have to lose. Current commitments—to educational goals or to a career—are, in Box's words, bonds which tie an individual to the conventional order. This may be why crime is so overwhelmingly an adolescent phenomenon. Many adolescents have few commitments, but as they get jobs, embark on careers, get married, have children, this changes. Likewise, the schoolboy in the bottom stream has little to lose by a conventionally 'bad' reputation, but the boy in the top stream has considerable accumulated investments to protect and therefore a great deal to lose by risking such stigma. One implication of this is that as personal circumstances change so conduct will change; stability and consistency in moral conduct will persist only so long as commitments or investments remain at the same level.

We are now in a position to meet a possible objection to the self-presentational approach. Since moral behaviour is normally behaviour that is conventionally valued, it could be argued that everyone would want to appear moral. Apart from the fact that some people are apparently quite willing to give a quite unflattering socially undesirable impression of themselves, conformity to conventional moral standards is not indefinitely rewarding. It can become dull and unexciting. Matza and Sykes (1961) suggested that respectable, law abiding citizens who endorse conventional values will also be attracted to a set of 'subterranean' values based on a search for adventure and excitement, a disdain of routine work, admiration for conspicuous consumption, and approval of aggressive toughness. A similar observation has been made by Moscovici and Faucheux (1972) who point out that the non-conformist or deviant is often more popular and attractive than the person who adheres to convention or the majority view. Presumably what holds many in check and prevents them from acting upon deviant values is that they believe they have too much to lose.

Conformity, moreover, does not always enhance the individual's moral status. If everyone is engaged in a quest for a positive social identity, not all will suffer setbacks by being deviant. Those who already have low moral status or who find they are barred or handicapped in using conventional routes to success may have more to gain by deviating from conventional standards than by upholding them (cf. Homans, 1961; Lemaine, 1974; Moscovici, 1976).

A further circumstantial factor suggested by Box is attachments, which refers to firm and stable relationships with others. Box suggests that for adolescents these would be significant attachments to mothers, fathers, teachers, or other adults. When such attachments are absent or weakened delinquency is more likely. The evidence for this is mixed. Boys in lower streams of secondary schools are more likely than those in higher streams to be delinquent (see also Kelly, 1975). They are also more likely to reject the values of the school and the conventional order with which it is associated (e.g. Sugarman, 1967). This could reflect low attachment to teachers who are seen to represent the conventional order but it could also as noted above reflect weaker commitments, or the formation of an anti-conventional sub-culture in the lower streams Similarly, though there are indications that delinquency is linked to conflict with parents (e.g. West and Farrington, 1973), it is also clear that such conflict is not a necessary condition for delinquency. Kulik *et al.* (1968a) identified various patterns of delinquent behaviour, some but not all of which were associated with parental defiance.

The attachment variable can be interpreted in other ways, especially if we broaden this variable to include an individual's acquaintances and friends, the members of his effective immediate social network. If our social identities are managed and maintained in quite specific sets of relations, how we act will depend on who the audience is and what we have led them to expect of us. With one audience we may have established a reputation for toughness, cynicism, or wild, reckless behaviour, while with another decency, hard work, or considera-tion for others. In most cases, however, an individual's social networks overlap sufficiently so that his reputation will be substantially similar in all of them. There are uncommon circumstances and particular conditions in which this will not be true. The degree to which a person's social networks overlap should therefore underlie the degree of overall consistency in that person's conduct.

The audience can be a source of variation in another sense. Some individuals may find themselves among acquaintances with whom moral reputation is not enhanced by being conventionally moral or law-abiding. Others may simply not have acquaintances and therefore hardly any personally significant audience to maintain a reputation for. If we behave consistently because the people we know expect it of us then there may be little consistency when we are not around the people we know or when we find ourselves without friends or acquaintances. It has been observed that not only do delinquents tend to have acquaintances who are also delinquent (e.g. Short, 1957; Voss, 1964) but they also tend to be less popular among their peers (e.g. West and Farrington, 1973). It has also been observed that close and enduring attachments are critical to the stability of one's behaviour and sense of identity (Berger and Kellner, 1964).

The Definition of Morality

I avoided beginning this chapter with any definition of morality, hoping that without this initial encumbrance a definition might spontaneously emerge. If this has not happened at least some clues have arisen about the framework for such a definition. The discussion of moral character has revolved around the consistency of anti-social and delinquent tendencies. Although it is reasonable to expect that any definition of morality would include those standards according to which a community comes to regard some conduct as anti-social or delinquent, the moral domain is obviously broader than this. Rather than considering what the scope of this domain might be I want to highlight some of the implications of the self-presentational approach.

The most important of these is that morality, insofar as it is relevant to conduct in everyday life, must involve a degree of consensus. If each individual has a unique and private view of morality which guides his conduct, what he does will make little sense to others and he will have considerable difficulty making himself understood. If anyone does develop a private view, he nonetheless has the problem sooner or later of persuading others to accept his view. Consensus is, of course, always open to renegotiation and indeed seems to require that those concerned continually reconsider or reconfirm the standards that are to apply and the manner in which they are to be interpreted (Strauss, 1978).

It is instructive that measures of moral attitudes are so often prefaced with the disclaimer that there are no right or wrong answers to the questions that follow and that everyone has his own opinions. Such statements betray the moral assumptions of investigators but their subjects might find these assertions odd, especially if it is part of their moral beliefs that there are standards that are unconditionally correct and to which everyone ought to agree. Can it really be assumed that most people believe in anarchy in moral matters, supposing each individual's opinion to be as good as any other? It is common enough to find such an extreme relativism professed among the intellectually sophisticated but acting on such esoteric, philosophical conclusions is another matter. Communication—of a moral identity as of anything else—requires a context of consensus.

It is clear that consensus is not absolute, nor that any one person is aware of only one set of standards. But the problems posed by moral pluralism for self-presentation would take another chapter to discuss. One common-sense meaning of character is what is distinctive about a person. We often say a person displays moral character if he stands by his principles under the kinds of pressure that we would expect to cause most people to abandon theirs. In other words, his conduct is out of the ordinary unusual. The claim he stakes to moral character is more unmistakable the more distinctive it is. But as Goffman (1967) notes, such opportunities for dramatizing moral identity do not fall to us frequently and to some maybe hardly ever. Perhaps for some people the only opportunity they see to express 'self', to be distinctive, is to break the rules. If being bad is more distinctive than being good, if all the pressures are to be virtuous, then being bad is being somebody.

References

Adorno, T. W., Frenkel-Brunswik, E., Levinson, D. J., and Sanford, R. N. (1950). *The authoritarian personality*. Harper, New York.

Allsopp, J. F., and Feldman, P. M. (1976). Personality and antisocial behaviour in schoolboys. *British Journal of Criminology*, **16**, 337–351.

Argyle, M., and Little, B. R. (1972). Do personality traits apply to social behaviour? *Journal for the Theory of Social Behaviour*, **2**, 1–55.

Berger, P. L., and Kellner, H. (1964). Marriage and the construction of reality: An exercise in the microsociology of knowledge. *Diogenes*, **46**, 1–23.

Blackmore, J. (1974). The relationship between self-reported delinquency and official convictions among adolescent boys. *British Journal of Criminology*, **14**, 172–176.

Bowers, K. (1973). Situationism in psychology: An analysis and critique. *Psychological Review*, **80**, 307–336.

Box, S. (1971). *Deviance, reality and society*, Holt, Rinehart, and Winston, New York.

Broughton, J. (1978). The cognitive developmental approach to morality: A reply to Kurtines and Grief. *Journal of Moral Education*, **7**, 81–96.

Brown, D. W. (1974). Adolescent attitudes and lawful behavior. *Public Opinion Quarterly*, **38**, 98–106.

Clark, J. P., and Wenninger, E. P. (1964). The attitude of juveniles toward the legal institution. *Journal of Criminal Law, Criminology and Political Science*, **55**, 482–489.

Emler, N. P., and Fisher, S. (1981). Gossip and the nature of the social environment. Paper presented at the *Annual Conference of the British Psychological Society, Social Psychology Section, Oxford, September, 1981*.

Emler, N. P., Heather, N., and Winton, M. (1978). Delinquency and the development of moral reasoning. *British Journal of Social and Clinical Psychology*, **17**, 325–331.

Emler, N. P., and Ross, A. (1980). Attitudinal and personality correlates of self-reported solitary and group delinquency. Unpublished Manuscript, University of Dundee, 1980.

Endler, N. S., and Hunt, J. McV. (1968). S-R inventories of hostility and comparisons of the proportions of variance from persons, responses and situations for hostility and anxiousness. *Journal of Personality and Social Psychology*, **9**, 309–315.

Endler, N. S., and Magnusson, D. (1976). Toward an interactional psychology of personality. *Psychological Bulletin*, **83**, 956–974.

Eysenck, H. J., and Eysenck, S. B. G. (1975). *Manual of the Eysenck Personality Questionnaire (adult and junior)*. Hodder and Stoughton, London.

Farrington, D. P. (1973). Self-reports of deviant behaviour: Predictive and reliable? *Journal of Criminal Law and Criminology*, **64**, 99–110.

Fishbein, M., and Ajzen, I. (1974). Attitudes toward objects as predictors of single and multiple behavioural criteria. *Psychological Review*, **81**, 59–74.

Gibson, H. B. (1967). Self-reported delinquency among school boys and their attitudes to the police. *British Journal of Social and Clinical Psychology*, **6**, 168–173.

Gibson, H. B. (1971). The factorial structure of juvenile delinquency: A study of self-reported acts. *British Journal of Social and Clinical Psychology*, **10**, 1–9.

Goffman, E. (1955). On face work: An analysis of ritual elements in social interaction. *Psychiatry*, **18**, 213–231.

Goffman, E. (1959). *The presentation of self in every day life*, Doubleday, New York.

Goffman, E. (1967). Where the action is. In E. Goffman (Ed.), *Interaction ritual: Essays on face-to-face behavior*, Doubleday, New York.

Gold, M. (1966). Undetected delinquent behavior. *Journal of Research on Crime and Delinquency*, **3**, 27.

Golding, S. L. (1975). Flies in the ointment: Methodological problems in the analysis of the percentage of variance due to persons and situations. *Psychological Bulletin*, **82**, 278–288.

Gough, H. B. (1965). Conceptual analysis of psychological test scores and other diagnostic variables. *Journal of Abnormal Psychology*, **70**, 294–302.

Hardt, R. H., and Peterson-Hardt, S. (1977). On determining the quality of the delinquency self-report method. *Journal of Research in Crime and Delinquency*, **14**, 247–258.

Hartshorne, H., and May, M. A. (1928). *Studies in the nature of character, I: Studies in deceit*, Macmillan, New York.

Hartshorne, H., May, M. A., and Shuttleworth, F. K. (1930). *Studies in the nature of character, III: Studies in the organization of character*. Macmillan, New York.

Havighurst, R., and Taba, H. (1949). *Adolescent character and personality*, Wiley, New York.

Hindelang, M. J. (1972). The relationship of self-reported delinquency to scales of the CPI and MMPI. *Journal of Criminal Law, Criminology, and Police Science*, **63**, 75–81.

Hindelang, M. J. (1978). Race and involvement in common law personal crimes. *American Sociological Review*, **43**, 93–109.

Hogan, R., De Soto, C. B., and Solano, C. (1977). Traits, tests and personality research. *American Psychologist*, **32**, 255–264.

Homans, G. C. (1961). *Social behavior: Its elementary forms*, Harcourt, Brace, and World, New York.

Hood, R., and Sparks, R. (1970). *Key issues in criminology*, Weidenfeld and Nicholson, London.

Hook, J. G., and Cook, T. D. (1979). Equity theory and the cognitive ability of children. *Psychological Bulletin*, **86**, 429–445.

Johnson, J A. (1981). The 'self-disclosure' and 'self-presentational' views of item response dynamics and personality scale validity. *Journal of Personality and Social Psychology*, **40**, 761–769.

Jones, E. E., Davis, K. E., and Gergen, K. J. (1961). Role playing variations and their informational value for person perception. *Journal of Abnormal and Social Psychology*, **63**, 302–310.

Jurkovic, G. J. (1980). The juvenile delinquent as a moral philosopher: A structural-developmental approach. *Psychological Bulletin*, **88**, 709–727.

Kelly, D. H. (1975). Status origins, track position, and delinquent involvement: A self-report analysis. *Sociological Quarterly*, **16**, 264–271.

Kohlberg, L. (1964). Development of moral character and moral ideology. In M. L. Hoffman and L. W. Hoffman (Eds), *Review of child development research*, Russell Sage, New York.

Kohlberg, L. (1969). Stage and sequence: The cognitive-developmental approach to socialization. In D. Goslin (Ed.), *Handbook of socialization theory and research*, Rand McNally, Chicago.

Kohlberg, L. (1971a). Stages of moral development as a basis for moral education. In C. M. Beck, B. S. Crittenden, and E. V. Sullivan (Eds), *Moral education: Interdisciplinary approaches*, University of Toronto Press, Toronto.

Kohlberg, L. (1971b). From 'is' to 'ought': How to commit the naturalistic fallacy in moral development and get away with it. In T. Mischel (Ed.), *Cognitive development and epistemology*, Academic Press, New York.

Kohlberg, L. (1976). Moral stages and moralization: The cognitive developmental approach. In T. Lickona (Ed.), *Moral development and behaviour: Theory, research and social issues*, Holt, Rinehart, and Winston, New York.

Kulik, J. A., Stein, K. B. and Sarbin, T. R. (1968a). Dimensions and patterns of adolescent antisocial behavior. *Journal of Consulting and Clinical Psychology*, **32**, 375–382.

Kulik, J. A., Stein, K. B., and Sarbin, T. R. (1968b). Disclosure of delinquent behavior under conditions of anonymity and non-anonymity. *Journal of Consulting and Clinical Psychology*, **32**, 506–509.

Lemaine, G. (1974). Social differentiation and social originality. *European Journal of Social Psychology*, **4**, 17–25.

Matza, D., and Sykes, G. M. (1961). Juvenile delinquency and subterranean values. *American Sociological Review*, **26**, 712–719.

Meehl, P. E. (1945). The dynamics of structural personality tests. *Journal of Clinical Psychology*, **1**, 296–303.

Milgram, S. (1965). Liberating effects of group pressure. *Journal of Personality and Social Psychology*, **1**, 127–134.

Mills, C., and Hogan, R. (1978). A role theoretical interpretation of personality scale item responses. *Journal of Personality*, **46**, 778–785.

Mischel, W. (1968). *Personality assessment*, Wiley, New York.

Mischel, W. (1969). Continuity and change in personality. *American Psychologist*, **24**, 1012–1018.

Mischel, W. (1973). Toward a cognitive social learning reconceptualization of personality. *Psychological Review*, **80**, 252–283.

Mixon, D. (1972). Instead of deception. *Journal for the Theory of Social Behavior*, **2**, 145–175.

Moscovici, S. (1976). *Social influence and social change*, Academic Press, London.

Moscovici, S., and Faucheux, C. (1972). Social influence, conformity bias, and active minorities. In L. Berkowitz (Ed.), *Advances in Experimental Social Psychology*, Vol. 6, Academic Press, New York.

Nelsen, E. A., Grinder, R. E., and Biaggio, A. M. B. (1969). Relationships among behavioral, cognitive-developmental, and self-report measures of morality and personality. *Multivariate Behavioral Research*, **4**, 483–500.

Nelsen, E. A., Grinder, R. E., and Mutterer, M. L. (1969). Sources of variance in behavioral measures of honesty in temptation situations: Methological analyses. *Developmental Psychology*, **1**, 265–279.

Powell, G. E. (1977). Psychoticism and social delinquency in children. *Advances in Behavioural Research and Therapy*, **1**, 27–56.

Rest, J. R. (1975). Longitudinal study of the Defining Issues Test of moral judgment: A strategy for analysing developmental change. *Developmental Psychology*, **11**, 738–748.

Rettig, S., and Rawson, H. E. (1963). The risk hypothesis in predictive judgment of unethical behavior. *Journal of Abnormal and Social Psychology*, **66**, 243–248.

Rushton, J. P. (1976). Socialization and the altruistic behavior of children. *Psychological Bulletin*, **83**, 898–913.

Shapland, J. (1978). Self-reported delinquency in boys aged 11 to 14. *British Journal of Criminology*, **18**, 255–266.

Short, J. F. (1957). Differential association and delinquency. *Social Problems*, **4**, 233–239.

Singh, A. (1979). Reliability and validity of self-reported delinquency studies: A review. *Psychological Reports*, **44**, 987–993.

Strauss, A. (1978). *Negotiations*, Jossey-Bass, San Francisco.

Sugarman, B. (1967). Involvement in youth culture, academic achievement and conformity in school. *British Journal of Sociology*, **18**, 151–164.

Turiel, E. (1969). Developmental processes in the child's moral thinking. In P. H. Mussen, J. Langer, and M. Covington (Eds), *Trends and issues in developmental psychology*, Holt, Rinehart, and Winston, New York.

Voss, M. L. (1964). Differential association and reported delinquent behavior: A replication. *Social Problems*, **12**, 78–85.

West, D. J., and Farrington, D. P. (1973). *Who becomes delinquent?* Heinemann, London.

Wicker, A. W. (1969). Attitudes versus actions: The relation of verbal and overt behavioral responses to attitude objects. *Journal of Social Issues*, **25**, 41–78.

Wiggins, J. S. (1966). Substantive dimensions of self-report in the MMPI item pool. *Psychological Monographs*, **80**, (22, Whole No. 630).

Yarrow, M. R., Campbell, J. D., and Burton, R. V. (1964). Reliability of maternal retrospection: A preliminary report. *Family Process*, **3**, 207–218.

Yarrow, M. R., Campbell, J. D., and Burton, R. V. (1968). *Child rearing: An inquiry into research and methods*, Jossey-Bass, San Francisco.

Morality in the Making
Edited by H. Weinreich-Haste and D. Locke
© 1983, John Wiley & Sons, Ltd.

CHAPTER 12

'Personal Identity' and Personal Integrity

Tom Kitwood

> 'The community is a fictitious *body*, composed of the individual persons who are considered as constituting as it were its *members*. The interest of the community then is, what?—the sum of the interests of the several members who compose it.'
>
> Jeremy Bentham, 1789.

This chapter explores one of the more neglected aspects of the moral domain: what might be termed the 'social-psychological entailments' of a particular theory of ethics. The case to be studied is act-utilitarianism, a doctrine historically associated with the breaking up of traditional forms of life and the process of industrialization. My treatment will be discursive and speculative, but the core of the argument is as follows. The problem of 'personal identity', which social scientists of several different persuasions suggest is a characteristic feature of life in industrial societies, is highly relevant to our understanding of the contemporary moral predicament. Act-utilitarianism necessarily entails a deficient conception of the person; one aspect of this being that it implicitly ignores the question of 'personal identity'. Nevertheless, universalistic ethical claims are not to be abandoned on this account, but held in tension with particularistic considerations. There can be no logical resolution of this problem, though social-psychological theory can be used to illuminate what it means for the individual. One aspect of personal integrity is facing this tension and accepting responsibility for the manner in which this is done.

Industrialism and its Social Concomitants

The world has now undergone about two hundred years of industrialization. Beginning in small regions of Northern Europe, this movement has continuously advanced, transforming the life of whole nations. It has now penetrated almost every major area of the world, and even remote rural regions have experienced its effects indirectly, as people leave in search of work in the 'modern' sector. It is likely to make many further inroads, especially since the prevailing theories of development, both capitalist and socialist, give a central place to industrial production. The character of industrialism is evolving all the time, notably because of the use of new technology and as changes occur in the power struggles between management and labour. Whether a new kind of social formation, a genuinely 'post-industrial' society, can be glimpsed at present is a matter of controversy; and whether industrial capitalism contains within it the potential for radical transformation to socialism remains an open question. It is clear, however, that the break from 'traditional' to 'industrial' society is associated with profound changes to the human condition: to the pattern of social life, to the relation between the human and natural orders, to forms of thought and to the mental structure of individual persons. No moral theory can be judged adequate to the realities of the modern world if it ignores the scale and significance of these transformations.

We will turn our attention first to the social-psychological problem upon the analysis of which the later discussion depends. There are grounds for thinking that it is actually generated by the social conditions of industrialism, though whether it was present in some other form in earlier societies, and perhaps not recognized as such, is by no means clear.

The Problem of 'Personal Identity'

The first attempts to grasp the significance of massive and rapid social change for human consciousness appear in sociological rather than in psychological literature. By the latter part of the nineteenth century certain countries (notably Britain, Germany, and America) had had a sufficiently long experience of industrialism for it to be feasible to begin an evaluation of its effects and possibilities. In each of the major sociological traditions the problem of 'personal identity' emerges in some form. Marx and his followers, for example, were confident about the ultimate liberatory potential of industrialism, though they were strongly aware of the destructive effects of the system with which they were confronted. Under capitalism, so they believed, the inevitable condition of the labouring class was one of alienation—the estrangement of human beings from themselves and their creative powers. Durkheim saw another condition, that of *anomie*: the absence of clear guidelines for action, based on consensus and tradition. Yet he envisaged the emergence of a new and better kind of social integration, characteristic of the industrial mode.

There was however, another tradition of sociology, more conservative in its orientation, which was pessimistic about industrialism *per se*. Its most famous exponent was the German, Ferdinand Tonnies. In his *Gemeinschaft und Gesellschaft* (1889) (translated as *Community and Society*, 1957) two types of social organization were contrasted. The first, *gemeinschaft*, arises from the fact that communities have emerged through the sharing of common concerns, ultimately linked to the struggle for survival; since the fundamental interests of the members are in many respects the same, trust and cooperation are 'natural'. *gemeinschaft* is based on the ties of kinship, neighbourhood, and friendship. In contrast to this is *Gesellschaft*, the form of social life which has grown up around the market. Here each person tends to act on the basis of rational self-interest. Cooperation is not 'natural', but occurs when the individuals concerned believe that their interests coincide. One implication of the *gemeinschaft-gesellschaft* distinction was that the former tended to enhance a person's sense of well-being and security, through the existence of many mutual bonds and obligations; whereas the latter was conducive to personal disintegration. Tonnies' original formulation has been much criticized, not least for its tendency to idealize the past, and for its potential as a tool to justify reaction, dictatorship, and narrow forms of patriotism. Yet the ideas which he put forward are still very much alive, and the extent of the discussion surrounding them suggests that the matter may be one of prime importance. The contemporary German sociologist Arnold Gehlen, for example, has analysed the process of 'subjectivization' which occurs in industrial societies, and views this as a symptom of social and cultural decay. Peter Berger, who has been strongly influenced by Gehlen's work, also discusses the difficulties of maintaining a 'personal identity' when social life has become fragmented through industrialism (e.g. Berger, Berger, and Kellner, 1973).

The psychological discussion of topics related to 'personal identity' has a long history, going back to the work of Locke in the seventeenth century, and beyond that to the Greeks' debates about the question of permanence and change. But the psychologists' discovery of a *problem* of 'personal identity', afflicting some or possibly all individuals in industrial societies, has been a twentieth-century affair, coming mainly from work in psychoanalysis and psychotherapy. Some of those who had begun with the ideas of Freud—notably Jung and Horney—found that their clients were not commonly presenting the symptoms of the 'classical' hysterias and neuroses. The new symptoms were often to do with a sense of unreality, meaninglessness, emptiness, and deadness, the inability to take a consistent hold on life. In the attempt to analyse and treat problems here therapists turned increasingly to ideas of ego-development. One of the most comprehensive theories was that of Erikson (1963, 1968), whose aim was not only to explain personal growth, but also to relate personality to social and cultural conditions. His cumulative-stage scheme gave the question of 'personal identity' a prominent place; 'identity-formation' was proposed as the specific task of adolescence. Parallel concerns, though with variations in terminology, are to be found in the work of several other humanistic psychologists.

It should be noted in passing that there are logical oddities in the use of the term 'personal identity' in the way that I have decribed. For *identity* is a term applicable to a relationship rather than to a person or thing *simpliciter*. Philosophers have also been discussing a 'problem of personal identity' (e.g. Perry, 1975), and from their point of view the social scientists might even be accused on having made some kind of category mistake. The philosophers' main focus of attention has been on such issues as the following. What kind of relationship is specified by the term *identity*? Can the concept of identity be applied at all to persons, who are in a continual process of physical and psychological change? If so, how must the concept be modified as compared to its use in other contexts? If it is indeed legitimate to speak of the identities of persons, what are the logical criteria by which identity is established? Although this discussion has remained largely separate, and possibly even aloof from, the treatment of the problem of 'personal identity' by social scientists, there are important connections. It is not my aim to explore these here. In deference to the philosophers, however, I will distinguish the problem with which I am dealing by referring to it as that of 'personal identity', while allowing them the use of the term without contamination by quotation marks.

The Problem of 'Personal Identity' In More Detail

It is hard to find in the seminal literature a clear stipulative definition of the term 'personal identity'; Erikson, for example, deliberately refused to offer any, preferring to let his readers discover meanings from the way his terms were used. A person with a strong 'personal identity' would, he alleged, hve a rich sense of being alive, would be socially competent in a variety of situations, would be capable of sustaining deep and lasting relationships, and would experience a 'subjective sense of sameness and continuity'. The person would have found some unified way of organizing experience; and though this was not one of Erikson's central themes, the implication was that a strong 'personal identity' was a necessary condition of moral maturity. The failure to achieve a satisfactory 'personal identity' was attributable mainly to psychosocial antecedents, though constitutional factors were not excluded. A tentative examination of the use of the term by social scientists draws our attention to three closely related issues; and it may be argued that each of these has a special significance for (at least some) members of industrial societies.

(i) *Distinctiveness*

In an industrial society it may well be difficult for the lives of individuals to take on a colouring which is truly expressive of personal qualities. The technological-bureaucratic system tends to force people through standard processes, to treat them as mere numbers. Those who are constantly treated thus may even come to believe (at least for a while) that this is part of the truth about themselves. At any rate a contrary belief may be difficult to sustain, and may require support through dramatic forms of deviant action. Distinctiveness is particularly hard to establish in those areas of industrial work which require a person to carry out highly repetitive tasks, or to work within a framework of strict procedural rules. Where freedom is severely curtailed rituals of conflict, together with minor acts of Luddism, horseplay, and rule-breaking tend to become the principal means of self-expression.

The concept of ethnic 'identity' is closely tied to the matter of distinctiveness. The work of Epstein (1978) on the continuance of ethnicity in societies which either are industrialized or are in process of becoming so, is of particular interest in this respect. For in contrast to the predictions of theories of cultural assimilation, which suggest that ethnic distinctions should gradually disappear, Epstein finds that ethnicity is commonly re-worked in the industrial context. It becomes a means, not so much of maintaining a traditional culture, but of asserting qualitative difference against those social forces which might reduce people to a state of uniformity, and experience themselves as lost in an amorphous mass. Also, it remains the basis for some of the closest social bonds.

(ii) *Reality*

The constraints of industrial society tend, under certain circumstances, to make an individual's subjective sense of reality unsubstantial. Some of the roles which people are required to occupy have little direct or obvious meaning; yet they may well be unavoidable, simply for the sake of economic survival. One solution, therefore, is to occupy the role 'at a distance', to perform it cynically and with detachment, in the hope of maintaining a private self intact. The price of this may be a reduced sense of reality, even in extreme cases to the extent that a person comes to question whether there exists a being of whom it is possible to say 'myself'. In sharp contrast to this stands out the (no doubt often idealized) seventeenth-century conception of a 'calling': a pattern of life in which public and private are closely intermingled, to be pursued with single-mindedness and dedication, and unique to each individual. Vestiges of this conception survived until fairly recently in the idea that certain professions such as medicine, law, and teaching were to be called 'vocations'.

The problem of reality arises also in another, and probably more serious way. Since the 'human nature' of each individual is, to a very large extent, the result of social interaction, a person whose social milieu is impoverished may well experience a sense of diminution. In extreme cases such as solitary confinement or the loss of a friend or lover upon whom a person's social being largely depended, the result may even be acute ontological insecurity. Industrial societies, while allowing great personal mobility and provoking a high level of stimulation, often tend to restrict genuine social contact, common instances being travel by private car, shopping in a supermarket, high-technology medical treatment, work on assembly lines or in typing pools, life in a geriatric home. The condition of unemployment, which often means being cut off from one of the most vital sources of social relationships, is perhaps the clearest example of all. In contrast to this genuine sociality is constantly breaking out, violating the imperatives of industrialism: in demonstations, festivals, political and religious movements, cooperatives, and communes.

(iii) *Coherence*

Life in an industrial society is often highly fragmented. A person may occupy roles which are physically and socially separate from one another, and which may even involve mutually incompatible prescriptions. The information which a person receives from the reactions of others in a variety of social settings may contain discrepancies. There may be wide gaps between what a person wants to do, and what he or she is required to do. All this can be regarded as part of the tragic consequence, or as the great opportunity, of living in an industrial society, depending on one's viewpoint. But both pessimists and optimists can agree that some will find coherence difficult to attain.

One of the richest treatments of this matter of which I am aware is that given by Ruddock (1972). He builds up a model of the person by bringing together insights from several different traditions in the social sciences, and thus illuminates both synchronic and diachronic aspects of the problem of coherence. His scheme involves six components (the meaning of which must be carefully examined from his own use): self, perspective, role, personality, project, and 'identity'. The problem of 'personal identity' is conceived as that of achieving congruence between perspectives on the self obtained from others, the various roles which a person occupies, the residues from the past laid down as 'personality', and the project—that which a person is undertaking to become. In discussion with Ruddock I have suggested that for certain purposes the model could usefully be supplemented by adding a seventh component: social life-world (Kitwood, 1980). This concept comes from the phenomenological tradition in sociology, originating in the work of Husserl, and amplified by Schutz. It has been modified slightly by Berger to mean, approximately, a 'zone of shared meanings'. Thus the task of achieving coherence may involve, in addition to what Ruddock indicates, the bringing about of a resolution between different systems of meaning which at a first order level appeared to be unrelated or even incompatible.

The three problems of distinctiveness, reality, and coherence overlap one another, and in certain respects approximate to a quasi-developmental relationship. Thus, for example, a person might achieve some measure of distinctiveness without solving the problems of reality and coherence, perhaps by adopting an outlandish style of performance in a particular role. A person might derive a strong sense of reality from interpersonal perspectives, while living with many contradictions at the levels of role and social life-world. For the purposes of theory one advantage of the rather elaborate model of the person that I have outlined is that it illuminates the different ways in which coherence might be achieved, and hence what might be termed a strong 'personal identity'. In one case coherence might be based on a dominant role (a small town station-master, perhaps); in another on powerful elements in the personality (maybe Freud's anal character); in another on the meanings derived from a particular social life-world (as with some strongly committed religious persons). There are other kinds of coherence according to which a person's life appears at one level to be spontaneous and unpredictable, while only having consistency when viewed, so to speak, from a greater distance; here the main integrating factor may be a long-term project. If, as so many theorists seem to suggest, 'personal identity' is indeed a major problem in industrial societies, one may hypothesize that there will be a strong pressure towards solving it in some way, even if in the long run the solution is restrictive or destructive.

'Personal Identity' in a Tribal Society

In contrast to the above observations on the constraints and opportunities of industrial societies, let us now look briefly at a very different form of social organization. Sociologists have very rightly given many warnings about the dangers of making broad generalizations about industrialism; anthropologists also make it plain that there are many forms of 'primitive' society. Clearly there are great theoretical dangers in the simple contrasts I am suggesting. To illustrate certain points I will take one example, the Kikuyu people of East Africa. Their traditional way of life is well-documented, both by a member of the tribe who was brought up before colonialism had made a strong impact, and who later went on to study anthropology under Malinowski (Kenyatta, 1938); and by an observer who spent many years in close contact with the Kikuyu people, even to the extent of being initiated into the warrior class (Leakey, 1952). The fact that both of these authors are male does, of course, mean that there is the danger of sexist bias in their accounts. It is possible also to fall into the error of idealizing a form of social life that has largely passed away, while failing to notice its limitations. Nevertheless, even on the basis of the evidence which is available, a comparison such as this, between 'tribal' and 'industrial', is worth making.

In the tribal society production, leisure, education, entertainment, morality, and religion form a unified whole, whereas in an industrial society there tends to be a separation between these different areas of activity. In the tribal society there is some degree of division of labour (between the sexes, for example) but each person does several kinds of work; in an industrial society the labour process is often highly fragmented, and there is a strong tendency towards specialization. Tribal society establishes social control largely through the pressure of public opinion, though there are extremely severe penalties for violation of important social norms. There is little privacy, and life is pre-eminently social. There may, of course, be competition between individuals in certain legitimate spheres such as courtship, bravery, or athletic prowess. Under these conditions it is not so much that there is a problem of 'personal identity' to be solved, as that the very existence of such a problem is inconceivable.

The distinctiveness of each individual is established, from the earliest days of childhood, on the basis of family and clan relationships. A person is often addressed as 'son of . . .', 'daughter of . . .'—constant reminders that the individual belongs to the group in a particular way. There are, moreover, certain special relationships, which might be termed 'primary identifications': thus a boy comes to believe, in an almost mystical way, 'I am my grandfather', 'I am my brother'. The full application of this principle has highly complex entailments: a boy's father's brothers are also his father, and so on. From a modern, Western standpoint, backed by centuries of Aristotelian logic, such a conception of relationship might be judged conducive to 'identity confusion'. This, however, does not follow for those whose thought is structured by a different kind of logic, in which categories are inter-permeable. Each person partakes uniquely in the corporate essence; and before a strong sense of distinctiveness might be established on other (and to us more familiar) grounds, such as personal talent or achievement, it is embedded in the consciousness of each individual through the awareness of social bonding.

These factors alone might be thought sufficient to provide not merely distinctiveness, but also a powerful sense of reality. This is enhanced, however, by the fact that each person's progress through life is marked by a succession of stages. The beginning of childhood proper is celebrated by the minor ceremony of the 'piercing of the ears', and the culmination of adult life is becoming a senior member of the clan, one whose eldest child has been initiated into the class of young adults. Each individual can thus recognize his or her position in an accepted pattern of life-history; and since the highest respect is reserved for the elders, the process of growing older is also one of progress. The most significant rite of all is initiation, in which a person becomes a member of an age-set, a horizontal group; the social bonds are thus not only those within the clan, but extend throughout the tribe.

These contrasts to industrial society (at least its Western, capitalist version), are striking enough. But perhaps it is in the establishment of coherence that tribal society differs most. The life of each individual is very varied, calling for many skills: building, planting, hunting, fighting, child-rearing, praying, sing-ing, dancing, story-telling. The company in which these activities are pursued is, however, very much the same. In this way not only is a wide range of talents and personality characteristics called forth, but the nature of these becomes known to the social group. Thus the coherence of each person is not a matter to be settled individually, in private reflection or choice; it comes to be agreed by the community, in the extended process of observation and subsequent discus-sion of the performance of each member. As a result the 'perspectives' which any one person receives from others are unlikely to contain marked discrepan-cies; the different members of the community will come to tell much the same story, modifying it as new performances are observed. All this is very different from the fragmentation which is often held up as one of the most characteristic features of industrial society. The closest parallels, such as they are, are to be found in the traditional working-class communities that grew up in connection with industries such as mining and textile production.

A modern critic might find many faults with tribal society. It evolves only slowly; it restricts individual's freedom severely; its conditions are conducive to the wielding of the weapon of fear. Nevertheless, in certain respects it sustains the psychological well-being of its members very effectively; indeed, a major effort of the imagination is required for those who have been reared in an advanced industrial society to comprehend the sense of personal-social vitality which, at its best, it can impart. It is, however, extremely vulnerable to modernizing influences. Precisely why this is so, and why some tribal forms of life disintegrate more quickly than others, is far from clear. More is involved than the naked use of power, or envy of the 'white man's magic'. But when the change to an industrial mode has begun to gain momentum the problem of 'personal identity' soon appears, with all its classic symptoms. And once the process of modernization has started, there can be no return to the security of the tribal form of social life.

Industrial societies sometimes carry with them the vestigial remains of their earlier history. One of these may be the resources available for person-description. The English tongue, for example, contains an immense number of trait-names. Some psychologists have gone to great pains to extend this aspect of commonsense theory and construed 'scientific' views of personality, based on the postulation of a small number of basic traits. This approach now seems highly naive, and has been widely criticized. The historical significance of trait theory has, however, generally been overlooked. For it may be that trait concepts were well-justified in some non-industrial societies, where it was possible to observe an individual's behaviour in a variety of social contexts, and so to make valid inferences about the existence of 'enduring dispositions'. The extent to which these were genuinely constitutional, or the result of psycho-social processes, is beside the point. Once established and recognized by the social group, these became an important part of each individual's 'personal identity'.

The Emergence of Utilitarian Theory

In the discussion of the problem of 'personal identity' thus far I have made no reference to ethical theory. It is, however, very significant that a similar problem, though in this case without an experiential basis, has come to light in the critical examination of utilitarianism. This is the ethical doctrine most closely associated with industrialism, or at least its Western, capitalist forms, and it was formulated during those very social transformations which (so we are led to believe) gave rise in later generations to the psychological malaise I have been describing. The central proposition of utilitarianism may be summarized as: 'the rightness of an action is determined by its contribution to the happiness of everyone affected by it' (Quinton, 1973). We must now characterize this doctrine briefly.

One of the most commonly made points about utilitarianism is that it was an attempt to put moral thinking onto a sound empirical basis, and that here one can trace the influence of the scientific method. The simplicity of its initial assumptions, and the use of quantification, show at least a superficial resemblance to the approach of classical physics. Less obvious, but possibly of greater importance, is the fact that utilitarianism was advanced as a moral-legal theory which would come to terms with the vast social changes, and hence the anachronisms, of the late eighteenth and early nineteenth centuries: the great boom in English trade and manufacturers and the resulting irrelevance of traditional craft and monopolistic modes; the contrast between the conditions of life of the rich and the poor, the powerful and the powerless; the sterility of the older academic centres; the archaic character of much current legal practice, and the arbitrariness of those new aspects of law which were based on precedent rather than principle. The aim of the utilitarians, and Bentham in particular, was to bridge the gap between philosophy and law, and so contribute to the foundation of a new and more beneficient social order. The influence of utilitarianism has been very powerful: not only in academic moral theory, but also through its incorporation into legal and social reform, and more recently into such planning techniques as cost-benefit analysis. It must also be said that there is a very close connection between the assumptions of utilitarian thought and those of classical political economy, through which industrial capitalism was legitimated in its early stages.

During the two centuries of its history, and in response to fluctuating assessments of its acceptability, utilitarian doctrines have been advanced in a variety of ways. It is not my intention to go into this matter here, for it has been thoroughly treated by such authorities as Plamenatz (1958), Quinton (1973), and Smart and Williams (1973). Suffice to say that all forms of utilitarianism are consequentialist in character, asserting that the rightness of an action is to be determined in some way by its effects; thus the conception of rightness is objective, in that it does not depend in any strong sense on the state of knowledge or the intentions of the moral agent. There is some variation in the type of consequence which is held to have intrinsic value; the commonest view being that this is happiness, specified in some particular way. The most 'classical' versions of utilitarianism (as advanced, for example, by both Bentham and J. S. Mill) were consequentialist in a direct sense; that is to say, it is the effects of particular actions which are to be examined, rather than the rules under which they might be subsumed. Act-utilitarianism, as this form is sometimes termed, became unfashionable for a considerable period, though it has been revived during the last decade. Recent extensions have been concerned to assert the global scale of human responsibility, and the obligation not only to carry out beneficient actions, but also to prevent what is harmful (e.g. Singer,

1972; Glover, 1977). Smart (in Smart and Williams, 1973) provides a particularly clear exposition of utilitarian doctrine, though with the qualification that he commends it rather than claiming that it can be justified empirically.

The philosophical debates about and within utilitarianism have continued right to the present day. Among the most famous issues are that of 'naturalism' (whether utilitarianism necessarily entails deriving 'ought' from 'is', and whether or not this can be justified); the precise form in which the principle of utility should be expressed; the place for moral judgment of motives and intentions; how far utilitarianism is capable of generating an adequate view of justice; and whether the classical form can be qualified so as to accommodate certain major criticisms, as in the version known as rule-utilitarianism. All this is clear evidence of the vitality of this body of theory, and of the wide recognition of its potential in illuminating ethical problems at both the personal and social levels.

To those who look for sociological clues, one of the most revealing of all the statements of the leading utilitarians is that of Bentham which was quoted at the beginning of this chapter. This comes from the second page of his *An Introduction to the Principles of Morals and Legislation*, first published in 1789 (Burns and Hart (Eds), 1970). For here Bentham appears to deny the existence of the human community as an entity in itself, and to assert that there are merely atomic individuals. This conception of social existence, which is (in Tonnies' terminology) one of pure *gesellschaft*, lies at the heart of utilitarian doctrine. It had great pragmatic value in helping to expose the meaninglessness of bland generalizations about 'the national interest' or 'the welfare of the labouring classes', and in drawing attention to the ways in which the needs and interests of certain types of person in society were being neglected. If it is taken literally and exclusively, however, it has profound social-psychological implications. These, it seems, were not recognized by any of the major exponents of utilitarianism, and were voiced only ineptly by the early critics.

The Concept of the Person in Utilitarian Thought

Bentham's remark implies that it is methodologically necessary, at least for the version of utilitarianism that he advanced, to look upon the human being as without tradition or social ties, and hence as de-personalized in many respects. It is only when people are, so to speak, theoretically stripped of their individual character and quality that it becomes possible to apply the technique for calculating benefit and harm. This suggests (though it does not prove) that something may be amiss with the doctrine as commonly presented if it is to provide a comprehensive basis for ethics. A similar point may be made, of course, about any theory that finds it necessary to look upon the person in this kind of way.

A useful beginning to a critique of utilitarianism along these lines is made by Williams in his debate with Smart. He concentrates his attention on the purest form, the 'act' version, and argues as follows. Utilitarianism derives much of its strength and compelling character from its claim to be absolutely impartial. It allows no distinction between persons, and implies that it does not matter who brings about a certain desirable state of affairs, so long as it actually comes to pass. But this effectively reduces each person to a kind of non-entity, whose main moral significance is that of being a source of causal intervention in the world. There is no place, and logically there cannot be, for the idea that each person has special ties, commitments, and responsibilities; at least there is no way of allowing that these constitute important moral considerations. Utilitarianism even implies that a person should give very little heed to private moral intuitions or scruples, since these would contribute so small a part to the total calculation of utility. Thus it requires a person to be alienated from his or her individual essence, disregarding or even violating what Williams calls 'personal integrity' or, perhaps less aptly, 'moral identity'. Ultimately, then, act-utilitarianism seems to be consistent with the existence of people whose moral characters lack distinctiveness, and who (beyond the principle of utility) have no moral convictions of their own.

From the standpoint of social psychology the main function of the concept of personal integrity here is to challenge the basic methodological requirement that people be regarded as mere atomic individuals, and to suggest that the uniqueness of persons and hence the diversity between them is an ineluctible moral consideration. But considering how the greater part of that diversity arises, this is to imply that the fundamentally social nature of human existence must be acknowledged at the very core of ethical theory. There is no way of acquiring the definitively human attributes, including those conventionally regarded as moral, other than through participation in social life; no arena for the exercise of moral choice except in particular human contexts; no means of comprehending (in a practical rather than a merely theoretical sense) the meaning of obligation except in relation to specific human beings. And since people vary enormously in the nature and extent of their morally formative experience, their moral strengths and weaknesses, the character of their social relationships, it is disastrous reductionism for an ethical theory to view them as essentially the same.

In developing his critique of utilitarianism Williams refers to some of the aspects of social existence that confer individuality upon each person. He points out that people take on commitments and projects that matter to them deeply; they have firm attitudes and convictions; they have some specially intimate relationships that sustain them as social beings; some parts of their lives are enacted within the framework of societal institutions. There is here the faint adumbration of a comprehensive model of the person relevant to the conditions of existence in a modern (i.e. industrial) society. In this context Williams does not articulate his implicit social psychology clearly, nor is it necessary for the point he is making.

Our understanding of the uniqueness of persons becomes deeper, however, if it is based on a carefully worked-out conception of the person as a social being, one which takes both psychological and sociological theory into account: the kind of model to which I made reference on page 218 in outlining the problem of coherence. Individuality can then be seen to involve a number of aspects, such as the following: personality, with its antecedents both biological and experiential; the social life-worlds in which a person participates; the roles which a person occupies, and the style with which he or she enacts them; the close relationships in which interpersonal perspectives are exchanged; the projects, both large and small, which a person undertakes; and the extent to which some kind of coherence has been achieved between all of these, to establish a 'personal identity'. Of course this is only the briefest outline, because each of the components can be further analysed, and a diachronic dimension has further to be added. This model, moreover, is only one of several that would serve the same function. But the main point is clear enough: despite superficial appearances, there are very great differences between persons at a social-psychological level. And in view of the diversification of the social sciences it requires not a unitary theory (based, for example on a concept such as personality or role), but a synthesis of several theories, to specify that in which individual differences consists.

To introduce considerations such as these is, then, to move away from the under-socialized conception of the person which has been such a marked characteristic of several Western theories: for example utilitarianism itself, and the closely related idea of economic rationality; much of humanistic psychology; certain accounts of persons and their 'values'; some of the major psychological theories of morality, of which Kohlberg's is a particularly clear example; and the greater part of the philosophers' discussion of personal identity to which I have made brief reference on page 216. The full significance of this for ethical theory has yet to be worked out. But at least one can say that a doctrine which fails to take account of individuality and the essentially social nature of human existence, and which has consistently failed to do so, must be regarded as inadequate; at least in its existing form.

How is it possible, then, that this deficient conception of the person has gained such a wide acceptance in Western theory? To do justice to such a question would require a major excursion into the sociology of knowledge, but here I wish to offer a single speculation. The main doctrines which view society as if it were made up of atomized individuals were formulated at a time when a great deal of 'social fabric' (kinship, community, tradition, etc.) was still intact. This, however, was not recognized; it remained part of the taken-for-granted background. Only gradually, as social fabric began to disintegrate on a large scale, was that background problematized. The formulation of a problem of 'personal identity' by psychologists was one attempt to grasp this at a theoretical level. By the time that the importance of this matter was being appreciated widely, however, the idea of the atomized individual was well-entrenched; several major theories embodying this conception had acquired paradigmatic status, leading to the spawning of other smaller theories on the same lines. Now we are in a paradoxical situation. In the light of a great body of evidence we can understand quite well the essentially social nature of human existence, and the meaning of individuality; yet we are confronted with established paradigms which do not take this into account.

In conclusion to this section one might press the general argument further, perhaps somewhat unfairly, with a hypothetical suggestion. Suppose that the atomized conception of the person as found in act-utilitarianism were adopted, literally, rigorously, and exclusively, in some society; what would be the result? Particular ties and intimate relationships would necessarily have to be devalued, and the social fabric of groups, movements, and communities loosened to a common level. Many personal projects would have to be dismissed as irrelevant. Far less attention would have to be given to the nurture of children, whose needs would be taken into account only on the same basis as those of all others. Under such conditions it is conceivable that within two or three generations social life in the sense that we now know it would have ceased, and the main surviving link between humans would be language. The creatures that emerged, despite their appearances, would be like feral children, devoid of many of the reactions that we take for granted as human. Act-utilitarianism, insofar as it embodies this conception, seems to be incompatible with the very conditions under which we are formed and sustained as genuinely human beings. It cannot, therefore, suffice as a basis for personal ethics.

A Place for Utilitarianism

It might be claimed that the empirical basis on which the argument thus far rests is not particularly well-established. But if it is sound, it seems that we are brought to a serious impasse. Act-utilitarianism, considered as the sole basis for a system of morality, is highly implausible, for reasons derived from social-psychological evidence. Yet universalistic ethical claims, which this theory commands us to consider as of prime importance, are both logially and intuitively compelling. They extend the moral horizon beyond mere parochialism; they invite us to serious reflection upon our responsibilities as citizens in a world that is economically and culturally interlocked. They surely have some part to play in the guidance of action in the modern world. It is not for nothing that utilitarianism has undergone a revival of late, as an expression of global moral concern.

Conversely, to reject universalistic claims on the kind of grounds I have been outlining is highly dangerous. For it must be admitted that any re-assertion of the importance of tradition, of solidarity with existing groups or communities, of the validity of special ties and obligations, could open the door for reaction. If we allow that such considerations do have moral weight we run the risk of providing the legitimation for many kinds of special pleading, for corruption in public life, for the labelling of non-members as sub-human and therefore outside the scope of ethical concern: indeed, for modern versions of the very kinds of practice that the early utilitarians were opposing. Ultimately we might be giving grounds for justifying the social system of fascism itself.

The problem, then, is this. A 'merely theoretical' examination of the contemporary moral situation suggests strongly the rightness of a universalistic doctrine of ethics such as act-utilitarianism; but history and social psychology imply that, in the long term, this is impracticable.

One possible response to this would be to relinquish the strongest form of utilitarian doctrine, which considers specific acts, and adopt some form of the rule version, which is less vulnerable to criticism on social-psychological grounds. The great objection to such a move, however, would be that we would be deprived thereby of one of the most incisive means of making moral judgments on novel or non-recurrent acts, and of carrying out ruthlessly direct assessments of benefit and harm to human beings. In a world of rapid social and technical change, it might be argued, an ethical tool of this kind is vitally needed, and it is this that act-utilitarianism specifically supplies.

Another response would be to advance a kind of cognitive-developmentalism, analogous to that of Kohlberg in relation to the theory of Rawls: that is, to postulate an ascent from particularistic to universalistic ethics as an individual matures. In this way it would be possible to acknowledge the importance of special ties and commitments in the earlier stages, while claiming that these are gradually laid aside as a person approaches the principled level of moral thought. This move would be open to many of the criticisms that have been made of Kohlberg's own ideas, and it would have to face a further objection which has not, so far as I am aware, been applied as yet with full force to his scheme. It appears to be necessary for the morally principled person to take a stance outside any community, to have no strong particularistic ties, to attach little importance to private projects: to avoid all forms of commitment that might compromise impartiality—to become in reality the atomized individual that the theory requires. Perhaps this might be feasible for a while, at least in certain cases; residues of past sociality remain in the personality and can provide some kind of sustenance. One might suppose, however, that in due course some of these rigorously principled moralists would begin to suffer from problems of 'personal identity', caused by precisely the kind of deprivations that I have discussed earlier in this chapter; and so, despite the rectitude of their theoretical position, become ineffective as practical moral agents. If so, this account of principled morality is implausible.

A third possible response would be to acknowledge that act-utilitarianism does indeed have a vital part to play in a system of ethics applicable to the modern world; but that this is not in the domain of pesonal morality, as some of the main modern exponents assume it to be. One might argue that the proper place for act-utilitarian thought is in public rather than private life: to provide the moral under-pinning for legislation, the basis for the criticism and hence the reform of institutions, the guidelines for social planning and allocation of resources. This, of course, would be faithful to one aspect of Bentham's own vision. One could then claim that moral considerations of a different kind are relevant to private life, where it is valid to give heed to particularistic concerns, and to recognize the importance of keeping social fabric in good repair. This move looks attractive, but it also has its problems. In reality the boundary between public and private life is far from clear. It is also extremely dangerous to accept a double moral standard, as many historical examples make plain: public atrocities carried out by people whose private lives were affectionate and 'decent', and private cruelty and corruption on the part of people who were models of public rectitude. Certainly one can accept the proposition that act-utilitarianism has an important function in public life; but is it possible to go further, and allow it a place in personal morality, while taking into account the social-psychological problems I have outlined?

I believe that it is, though the result is not likely to please those who like neat solutions. The starting-point is the recognition that there now exists a fundamental tension between universalistic and particularistic ethical claims; both are valid, but in different ways. The tension has always existed to some extent. Even 'primitive' people had to decide how to treat the 'stranger', whether as a non-person or as a human being like themselves. For most purposes, however, some form of particularistic morality applicable to groups small enough for all members to know each other was sufficient. The tension is stronger for those who live in societies that have undergone some degree of industrialization, accompanied as it is by the break-up of traditional forms of life and the expansion of social horizons. It has become most acute for those to whom modern means of travel and telecommunication have given some awareness of the world as a whole, and some understanding of the enormous discrepancies in well-being, power and wealth that it contains. The tension has largely arisen, then, as a result of the related processes of social and technical change; universalistic systems of ethics emerged as an attempt to face up to the consequent moral implications. Their claims cannot be reconciled with those of particularism. To be morally aware in the modern world is to recognize this tension and to live with it.

It is vain to try to escape this tension by looking for some second-order technique that would allow the one set of claims to be weighed objectively against the other, thus relieving the moral agent of the final burden of decision. For the tension presents itself in a different way to each person. On the one side there is the utilitarian calculus, which attempts to be absolutely impartial, and so makes the same kind of claim on everyone. But on the other side are the particularistic concerns, which are specific to each individual; and as any comprehensive social-psychological model makes plain, this is an area where interpersonal differences are very great. Once this is recognized, it becomes clear why a general logical solution is impossible. In any case, would it be desirable for the tension to be resolved in that kind of way? It can be argued that one of the most essential features of being human is having to make choices and take responsibility, and that this is one of the most valid ways in which we assert our freedom.

In terms of the model of the person to which I have referred at several points in this chapter, it might be said that universalistic moral considerations constitute a zone of shared meanings in its own right—virtually a social life-world. However, even though the full-blooded act-utilitarian can assert that the moral obligations derived from it are completely objective, it is bound to have a different salience in the consciousness of each individual: partly, no doubt, in relation to cognitive development, but also, and more directly, in relation to the vicissitudes of life. For one person the claims of universalistic ethics are little more than abstract theory, lacking real substance, whereas for another, with very wide social experience, they might become the most significant set of meanings of all. Even on this side, then, the sense of tension will vary greatly from one individual to another.

Social-psychological aspects such as these have to be taken into account in any realistic attempt to specify the nature of moral obligation. This, however, does not justify a rejection of universalistic claims, and an assertion of particularistic attachments to the exclusion of all else. Even if so doing would serve to enhance the subjective sense of distinctiveness and reality, it would be an inadequate moral response to the modern predicament. A concept of personal integrity which implied the necessity for this would be seriously deficient. We might assert, rather, that it is incumbent on each individual to carry out a personal synthesis: to establish a relationship between universalistic moral considerations and the meanings derived from the social life-worlds in which he or she participates, to accept the role of world citizen alongside other roles, to integrate all other projects with that of universal benevolence, and so on. The form of that synthesis will change throughout life, as experience grows and horizons enlarge, and there will be great variation from one person to another.

This has implications for the nature of society, if it is to be one that promotes the formation of effective moral agents, and is to remain so over many generations. For its institutions and processes must be conducive, inter alia, to the establishment of distinctiveness and reality in such a way that a person can in due course transcend particularism without a crisis of 'personal identity'. It appears that some of the main tendencies of the capitalist industrialism of the West work against this possibility. *Gemeinschaft*, in the old sense, cannot be recreated, nor would it be desirable to do so. But *gemeinschaft* did fulfil some vital psychological functions; and the discovery of forms of social existence that provide these without constricting personal development is one of the greatest moral issues of our age.

The social-psychological problem of coherence, then, has a specifically moral aspect. The achievement of coherence implies not only attaining congruence between various particularistic concerns, but also a synthesis of these with the demands of universalistic ethics. To undertake this is to face the inevitable prospect of some degree of inner tension, and a recurring tendency to subjective dissonance. It is necessary, however, to accept this, and to take responsibility for the synthesis that results. Here, in the modern world, is one of the most important meanings of the term *personal integrity*. And at this point personal integrity and 'personal identity' coincide.

References

Bentham, J. (1970). J. H. Burns and H. L. A. Hart (Eds), *An Introduction to the Principles of Morals and Legislation*, Athlone Press, London. (Originally published in 1789.)

Berger, P., Berger, B., and Kellner, H. (1973). *The Homeless Mind*, Penguin, Harmondsworth.

Epstein, A. L. (1978). *Ethos and Identity*, Tavistock, London.

Erikson, E. (1963). *Childhood and Society*, Norton, New York.

Erikson, E. (1968). *Identity: Youth and Crisis*, Faber and Faber, London.

Glover, J. (1977). *Causing Death and Saving Lives*, Penguin, Harmondsworth.

Kenyatta, J. (1938). *Facing Mount Kenya*, Secker and Warburg, London.

Kitwood, T. M. (1980). *Disclosures to a Stranger*, Routledge and Kegan Paul, London.

Leakey, L. S. B. (1952). *Mau Mau and the Kikuyu*, Methuen, London.

Perry, J. (Ed.) (1975), *Personal Identity*, University of California Press, Berkeley.

Plamenatz, J. (1958). *The English Utilitarians*, Blackwell, Oxford.

Quinton, A. (1973). *Utilitarian Ethics*, Macmillan, London.

Ruddock, R. (Ed.) (1972). *Six Approaches to the Person*, Routledge and Kegan Paul, London.

Singer, P. (1972). Famine, affluence and morality. *Philosophy and Public Affairs*, **1**, 229–243.

Smart, J. J. C., and Williams, B. (1973). *Utilitarianism: For and Against*, Cambridge Univerisity Press, Cambridge.

Tonnies, F. (1957). *Community and Society*, translated by C. P. Loomis, Harper and Row, New York. (Originally published in 1887.)

Morality in the Making
Edited by H. Weinreich-Haste and D. Locke
© 1983, John Wiley & Sons, Ltd.

CHAPTER 13

Moralities and Conflicts

GLYNIS M. BREAKWELL

Psychologizing about moral development and about intergroup conflict have been distinct enterprises—practitioners of neither theoretical tradition darkening the others' door. The object of this chapter is to examine what each could gain by welcoming the others in.

The Social Psychology of Intergroup Conflict

The major obstacle to any attempt at bringing two distinct traditions of theory together is the fact that they are likely to make very different assumptions about the nature of the problems they approach, be founded upon very different ideologies and have very different terminologies. In short, they differ in premise, purpose, and prose. Since other chapters in this volume discuss the premises, purposes, and prose of theories of moral development, it is not necessary to reiterate them here. However, it is necessary to describe in brief the fundamentals of intergroup theories.

No claim will be made here that there is a single theoretical monolith which is commonly called 'intergroup theory'. The term symbolizes an orientation to the study of intergroup relations. Analogous to labels like 'learning theory' or 'psychoanalytic theory', it connotes a way of viewing a problem area and a way of phrasing questions rather than a unitary solution to them. It prescribes the routes but not the destination and many fall by the wayside.

Israel (1972) called the assumptions from which empirical theories are derived 'stipulative statements'. His main thesis was that such statements, having the status of normative constructs, serve a regulative function, determining the content of empirical theories and, together with formal methodological rules, influencing procedures of scientific research, which themselves affect theory. Intergroup theory seems to involve two such statements:

(i) the behaviour of individuals acting as group members, if not always manifestly different from that of individuals acting as autonomous agents, always has to be *interpreted* differently. Thus explanations centring on the psychodynamics of the individual can never predict or explain the subtleties of intergroup behaviour.

'We cannot do justice to events by extrapolating uncritically from man's feelings, attitudes, and behaviour when he is in a state of isolation to his behaviour when acting as a member of a group. Being a member of a group and behaving as a member of a group have psychological consequences. There are consequences even when the other members are not immediately present. The orthodox custom of taking these consequences for granted amounts to ignoring them. It has resulted in serious miscalulations of behavioural outcomes . . .'

(Sherif, 1966, pp. 8–9)

The notion that individuals act as group members even when not acting in unison with other group members or in explicitly intergroup contexts introduces the corollary assumption that group membership has a pervasive influence upon self-definition. The implication is that the individual carries the group—its prescriptions, prohibitions, and purposes; its status structure and social role—around *within* himself. The group permeates the member, shaping his sense of self and then his behaviour. Moreover, it is hypothesized that this is true of every element in the group matrix: each membership creates its own reflection modified by and coalescing with the images of other memberships. Consequently, it is questionable whether an individual ever acts as an 'autonomous' agent: there are merely variations in the intensity with which any one group affiliation is evoked by any single context.

(ii) predictions about *inter*group relations based on the knowledge of relations between people *within* groups are likely to be fallacious. Therefore, relations between groups must be studied in their own right for only within this framework can the intergroup behaviour of individuals be properly interpreted.

'Though not independent of the relationships within the groups in question, *the characteristics of functional relations between groups cannot be deduced or extrapolated solely from the properties of relations that prevail among members within the group itself.'*

(Sherif, 1966, p. 12—original italics)

The close connection of this stipulation to the first is obvious; it signifies the further rejection of the primacy of explanations of social behaviour which rely on intra-individual and inter-individual dynamics. In the climate of the 1960s, when dissonance theories, game-playing, and various formulations of the frustration-aggression hypothesis reigned supreme, such a stance was somewhat incongruous—like a piece of Wedgwood in a collection of Ming.

Current collectors of china are more eclectic, at least they are in Europe. Intergroup theory has become respectable with the work of Tajfel (1978), Moscovici (1976), and Doise (1978) and the 'individualistic' social psychology which Steiner (1974) bemoaned has been tempered. But intergroup theory, as it is envisaged here, is too concerned with the social system of grouping and groups to be a thoroughbred theory of social psychology. Dealing with relations between groups, focusing upon relative status and the instability of power structures, intergroup theory has to be continually justifying its claim to be a social psychological theory. Simultaneously, it has to justify the value of social psychological explanations of phenomena which are intimately tied to wide-scale social, economic, and political processes. Tajfel (1974) typified the response of intergroup theorists when he said that they do not assume 'explicitly or implicitly, some kind of primacy or priority of social psychological explanations of intergroup behaviour.' Instead, Tajfel argues that variables, which might be aptly called social psychological variables, are bred of the social, political, and economic context and that these variables acquire a functional autonomy which enables them to reflect the course of those processes which generated them. For example, Klineberg (1950, 1964) marshalled evidence that group stereotypes are the products, not the initial causes, of rivalry between groups; he also pointed to the fact that, once evolved, stereotypes can channel and compound conflicts. Intergroup theory requires that levels of analysis and explanation ranging from the psychological to the materialist be used in concert to explicate the functioning of these social psychological variables in terms of socio-psychological processes.

The overwhelming concern of intergroup theory is conflict. It is as if relations between groups can only be conceptualized in terms of conflict. Hostility is the norm and there is the hint that conflict is the defining essence of the group. A group calls into being its boundaries only through conflict with other groups.

This emphasis on conflict is paralleled by an equal emphasis on explanation. The enterprise has largely entailed explaining conflict rather than describing it. The explanations of intergroup conflict fall into roughly two classes: the conflict of interests model and the social comparison model. Sherif, in many works, proffered the notion that groups come into conflict only where they compete to attain the same goal: hostilities occur only when both strive to get something which can belong to only one at a time. The experimental work which Sherif (1966) used to support this proposition has been criticized on many fronts (Billig, 1976) and later empirical studies (for example, Tajfel and Billig, 1974; Turner, 1975) have shown that hostilities between groups can be engendered where there is no objective conflict of interests. The second sort of explanation is more fundamentally psychological. This is based on the notion that people gain a sense of their own personal worth only by continual comparisons of themselves with others. Since social identity is believed to be derived from group membership, the value of this social identity is intimately related to the social position and status of those groups from which it is distilled. The need for a positive social identity, according to Tajfel and many of his co-workers, motivates comparisons of one's own group with others and ultimately will result in attempts to better the relative position of one's group. It is this desire to differentiate one's group from others which is considered to be the source of intergroup conflict. In the strictest logical sense such an explanation of conflict treats it as inevitable: as long as people want a positive social identity (and this is given the status of a stipulative statement) then they will seek to differentiate between groups, both subjectively and objectively, and there will be conflict.

The purpose here is not to relate the many methodological and logical criticisms of this type of explanation (see Breakwell, 1978a, 1979), though it should be mentioned that much of the weaknesses stem from the inadequate concept of social identity that is the motivational foundation of the theory. In fact, the prime objective here is to point out that *conflict is seen as an outcome* to be explained but this outcome is not itself seriously analysed. The complex conditions under which conflicts occur are delineated but no one says *what conflict is.* A phenomenology of conflict is missing. Bald statements like 'when such and such coincide social mobility will be sought' and 'if this and that prove ineffective then social change will be demanded' abound. But the structure and processes of conflict, as it mediates individual mobility or social change, and, indeed, the very composition of these events themselves, is left unconsidered. Of course, this is no bad thing in itself: every sensible theorist sets boundaries around those things that are to be approached and leaves the rest to others. However, this traffic in the causes rather than the substance of conflict is a problem. Things that go on in conflicts between groups (and, for that matter, at the interpersonal level) are left to strategists and politicians and journalists and others who are interested less in theory and more in practice. This is unfortunate because it means that social psychology has a simplistic picture of conflict—stationary, without sound, and in monochrome.

The bifocal image of conflict which is implicit in its explanations consists of two global notions: physical hostility and attitudinal hostility—an analytic rather than substantive dichotomy echoing that between action and thought where talk fluctuates between the two. Such notions of hostility are so global as to include everything and explicate nothing. Physical hostility can include everything from the neutron bomb to economic protectionism; attitudinal hostility can cover anything from ideology to the crudest minutiae of stereotypy.

Attitudinal hostility and the rhetoric of conflict which reflects and encapsulates it are concepts which deserve unpacking since it is in them that moralities play such an important part. A little story might help here. John 'loves' Julie. Julie 'loves' John but also 'loves' Gordon. Not wishing to two-time (deceive) John, Julie 'loves' and leaves him. John is not too happy about this. He would like to gut and fillet Gordon but Gordon is tough and has a few rough friends. On seeing Julie with Gordon, John begins a tirade of verbal abuse. 'She's a whore; he's a creep. He's a twit; she's a tart.' And 'Gordon is a moron' becomes a refrain. Moreover, this process of stereotyping which acts to devalue the others is accompanied by repeated appeals to the injustice of it all. John declares that it is not fair that she should 'pack him' (give him up) for Gordon. In the end, he gets through by creating a forced nonchalance which is really very unconvincing. (Any resemblance of this little tale to the story of the punk pop song 'Jilted John' by the group of the same name is purely intentional.) All of this rhetoric, both the name-calling and the lamentation of the injustice, are directed, not to the culprits, but to a generalized other. John does not appeal to the other actors in the drama but to an independent and presumably persuadable audience. Though it should be noted that appeals are not always made to an independent third-party. The audience, whatever its structure, is to see the crime even if any verdict it pronunces can never be implemented. Indeed the audience can be totally silent, and in some cases it can be purely imaginary: it is the assumption which John makes that it hears which is of importance to John.

The Jilted John example is at the interpersonal level but it points to processes of rhetoric and reference to justice which operate at the intergroup level. It also indicates that the *power* of the actors plays an important part—if not necessarily an overt or consistent part—in the ways that rhetoric and appeals to justice can be used. If Gordon had not been tougher or had no friends or had been perceived as open to fairness arguments, then rhetoric may have given way to physical violence or justice appeals may have been made to him rather than to some generalized and ineffectual audience. The point is that Gordon's characteristics limited the options available to John. This capacity to limit the definitions of the situation and limit the range of potentially effective actions within the defined context represents power. As such, power is amenable to no generalizable operational definition; it can be expressed in any number of social structures and relationships. The abstract and generalizable feature of power is the capacity, which can be invested in individuals or institutions, to draw the boundaries around legitimate action, legitimate means of production and destruction, and legitimate originality. Of course, the boundaries of legitimacy can be challenged; the infrequency of attempts to do so or the frequency with which these attempts fail represent an index of the degree of power involved.

The phenomenon of tailoring rhetoric and justice-appeals in reponse to the power structure is exemplified by a series of experiments (Breakwell, 1976) conducted for a very different purpose. The subjects in these experiments were made to feel that their social identity was threatened. To be precise, teenage lads, who claimed to be football supporters, were told that by any objective criteria they were not supporters because they did not go to matches (thus depriving their team of 'financial and spiritual' support). In the first of two experiments, these threatened lads and another group of lads whose claims to supporterdom had been accepted (since they attended matches regularly) were asked at the end of the experiment to rate how fair they thought the experimental criterion of supporterdom to be and to evaluate the experiment as a whole. It was predicted that the threatened lads would claim that the criterion was unfair and that the experiment was rubbish, while it was expected that the unthreatened lads, who had been accepted as genuine supporters, would regard the criterion as reasonable and righteous and the experiment worthwhile. In fact, there was no significant difference between the responses of the threatened and the unthreatened. Now, in this first experiment, it had been the experimenter who had asked for the evaluations and both the criterion and the experiment were said to be fair and valuable by all subjects. In a second, later, experiment, these evaluative questions were addressed to the subjects by a member of the teaching staff at the school where the experiment took place and subjects were led to believe that the experimenter would not be made aware of their responses. In fact, the school passed on the comments to the experimenter. On this second occasion, the threatened subjects decried the criterion of supporterdom and the experimenter in the strongest possible terms. The removal of the experimenter (and whatever authority and power that she represented) meant that she could be attacked. Whatever moral this might offer those researchers who believe that respondents will tell them truly what they believe or feel can be left for the reader to decide. The important thing for the present argument is that the rhetoric of hostility and the originality which this often implies can be very carefully and precisely controlled by the power relations in the immediate context. Redress to notions of fairness were not used with the source of the injustice. This is not to say that fairness arguments are never used with those who create the perceived injustice. It depends on the perceived feasibility of the plea to justice having any effect and that prospect is probably least feasible when the source of injustice is the sole audience for the pleas. The nature of the audience for the rhetoric involved in conflict is of great importance—the audience will shape the strategy of rhetoric, just as the reaction to the experiment is contingent upon the context in which it is expressed. This is also to admit that none of the reactions expressed are the total truth. There is no absolute truth in this respect, merely truths relative to audiences. The irony lies in the fact that one is never really sure who is in the audience.

Moral Rhetoric and the Generation of Moralities

The term 'rhetoric' in the argument that follows carries no pejorative connotations. Rhetoric is merely the label given to language used by a group to support itself in a conflict. Moral rhetoric is therefore essentially propaganda, representing a group within a confict in a biased way to the group's advantage, which involves moral notions and codes. The actual structure of rhetoric, whether moral or not, is derived from the ideology of the group. Rhetoric and ideology feed off each other. Where ideology is a group's coherent, persistent, and avowed system of beliefs, rhetoric tends to be the transient embodiment of longer-lasting ideological stances. Rhetoric can be directed at some independent entity outside of the conflict, it can be directed at the opponent group, or it can be meant for the members of the group which formulates it. Wherever it is consciously directed, it will be out of control once it is employed. At least, it will be out of control to the extent that audiences which were never envisaged may evolve. Ultimately, the nature of the audience and its reaction is a function of the structure of the rhetoric and the power of all participants.

Rhetoric, insofar as it reflects and encapsulates ideology, might be regarded as attitudes in action. Like attitudes, rhetoric has two elements which are totally interdependent: the cognitive content and the conative evaluation. Which is to say that rhetoric labels a group as having certain characteristics and simultaneously labels these characteristics as good or, more frequently, bad. In fact, it most often happens the other way round: the group is labelled bad and characteristics which suit that appraisal are sought. Implicit in the bad label is an entire moral code—the rhetoric is based on knowing what is good and what is bad; what is right and what is wrong. Of course, this assumes that a moral code is simply (or not so simply) a specific type of bundle of social rules for evaluation, which is arguable. Since this question is considered elsewhere in this book, it seems unnecessary to argue it here. Whatever the precise definition of a moral code, the main thrust of the present argument remains the same. The main assumption required is that moral codes are derived from a total history of social life and, in particular, from the history of intergroup conflict.

It should be added that the question of which came first—morals or conflicts—is unanswerable in any evolutionary sense. Morals and conflicts evolve in time. If we take a look at them at any *one* time, then the existing moral codes will be derived in large part from previous conflicts and their aftermath. But, in such a single slice of time, it would be equally true to say that the nature of conflicts (or specifically rhetoric employed in the course of conflicts) is derived partly from the cumulative record of moral codes. The argument is not one of causal primacy but merely of total interdependence. The issue of evolutionary primacy is irrelevant to understanding current conflict structures.

On the one hand, the rhetoric can have this implicit moral component due to the process of evaluation being often based on moralities. On the other hand, it can also have an explicit moral component: one group can simply argue that the other group is immoral. Implicit moral rhetoric leaves the imputation of immorality to the audience for the rhetoric. Consequently, it is possible that the group to whom these 'bad' characteristics are attributed will not recognize any accusation of immorality in the characterization. Implicit moral rhetoric only works if the rhetoricians and their audience share a consensual understanding of a single moral code. Hinting at a truth only works if the truth is already appreciated and the symbols which represent it are well known. Explicit moral rhetoric requires no such mutual symbolic representation since it involves an overt categorical verdict that the actions of the other group are immoral. Explicit moral rhetoric tends to be involved with groups' actions rather than their attributes.

An example of explicit moral rhetoric can be seen in much of the argument which surrounds any strike by any one the essential services (firemen, doctors, even lecturers). The arguments against strike action by such groups question the morality of such acts. The main thrust of the moral rhetoric is to remove the strikes from the economic arena and lift them onto a 'higher' plane where—coincidentally—the strikers have less chance of justifying themselves. The actions of the doctors and the firemen are immoral because they risk the life and limb of their clients; lecturers should mark exams because a delay in the publication of finals results would jeopardize he livelihood of their clients. It is worth noting that when these strikes occur, those involved are not regarded as immoral because they want more money (though even this can become 'immoral' in certain economic and legislative contexts); they are immoral because they strike for it. The fact that more money is not forthcoming without industrial action based on the withdrawal of labour is never considered within moral rhetoric. It is not surprising therefore that the blame for the 'immoral' nonchalance about the life prospects of the clients of these professions sticks with the practitioners and not with those who refused to submit to their pay demands. Blame seems to be incurred by those that moral rhetoric most immediately associates with the 'immoral action'. The true origins or more distant originators of the conflict are of peripheral concern to the moral rhetorician. It is easier to muster moral rhetoric against those nearest the scene of the 'crime'. This may be because explicit moral rhetoric needs to be simple in its attribution of responsibility if it is to be effective.

Such overt simplicity of moral rhetoric at the manifest level should not be allowed to mask the complexity of the processes involved in it. Certainly, one complexity which needs to be considered is what might be called the 'double standard' of moralities. All moral rhetoric has at least two audiences: the ingroup and the outgroup (and this applies no matter how a group is defined). The moral which defends the ingroup simultaneously acts as a tool against the outgroup. This means that the same moral is frequently differentially used in relation to the ingroup and the outgroup. A nice example of this emanates from the New International Economic Order and the campaign which Third World countries are mounting. Certain Third World countries have claimed that the more developed nations should provide aid for them, invoking some concept of distributive justice with the accent upon international interdependence and equality. These same states simultaneously refuse to accept that the same principle of equality should operate within their national boundaries and reject external attempts to impose human rights legislation as an attack on their national sovereignty. The same moral imperative is involved; the only difference is that in the first instance it is being employed to get something for the ingroup; in the second, it is being rejected in order to maintain a regime which the ingroup has already imposed.

The interesting thing here is that the ingroup is flexible: first it includes all the nation (even a cartel of countries) and then it shrinks so as to include only the most powerful in that nation. There is an echo of that dichotomy which every child learns through, often bitter, experience—the powerful can always say 'do as I say, not as I do', they can demand that others adhere to principles which they disregard in their own behaviour. What is perhaps more interesting is the fact that the proclaimed size of the ingroup seems much more a function of the requirements of the rhetoric than it is related to who will really benefit from the success of the rhetoric. If a large ingroup is required to accentuate the potency of the rhetoric it will be conjured up (probably full of orphans, widows, waifs, and strays—and any other emotion-reaping menagerie). The same ingroup will dissipate quite miraculously when the spoils are shared out. This elasticity of the ingroup, of course, is only understandable if the group is defined in cognitive as well as social terms (Breakwell, 1978b).

If this process of moral rhetoric went no further than has been outlined above, it might be regarded as merely another way of devaluing and attacking the outgroup and its form and consequences might be predicted on the basis of any of the current theories of intergroup behaviour. Moral rhetoric should obviously not be treated as if it were dissociated from these other dimensions of intergroup conflict. However, it is unique since it can operate in a way which establishes new moral codes and new applications of old codes.

To deal with the latter phenomenon first. Take the case of the tribe who found that the tribe down the road were capturing any of their number who meandered over that way and eating them. They might retaliate: eating any of the other tribe who came their way. But let's say that they found that they were losing out in the tally at the end of the week—they were losing more people than they could eat (and, of course, this is a progressive problem—the fewer people you have, the fewer you can eat). So they decide that a different strategy is called for. They cannot simply attack the others because by this stage they are seriously outnumbered. They, therefore, try peaceable measures: a campaign of moral rhetoric. Witchdoctors are sent to the other side under a skull of truce and they deliver the great truth: 'IT IS WRONG TO EAT YOUR NEIGH-BOURS'. Now this is a new idea; everyone knew that it was wrong to eat your own family or any of your own tribe but now it is wrong to eat people from other tribes (at least those who live just down the road). The witchdoctors' task really varies in difficulty according to the power of the opponent tribe—if they feel confident that they can feed off their neighbours without suffering any dire consequences the moral argument is likely to fail. Why should they choose to extend their tribal allegiance if they get nothing in return? However, if their superiority is a little less secure, then the persuasive witchdoctor stands a chance. Where mutual benefits can be grasped from the change in the application of the moral code it is likely to be changed.

The important thing here is that the code itself is not changing, the social entities to which it was applied are changing. There is an extention of what Vine (Chapter 2) has called the 'moral ingroup'. Vine has said that this extension of the 'moral ingroup' occurs as groups evolve historically towards greater interdependence. The present argument would, however, lead to the conclusion that interdependence, of whatever sort, is only one influence which may propel movements of the moral ingroup boundaries. In fact, the direct opposite—intergroup conflict and growing independence—can result in the extension of the moral ingroup. For example, the movement against slavery coincided with a decline in demand for slave labour in the abolitionist economies. Similarly, the extension of the rights and protection of children parallels their redundancy as a workforce. In these cases, the extension of the group regarded as worthy of human rights occurs not because the superior morality-defining groups are becoming more reliant on slaves and children but because they are actually less dependent upon them as elements of the workforce. Similarly, the extension of civil rights to blacks in the United States or emancipation to various religious minorities in the United Kingdom cannot be seen as a result of growing interdependence. As a matter of historical fact, these things have been brought about by intergroup conflict. The whole notion of interdependence can only stand if it is bolstered by putting into the context of a general intergroup theory.

A parallel to the sort of change in the application of a code described above can be seen in the way in which the characteristics of groups may be re-evaluated according to new material or psychological contexts. For example, the 'Black is beautiful' campaign of négritude. This movement called upon blacks to recognize that there is nothing shameful in Blackness and advised that blacks should no longer emulate whites. As Fanon (1967) pointed out the movement accepted that blacks have 'curly hair, flat noses and thick lips' and fought to have these characteristics re-evaluated. This avowed objective rather than seeking to diminish nationalism or ethnocentrism fanned their fire. These leading principles were left intact and reaffirmed. Leaving the principle intact and merely changing its application is just what the cannibals were doing when they agreed that more people should fall under the gastronomic taboo.

Fundamental changes in moral codes are rare. The one which springs most readily to mind is where the ethic of retribution was supplanted by that of humanitarian care (instead of an eye for an eye, two cheeks for none). The problem with using this example is the confusion of religious and social movements. The two are not easily differentiated at the best of times. A religious movement may be considered to be a specific type of social movement. Indeed, it is noticeable that social movements which seek to change the moral code rather then its sphere of application often get daubed with the religious tar.

Where new moral codes are introduced it seems characteristic that the old remain and make comeback bids now and then. It is as if they remain in the repertoire and lurk while waiting for an airing. So that there is not simply the question of to whom the moral code is applied but also the time when it is applied.

The entire question of time is very interesting. Both morals and the facts attached to them can be reconstructed retrospectively. Current moral standards can be imputed to the past thus condemning the actions of others in the past. For instance, our erstwhile cannibals might be repelled by their ancestors who ate people when they now know that it is wrong to eat people. The fact that it was not wrong to eat people in the past is somehow forgotten amidst the 'tempocentrism' of today. Also time can rewrite the past. The facts can be reconstructed according to current moralities—which is merely to reiterate the adage that every present creates a new past. For instance, in the moral indignation of the present, our cannibals may well come to believe that their ancestors were totally indiscriminate in their eating habits. They might even come to believe that they would have eaten members of their own family or tribe. This reconstruction of the past does not normally occur if it means the ingroup will be seen to have a negative history but it can occur if the ingroup is currently in a subordinate position and the dominant group's ideology propels the inferior group into self-depreciation and self-denial. By far the most frequent incidence of the reconstruction of the facts of the past occurs where it is designed to deprecate the outgroup or, at the interpersonal level, the outsider.

There is a nice, if irreverant, example of how moral perspectives can change facts and their import in a film called 'The Big Bus'. The hero was the fearless bus driver of the first atomic-powered bus, but like all heroes he had a tragic past to live down: on one trip he had been stranded in the mountains with an entire busload of passengers—as the days went by, the food ran out and his co-driver went mad, killing and eating the passengers in order to stay alive. The hero had survived by eating the leather of the bus-seats, etc. and had studiously avoided eating any of the passengers. But his attention had wandered one night when his co-driver had made a stew. Our hero knew nothing, we must believe, of the foot of the business magnate which was the prime substance of that stew. He ate the stew and only later learnt that he had eaten a human foot. For this unintentional act of cannibalism he was blackballed from all drivers' bars and could not get a job anywhere when he finally managed to get back to civilization. No one would accept that it had been, in our hero's own words, 'just one measly foot and by mistake'. People did not care whether it had been intentional or not, or even whether it had been one toe or a whole torso, the man was labelled cannibal. Fanciful maybe, but a nice example of the way morals change the perception of facts. It did not matter that he could prove it had only been a foot—that truth would not be accepted. Our hero might be manifestly not culpable, but morality was avenged. Moral indigation is an enemy to objectivity—even when this is only consensual subjectivity.

This business of intention as applied to groups is interesting. Some argue that moral action can only occur where action is voluntary—accidental or forced actions can never have moral connotations. Groups are never *seen* to act accidentally though the consequences of their actions may be understood to be unforeseen. They are always *seen* as conscious actors or else they are redefined as mobs or some such conglomerate: they are always acting within a possible moral domain. Not that actual intention has much to do with moral imputations; intentions can always be conferred from outside by those who would like to moralize about an act.

Social Identity and Moral Rhetoric

It must be stressed that there is a difference between moral rhetoric, moral action, and the imposition of moralities by one group upon another. The actual negotiation of moralities which occurs in intergroup conflicts is very different from attempts to merely reconstruct moral values in retrospect. The former is dependent upon the relations of the negotiators; the latter can be done in virtual isolation. Historical reconstruction of moral codes, their re-representation, is not inevitably social insofar as a single group can revamp the past unilaterally frequently without fracturing current social relationships. The change of current moralities is quite another thing. Changes in current moralities need to be subjected to social negotiation. The object of negotiation is not just to decide the content of a moral code but also to establish its legitimacy. Obviously, the power of the negotiators will influence what is regarded as legitimate and what is not. Often there will be a disparity between what is officially regarded as legitimate and what is regarded as legitimate by the least powerful—even though they may have agreed to the official version.

In these negotiations, and by that it is not intended to imply that representatives of the concerned groups get round a table to consciously dispute pros and cons of any particular morality, the moral rhetoric which has been evolved to further the cause of particular intergroup conflicts may shape changes in moralities. The specific origin of the moral rhetoric is shed and the principle it embodies may be adopted as a moral rule. The dictum that started as a tool of conflict can thus become enshrined as a moral dictate. But this is not to say that it is thereafter no use as a tool of conflict. The enshrined dictum is normally the one which has proven most successful for the dominant group; it has previously served to further their ends in the intergroup context, as a corporate morality it will serve to legitimate the advantages it has already aided to confer. In other words, the rhetoric which helped them get there becomes the morality which helps to keep them there.

Questions of legitimacy are important for the impact that changes in moral codes will have on individual morality and thus upon individual social identities. Legitimized moralities build-in group obligations for members. Some moralities actually demand the individual's self-subjugation to the group explicitly. More frequently moralities specify tenets of behaviour which the group member must not challenge if membership is to be maintained. If one's group is currently lauding the value of human life and one wishes to remain a legitimate member it is wise not to take to mass murder. If one did take to mass murder, one would not only discredit oneself: the group as a whole might also be discredited.

Just as moral rhetoric can be used to manipulate relations between groups, group moralities can operate against individual rebellion to control members and reinforce the status quo. As agents of the status quo, moralities may serve to legitmate inequalities of power and status within the group. Where change in material circumstances result in changed perceptions of the relations within the group and some come to be perceived as illegitimate then not only can these relations be challenged but also the moralities which were supporting them may be threatened. It becomes most interesting when the challenge takes the form of an individual morality that turns the old code against itself: like the revolutionary who will kill in order to prevent killing.

If one wanted to tie the notions of morality propounded here into a theory of social identity, it would have to be through the concept of legitimacy. Moralities legitimize and rationalize relations within and between groups. The moral ideology of a group, encapsulated frequently in its rhetoric, sets the bounds of legitimate action; it establishes codes of practice. It is within these codes of practice that social identity has to be forged, and if not within them then against them: either way their impact is immense. Identity is immutably tied to moralities which are evolved through the contingencies of intergroup conflict. The morality tells the aspiring social being what to look for in an identity, where to look for one and how to acquire it.

Conclusion

In conclusion, what has been argued above leads to three claims:

(i) Individual morality derives from group (i.e. socially prevalent) moralities—a fact which Piaget and Kohlberg may both assume but which both fail to explicate.
(ii) Morality can be a weapon of intergroup conflict and will be evolved within conflict—a fact not discussed by intergroup theorists.
(iii) Intergroup moralities lay the boundaries in relation to which social identities are crystallized—a fact not discussed by identity theorists.

It would be nice to see theorists in these three domains moving freely across the frontier between their own level of analysis and explanation and that of others. The real complexity of the problems can only be understood when they can be viewed from levels of analysis ranging from the intrapersonal to the intergroup.

References

Billig, M. G. (1976). *Social Psychology and Intergroup Relations*, Academic Press, London.

Breakwell, G. M. (1976). The Mechanisms of Social Identity in Intergroup Behaviour. Unpublished PhD Thesis, Bristol.

Breakwell, G. M. (1978a). Some effects of marginal social identity. In H. Tajfel (Ed.), *Differentiation Between Social Groups*, Academic Press, London.

Breakwell, G. M. (1978b). Groups for Sale. *New Society*, 13th July.

Breakwell, G. M. (1979). Illegitimate group membership and intergroup differentiation. *Brit. J. Soc. Clin. Psychol.*, **18**(2), 141–149.

Doise, W. (1978). *Groups and Individuals*, Wiley, London.

Fanon, F. (1967). *Blacks Skins, White Masks*, Grove Press, New York.

Israel, J. (1972). Stipulations and constructions in the social sciences. In J. Israel and H. Tajfel (Eds), *The Context of Social Psychology*, Academic Press, London.

Klineberg, O. (1950). Tensions affecting international understanding. *Soc. Sci. Res. Council Bulletin 62.*

Klineberg, O. (1964). Intergroup relations and international relations. In M. Sherif (Ed.), *Intergroup Relations and Leadership*, Wiley, London.
Moscovici, S. (1976). Social Influence and Social Change, Academic Press, London.
Sherif, M. (1966). *Group Conflict and Cooperation*, Chicago University Press.
Steiner, I. D. (1974). Whatever happened to the group in social psychology? *J. Exp. Soc. Psychol.*, **10**, 94–108.
Tajfel, H. (1974). Intergroup Behaviour, social comparison and social change. Katz-Newcombe Lectures, University of Michigan.
Tajfel, H. (Ed.) (1978). *Differentiation between Social Groups*, Academic Press, London.
Tajfel, H., and Billig, M. G. (1974). Familiarity and categorisation in intergroup behaviour. *J. Exp. Soc. Psychol.*, **10**, 159–170.
Turner, J. (1975). Social comparison and social identity: some prospects for intergroup behaviour. *Eur. H. Soc Psychol.*, **5**(1), 5–34.

Author Index

Subject Index

249